ROMANS
"The Clearest Gospel of All"

By Jack Sequeira

JACK SEQUEIRA MINISTRIES

Romans "The Clearest Gospel of All"
Jack Sequeira

Edited by Edwin A. Schwisow
Cover and Layout by Ron Burgard, Macmouser Graphics

Copyright © 2005 by E. H. Jack Sequeira
Contents and/or cover may not be reproduced in whole or in part in any form without the express written consent of the Publisher.

Published by Jack Sequeira Ministries
PMB #244, 3760 Market Street NE
Salem, OR 97301
www.jacksequeira.org

Unless otherwise indicated, Scripture is taken from the
New King James Version.

Printed in the United States of America
Third printing 2016

ISBN: 0-9769168-0-0

Acknowledgements:

I am deeply indebted to family, friends, and supporters of the Good News for making this reprint financially possible. Thank you!

January 2016

Table of Contents

Preface 5
1 .... The Clearest Gospel of All *(Romans 1:1-17)* 7
2 .... The Wrath of God *(Romans 1:18-32)* 14
3 .... The Sin of Self-righteousness *(Romans 2:1-29)* 22
4 .... The Universal Sin Problem *(Romans 3:1-20)* 29
5 .... The Gospel Introduced *(Romans 3:21-23)* 36
6 .... The Law and the Gospel *(Romans 3:24-31)* 44
7 .... Justification by Faith Alone *(Romans 4:1-25)* 51
8 .... Fruits of Justification by Faith *(Romans 5:1-5)* 59
9 .... God's Unconditional Love *(Romans 5:6-10)* 66
10 .... Adam—A Type of Christ *(Romans 5:11-18)* 73
11 .... The Two Adams *(Romans 5:11-18 - Continued)* 80
12 .... The Reign of Sin and Grace *(Romans 5:19-21)* 87
13 .... Dead to Sin, Alive to God *(Romans 6:1-13)* 94
14 .... From Law to Grace *(Romans 6:14-23)* 101
15 .... Slaves of Sin *(Romans 6:14-23 - Continued)* 107
16 .... Liberated from Under Law *(Romans 7:1-6)* 113
17 .... Our Utter Sinfulness *(Romans 7:7-13)* 120
18 .... Wretched Man that I Am *(Romans 7:14-25)* 127
19 .... Delivered from Sin's Bondage *(Romans 8:1-4)* 134
20 .... Life in the Spirit *(Romans 8:5-14)* 141
21 .... The Blessed Hope *(Romans 8:14-30)* 148
22 .... God is on Our Side *(Romans 8:31-39)* 155
23 .... The Jewish Tragedy *(Romans 9:1-33)* 161
24 .... Who Constitutes True Israel? *(Romans 10:1-21)* 168
25 .... God Keeps His Promise *(Romans 11:1-36)* 175
26 .... Living the Christian Life *(Romans 12:1-8)* 182
27 .... Into His Likeness *(Romans 12:9-21)* 189
28 .... Loyal Citizens *(Romans 13:1-7)* 196
29 .... Fulfilling the Royal Law *(Romans 13:8-14)* 202
30 .... Christian Relationships *(Romans 14:1-23)* 209
31 .... Burden Bearing *(Romans 15:1-33)* 217
32 .... One in Christ *(Romans 16:1-27)* 225

Preface

The apostles "turned the world upside down" with "good news of great joy for all the people." God in Christ reconciled the entire human race to himself (2 Corinthians 5:19)! That good news was proclaimed in its fullness early in the Christian era. A great Church Father, Athanasius (293-373 AD), believed and taught that Jesus Christ had purchased salvation and granted it to all—without any exception. Sad to say, this incredible good news of salvation is often lacking in present-day proclamation of the gospel.

When Jesus Christ came to this world some 2,000 years ago, he lived out the gospel in His own life—the incredible good news of salvation for all mankind (Titus 2:11). But it is the apostle Paul whom God set aside to explain "the unsearchable riches of Christ" (Ephesians 3:8). This is why Paul's epistles fill almost half of the New Testament.

No other book in the Bible so clearly and masterfully explains the gospel of the Lord, Jesus Christ, as Paul's epistle to the Romans. Here the great apostle sets forth the whole counsel of God regarding salvation in Christ. Paul's purpose in writing this somewhat lengthy letter is to fully establish his readers in their Christian faith (Romans 1:11). Today, in this "time of the end," it is even more vital for believers be fully established in Christ.

Understanding justification by faith, so clearly set forth in Romans, delivered Martin Luther from his earlier bondage to legalism (salvation by human effort) and installed him as the leader of the Protestant Reformation. No wonder he labeled Romans "The Clearest Gospel of All." Years later, as John Wesley listened to a man reading from the preface of Luther's Commentary on Romans, his heart was "strangely warmed" the evening of May 24, 1738—and thus was born the great 18th-century English revival.

Were Paul living today, he would be as concerned about today's believers as he was about the Roman Christians. Their future under persecution looked bleak, as terrorism threatens ours. While the substance of a gospel written specifically for Christians today would be the same, the style would be different. Christians of Paul's day belonged to a far different culture, background, and mindset. Perhaps this is why many today find Romans hard reading. This book of expository studies tries to bridge the gap between Paul's day and ours and make Romans more meaningful and bring revival and reformation to modern readers. The Lord declared, "you shall know the truth, and the truth shall make you free" (John 8:32). Jesus also made it clear that before the end comes "this gospel of the kingdom will be preached into the entire world for a witness" (Matthew 24:14).

To receive full benefit from each chapter of this book, I suggest first reading the passage in Romans cited at the beginning of each chapter—preferably from more than one translation. Every attempt has been made to be absolutely true to Paul's thoughts in each text. I do not claim infallibility, however, and the best I can hope for is that readers will be stimulated to deeper and more prayerful study of Romans, while drawing closer to "Jesus Christ our Lord, through whom we have received grace" (Romans 1:4 and 5).

Pastor Jack Sequeira
www.jacksequeira.com

Chapter 1
The Clearest Gospel of All

Romans 1:1-17

No book or section of Scripture presents so masterfully the plan of salvation and doctrine of righteousness by faith as Paul's Epistle to the Romans. Indeed, Martin Luther describes Romans as the clearest gospel of all, for it was in understanding Romans 1:17 that he shook off the bondage of legalism and became the great leader of the Protestant Reformation.

The same doctrine led to the conversion of John Bunyan, commonly known in Great Britain as the immortal tinker of Bedford and in America as the author of *Pilgrim's Progress*.

And it was by listening to the preface of Luther's *Commentary to Romans* that John Wesley, the founder of the Methodist Church, felt his heart strangely warmed the evening of May 24, 1738. Thus was born a great revival in Great Britain during the 18th century. The Epistle to the Romans, in fact, has been the basis of most revivals in the history of the Christian church.

What makes Paul's Epistle to the Romans so special?

There are at least two reasons, one general (the author, Paul the apostle) and the other more specific (its unique audience).

From Saul to Paul

We begin with Acts 9:1-12 where we find the wonderful account of how Saul, a great persecutor of the Christian church, meets Jesus Christ while traveling from Jerusalem to the city of Damascus. God then appears to a believer, Ananias, and tells him that he must go to the street called Strait and meet a young man named Saul, bless him, baptize him, and open his eyes.

Ananias thinks God has made a mistake, for Saul has done great harm to the early Christian church. But notice how God responds to Ananias in Acts 9:15: "But the Lord said unto him, Go, for he is a chosen vessel of Mine to bear My name before Gentiles, kings, and the children of Israel." After Saul receives his vision and is baptized, he immediately proclaims Jesus Christ, saying, "He is the Son of God."

When Christ came to this world 2,000 years ago, He came that there might be a gospel (good news) to be preached. But it was Saul (later known as Paul) whom God chose to be the instrument to explain the incredibly good news of salvation to the whole world, in Jesus Christ.

Opening Romans

With this in mind, we turn to the book of Romans itself. We notice in Chapter 1, verse 1, how Paul introduces this epistle to the Christians at Rome: "Paul, a bondservant (*the Greek means slave*) of Jesus Christ, called to be an apostle, separated unto the gospel of God." Paul is the dominant theologian of the New Testament and writes almost half of it. Without Paul's writings, the Christian church would be at a terrible loss.

So, the first reason Romans is so special to every Christian is that Paul is God's chosen vessel to explain the gospel to the world. But the second, and more specific reason, is that unlike any other epistle Paul writes, this is a letter to a body of Christians he has not personally established or even met, as a church.

When Paul writes his epistles to the Corinthians or the Ephesians or the Philippians or to individuals like Titus or Timothy, he is addressing Christians to whom he has already presented the gospel. But in the book of Romans, he writes to Christians he has never met before—as a group. So he explains the full message of the gospel, as he would if he were speaking to them verbally for the first time.

In Romans 1:11 Paul himself says that his purpose in writing his letter and later in visiting Rome is to impart some spiritual gift, that they may be established. In Romans 1:13 he says, "Now I do not want you to be unaware, brethren, that I often planned to come to you (*but was hindered until now*)." He was hindered, he says in Romans 15:22, 23, because God has told him that he is not to go to Rome until he has visited every unentered area in the Middle East. Now having done so, he is ready to go to Rome.

But in holding Paul back from visiting Rome, God has compelled the apostle to write this gospel message in clear, distinct tones for all time. Paul explains the gospel in all its clarity for a first-time audience—making it, as Luther calls it, "the clearest gospel of all."

We will spend 32 studies going step by step through this epistle, to discover what Paul is telling us about the whole plan of salvation.

The Theme

The great theme of Romans appears in Romans 1:15-17. Paul has already told the Roman Christians that he wants to come to Rome, and then, in verse 14, he says he is a debtor, both to the Greeks and to the barbarians, both to the wise and to the unwise. He wants to preach this gospel to everyone in Rome—to the captain as well as the slave.

Rome, of course, was regarded as the capital of the world in those days, and Paul is saying to these Roman Christians in verse 15: "As much as is in me (*with every ability that I have*) I would like to come to Rome and preach this gospel to those who are residing there." He already has preached the gospel in the Middle East. Now having finished his work there, he wants to come to Rome. His epistle will prepare them for his arrival.

In his introduction to the epistle/gospel, Paul says in Romans 1:16: "For I am not ashamed of the gospel of Christ, for it is the power of God to salvation for everyone who believes, for the Jew first and also for the Greek (*that is, the Gentile*)."

It was quite customary in Paul's day to put things in the negative, as a way of showing emphasis. Paul uses the negative in verse 16 to emphasize the positive. If Paul were living today, he would have put the whole thing in the positive, perhaps writing: "I am absolutely and completely excited and would like to know nothing among you except the gospel of our Lord, Jesus Christ—Jesus Christ and Him crucified. I have nothing else to proclaim except this message."

Paul is not ashamed of the gospel, though the Romans of his day look on the Christians as third-class citizens. The Romans consider themselves first-class citizens: They are the rulers of the then-known world. They look upon the Jews as second-class citizens. But Christians—both Jews and Gentiles—are seen as third-class citizens, because they worship a man who has been crucified on a Roman cross—a symbol of shame and degradation.

Rome is a proud city—no doubt about it. All kinds of philosophies are being proclaimed there. It boasts military power, architectural power, and economic power. But Paul says he wants to come to Rome, not to add yet another human philosophical invention, but to bring the gospel. The reason he is not ashamed is that the gospel is not man's, but God's power unto salvation. Rome, with all its pride and accomplishments, has failed to do one thing—it has failed miserably to conquer sin. Sin in fact will eventually bring the downfall of this great empire.

Paul says he wants to make the power of the gospel available to those in Rome. Ashamed of it? Why should he be? It is the only power that can save man. As long as we accept salvation and believe—whether Jew or Gentile—we have the power of God, who is able to save both the wise and the unwise, the rich and the poor, the noble and the slave. It does not matter to which class or category we belong. It does not matter in which time of the world's history we are living, in the first century of this Christian era or the 21st century. For man is always a slave to sin, and the only power that can liberate him from sin is the gospel of our Lord, Jesus Christ.

The New Testament tells us it is God who takes the initiative for our salvation. This is why, having announced in Romans 1:17 his full confidence in the gospel, Paul defines it as the "righteousness of God."

By this Paul means that the gospel is a righteousness *planned* by God. Second, it is a righteousness *prepared* by God. And, finally, it is a righteousness *made available* to mankind by God. Man has made no contribution to this salvation; it is unexpected, incredibly good news. In Romans 5 we will discover that while we were helpless, incapable, ungodly sinners—and, worse still, God's enemies—we were reconciled to God through the death of His Son. God took the initiative.

Our salvation in Jesus Christ is a salvation that comes entirely from God, based on His unconditional love for mankind. God so loved the world, we are told in John 3:16, that He gave us His only begotten Son, that whoever believes should not perish but have everlasting life. God commissioned Paul to preach this gospel to the world and commissions us to do the same, today. Hence this book.

An Overview

In this Epistle to the Romans Paul presents the incredibly good news of God's salvation, prepared in Jesus Christ for all humanity. This, of course, is the grand theme of the Bible, Old and New Testaments alike. But in no place is this message of salvation set forth so clearly and explained so masterfully as in the Epistle to the Romans. Here Paul unfolds for us the whole counsel of God. He presents our sin problem—something we will study in depth later on. The gospel is God's solution to our sinful condition.

But before he presents the gospel, Paul must convince us that we are sinners—100 percent sinners in need of a Savior. Once he accomplishes this, he describes the truth as it is in Christ—His birth, His life, His death, and His resurrection. Christ is humanity's Righteousness. He came to this world as its Representative, Substitute, and Surety.

Paul then goes on to describe the human response necessary if the righteousness of Christ is to have any effect. Faith in Jesus Christ, Paul says, is the only basis for making that salvation effective.

Paul then describes the role of the Holy Spirit in sanctification. God has not left humanity on its own. After accepting Jesus Christ, Christians receive His Holy Spirit so that they may experience the power of the gospel in their personal lives.

Finally, in the last chapters of Romans, Paul applies the gospel to daily Christian living. When applied to sinful human beings, the gospel is defined as righteousness—or justification by faith. The just shall live by faith and, having been justified by faith, the question is, "How shall we live"? Paul in Romans chapters 12-16 describes practical Christian living—Christian ethics.

Everything a Christian needs to know about the plan of salvation is found in the Epistle to the Romans. It is a difficult book to understand, not because Paul wrote it for scholars, but because he addressed it to a people whose mind-set was so different from ours today, in the 21st century.

The purpose in this book is to bridge the gap between Paul's day and ours, so that the gospel of Jesus Christ as presented in Romans may come to us as the clearest gospel of all. We will study it in detail, because here we have the most extended treatment of the entire range of Scripture on the crucial doctrine of justification—or righteousness by faith.

The devil does not want this message to be clearly understood. He wants Christians to believe that "they" have to "do" something to attain salvation. He trapped the Galatians in this mixed-up idea of salvation and wants to do the same today.

This is why understanding this message of righteousness by faith is so important. It was this message that turned my ministry around. I spent five years of my ministry in legalism, trying to work my way to heaven. I became so discouraged that at the end of those five years I was ready to give it all up. But then God stepped in and turned me around, as He opened to my mind this wonderful message of salvation by grace alone, through faith alone in Jesus Christ. Now I enjoy preaching from the pulpit, though by nature I am an introvert.

In concluding this chapter, let us briefly review what Paul is telling us in Romans. We can divide the Epistle into four major parts. The first part tells us that God has already, unconditionally redeemed all mankind in the holy history of His Son, Jesus Christ. Therefore lawfully (*or forensically*) all humanity has been reconciled to God and stands justified before a holy God. Paul brings this out, especially in Romans 5:18. This is the unconditional good news of salvation introduced in the first section of Romans.

Paul next tells us that this legal, forensic justification that applies to all men has to be made effective. All mankind will not go to heaven—not because Jesus has not redeemed humanity, but because God has created mankind with a free will. He will not force salvation on any human being. This objective justification which He obtained for the entire human race has to be made effective. This is not done by going on a pilgrimage to the Holy Land, by doing some good works, or by keeping the law. It is made effective by faith alone. The gospel and human response to it—put together—sum up the doctrine of justification by faith alone. Luther's greatest discovery (justification made effective by faith alone) turned Europe upside down, as he proclaimed it in Germany and beyond.

The third point Paul makes in Romans is that justification by faith does not stop at giving us peace and assurance of salvation. Yes, it does that. But thank God, it goes beyond that! Romans teaches that because we have become children of God, God sends His Holy Spirit to dwell in us, that we may become partakers of the divine nature. Through this indwelling power, we may escape the world's corruption.

What is this corruption? In 1 John 2:16 we find how John defines it. He says it is the lust of the flesh, the lust of the eyes, and the pride of life. These are three basic drives that control the sinful man. Paul tells us that through the indwelling Spirit we may escape this corruption and live lives pleasing to Him.

Remember what Jesus reminded His disciples in John 15:4: "Abide in me and I in you." Here He is talking to born-again Christians—to His disciples who had already accepted Him as the Messiah. This statement also applies to us who have accepted Him. Jesus tells us, "Without Me you can do nothing, but, if you abide in Me and I in you, you will bear much fruit and My Father will be pleased."

Again, in Matthew 5:14 Jesus addresses the disciples by the Sea of Galilee in the Sermon on the Mount, and says: "You (*Christians*) are the light of the world." The word "light" in the original Greek text is in the singular, but the word "you" is in the plural. The English translation does not bring this out. Jesus is saying that Christians, who are many, are but one light, and that light is "Christ in you, the hope of glory" (Colossians 1:27).

When Jesus came to this world, He brought light into darkness. Jesus is no longer here: He's in heaven. But His body, the church—the called-out people—are still living on this earth. Jesus says, "You are My representatives. You are to be the instrument through which I am going to shine." Then in Matthew 5:16, He says, "Let this light shine so that men may see your good works and glorify your Father in heaven." This is the final purpose of the gospel.

But there is still a fourth point in Romans. Even though Christians have accepted Christ and can stand justified, perfect in Christ as born-again Christians, their human nature is still sinful and will remain so until the Second Coming of Christ. Paul brings out in Romans the wonderful news that one day Christ will come and redeem humanity from the corruption that it inherited through Adam's fall.

One day the world will know the power of the gospel in its fullness. Until then, may God help us to know this truth as we study this excellent book, the Epistle to the Romans—the clearest gospel of all.

Chapter 2
The Wrath of God

Romans 1:18-32

Martin Luther describes Romans as the clearest gospel of all, and in our study of Romans 1:15-17, we find Paul telling his readers that he is now ready to preach the gospel in Rome—the metropolis at the center of the then-known civilized world. Paul then adds, "I am not ashamed of this gospel, for it is the power of God unto salvation."

The Sin Problem

Having said this, Paul directs his readers to mankind's universal sin problem—a topic that begins in Romans 1:18 and finally ends in Romans 3:20. Why such a lengthy passage on the sin problem? And why does Paul bring it up so early in the book?

To answer these questions, we must bear in mind that the gospel is good news, not for good people but for sinners; not for those who are 80-, or 90-, or even 99.9-percent sinners, but for those who are 100-percent sinners—from head to foot. Jesus Christ Himself came to save man from sin. He did not come for the righteous (Mark 2:17).

So Paul first has to convince us that in and of ourselves we have nothing good. Yes, man may be capable of doing many good things, but nothing that can save him. God has to convince us that we, in and of ourselves, are helpless—incapable of saving ourselves. He has to destroy in us every confidence in the flesh (our sinful human nature), because man's only hope is the gospel of Jesus Christ (Philippians 3:3). The hope He offers is only for those who recognize that they need a Savior. It will take us three studies to deal completely with this issue.

But be forewarned: In this passage Paul paints a dismal picture of the human race. It can be discouraging to study. But Paul has some wonderfully good news for us, beginning with Romans 3:21.

For after he has painted the dark, hopeless picture of mankind, he says, "But now. Do not give up hope. I have incredibly good news for you." The stars shine brightest on a pitch-dark night. It is only in view of our total sinfulness—our total depravity—that the gospel shines most gloriously.

This study and the two to follow are by no means pleasant ones. But we must first understand this long, dark passage before we can launch into our study of the glorious gospel of our Lord, Jesus Christ.

The key statement of Romans 1:18-32 is verse 18. The rest of the passage—verses 19-32—simply explains verse 18: "For the wrath of God is revealed from heaven against all ungodliness and unrighteousness of man, who hold the truth in unrighteousness" (KJV).

The Wrath of God

Paul begins discussing our sin problem with the phrase, "the wrath of God." When we read in the Bible about the wrath of God, we often become fearful because we tend to project human-style wrath onto God—something we must never do. James 1:20 tells us clearly that the wrath of God is unlike any human wrath.

Many today still read the Old Testament and think of God as a God of vengeance, a God of wrath, waiting to bring fire down upon us because of our sins.

But when Paul uses the words "wrath of God," he is talking about something very different than human wrath that lashes out against others with anger and loss of self-control.

Paul is talking about something far different, and Romans 1:18-32 offers one of the best explanations of God's wrath in all Scripture.

What, then, is God's wrath? In a nutshell, it is His hatred for sin. God hates sin. He hates sin because He loves us. God cannot love us sinners and love sin at the same time, because it is sin that kills us. As Paul mentions in Romans 6:23, the wages of sin is death. In 1 Corinthians 15:56 he says "the sting of death is sin." Sin kills us. God hates sin because He loves us. John 3:16 says He so loved the world that He gave His only begotten Son, that whosoever believeth in Him should not perish but have everlasting life.

We human beings, however, face a serious problem. We lack the ability to separate sin from the sinner. When somebody does something wrong or commits a crime, we shut him up in prison. We ostracize him from society. We condemn him as well as the sin he has committed. God, on the other hand, makes a distinction between sin and the sinner.

If a sinner refuses to separate himself from his sin, he will suffer the wages of sin. But God loves the sinner and hates the sin that kills him. There is only one sin God cannot forgive—the sin of unbelief. If we reject the gift of God, given at infinite cost, then we are in a position where God cannot save us.

Paul tells us that the wrath of God is revealed from heaven against all of man's ungodliness and unrighteousness. Notice two important facts in this statement: First, God sees ungodliness as the precursor of unrighteousness.

Ungodliness and Unrighteousness

The modern, secular view is that man's real problem is unrighteousness. We read about the terrible things taking place in our world, and we say that man's problem is his unrighteousness. Ungodliness is hardly mentioned. Yet in God's view, unrighteousness is the consequence—or fruit—of ungodliness.

Man's basic problem is not unrighteousness—it is ungodliness. When man turns his back to God, unrighteousness follows—sin, crime, or whatever we choose to call it. We need to bear this in mind, for during the past few decades, since the arrival of secular humanism in our society, nations have gradually begun to turn their backs on God.

We cannot solve our problem of unrighteousness by human effort, for we are slaves to sin. Many liberal theologians today are saying that what we need is dialogue. The world, they say, is torn into all kinds of factions. Sin is seen as a sickness—a disease that man must cure. They see sin as the remnant of our animal natures and feel that in time, as we develop and progress in life, we will get rid of this problem.

But all this is said by man, speaking in terms of men. The problem is elsewhere—the problem is man's estranged relationship with God. Paul is saying that God hates—He detests—sin. His wrath from heaven is revealed against all ungodliness and its fruits, mankind's unrighteousness.

Man's Resistance

Then he adds a second point: Mankind, because of its sinful state, deliberately wants to suppress the truth of God and His saving activity in Jesus Christ. Romans 1:28 says that man does not like to retain the knowledge of God, for he detests God.

Mankind resists the knowledge of God because human beings in their sinful state are egocentric (self-centered). Men and woman do not want to accept the fact that, without God, they can do nothing. Human beings do not like to be beggars. We hate to be given a gift for which we cannot pay.

Third World society teaches us that those who accept foreign aid from developed countries by and large hate those who provide that aid.

When Americans travel overseas, they often wonder why those they have helped most hate them. The answer is that America has shown them to be beggars, incapable of returning the favors it gives them.

Now Paul explains the situation as it applies to sinners. How is the ungodliness of mankind revealed from heaven? From Romans 1:21 onward, Paul says it is revealed through the history recorded in the Old Testament. Since the fall of mankind, human beings have tended to run away from God. Before Adam and Eve sinned, they happily welcomed God's presence. But immediately after they sinned, when God came to see them, they hid. Paul tells us in Romans 1:19 "because that which may be known of God is manifest in them; for God had shewed it unto them" (KJV).

If man lacks a knowledge of God, it is not because God has hidden Himself. It is because man has deliberately pushed God out of the picture. Man, Paul says, began with knowledge of God. If mankind has failed to know God, it is not because God has not revealed Himself to them.

Man and Nature

In Romans 1:20, we read, "For since the creation of the world his invisible attributes are clearly seen, being understood by the things that are made even His eternal power and Godhead, so that they (*the human race*) are without excuse."

God has revealed Himself in both man and nature. When Adam and Eve sinned, God's image was not completely obliterated. There was still left in Adam and Eve—in their consciences—a knowledge and desire to seek after God.

But, Paul says, even though He has revealed Himself through nature and through the conscience, man does not want to retain this knowledge in his heart. So, we now have many explanations about God and creation. How can we imagine that this complex, highly refined, highly planned, highly organized world could come about by chance? How is it that a mixture of gasses suddenly produced life and the urgings of evolution have developed and improved us until we are what we are today?

If we take some scrap metal, put it in a bag, and shake it for a million years—or even 50 billion years—will we produce a Cadillac? We know very well that all it will produce is worthless polished metal.

Creation is highly organized. We boast of our technology, but we can be sure that as the angels look down on us from heaven, they say, "Wait until they get to heaven and realize what more they still have to learn." Our knowledge with all our present accomplishments is nothing compared with what we will learn when we get to heaven.

But what does man do when he turns his back to God? The answer is found in Romans 1:21: "Although they knew God, they did not glorify Him as God, nor were thankful." Here is a God who is the Giver of all good things; yet, man becomes unthankful. Not only does he refuse to acknowledge God, but he becomes ungrateful for what God has accomplished for him.

No Right to Live

The moment Adam sinned, he had no right to live; the moment Adam sinned, he should have died. But God kept him alive because He had a plan of salvation from before the foundation of the world, through Jesus Christ, the Lamb of God (Revelation 13:8). He kept Adam and Eve alive for only one reason—that they and their children might turn back to Him and accept the gift of salvation in Jesus Christ.

But does man normally do this? No. Man is unthankful. He is not only ungodly but ungrateful.

In verse 21 Paul says that men become futile in their thoughts and their foolish hearts were darkened. When man turns his back to God, only darkness remains.

Godless Utopia?

Just one year after my family arrived in Ethiopia as missionaries, that country experienced a Marxist revolution. We were disturbed to see how many educated Christians fell for the Marxist philosophy. They disliked the practice of Communism but they fell for the ideology. They said to themselves, "There must be something attractive about Marxist philosophy." So they began reading *The Communist Manifesto*, authored by Karl Marx and Frederick Engels. They read Karl Marx's books and began discovering that the essence of Marxism is ungodliness. It is an atheistic philosophy.

Karl Marx says that the problem with man is selfishness. He recognized man's selfishness, but he calls it self-alienation. He argues that man is selfish, not by nature, but because of his environment. By environment, of course, he means capitalism.

So Marx's gospel becomes, "Let us change the political and economic environment. Let us force our people to share until it becomes natural."

He suggests that socialism should confiscate private ownership—the banks, the businesses—and then make equal distribution of the wealth.

The people in Russia said, "Wonderful!" The people in China, Cuba, and Ethiopia said, "Wonderful!" Marx teaches that once people have learned to share, they will share spontaneously and naturally. Man will be redeemed from selfishness. This in essence is what he means by Communism.

Russia tried this method. For 75 years, the Soviet Union forced its citizens to share—until today they have nothing to share. The problem with man is not his environment but his very nature. It is sinful, so he needs a Redeemer.

In Romans 1:22 and 23 Paul says: "Professing to be wise, they became fools, and changed the glory of the incorruptible God into an image made like corruptible man—and birds and four footed beasts and creeping things."

Encroaching Liberalism

Some say that this no longer applies to us in our sophisticated world. That may be true, but something is creeping into even the Christian churches—liberal theology, the historical-critical method of interpreting Scripture.

This term means simply that the human mind becomes the ultimate measuring rod of truth. Man must interpret Scripture by his own rationale—on the basis of the scientific method. But we cannot use the scientific method to interpret the Word of God, because the Bible through inspiration reveals a supernatural God who cannot be measured. It is the Holy Spirit who must enlighten us (I Corinthians 2:11-13).

But man believes he can solve all his problems. He does not want God in his life. How does God react to such stubbornness, such infidelity? How is God's wrath revealed from heaven against man's ungodliness? Romans 1:24, 26 and 28 gives us the answer in verse 24: "Therefore (*that is, because man insists on living without Him*), God also gave them up." Then in verse 26: "For this reason (*because man refuses the blessings of God*), God gave them up to vile passions." In verse 28 Paul continues: "And even as they did not like to retain God in their knowledge (*notice man's problem; he does not want to retain God in his knowledge*), God gave them over to a debased mind."

God says to mankind in other words, "All right, you think you can live without Me. Try it and see what happens." The moment we turn our backs on God, unrighteousness results.

The United States of America, which was established with the principle "In God We Trust" imprinted on its coins, today is turning its back on God. First it has stopped young children from praying in schools. Now there is talk of doing away with the inscription "In God We Trust" altogether. The result is crime and sin rampant in every city and even in the countryside.

God's Forbearance

One day my wife and I were preparing to go to church with our three-year-old son. My wife said to me, "Could you please tie Chris's shoelaces?" I went to help my son, but the boy would not let me do it. He said, "I can do it." So I allowed him to try to tie his own shoes. I did not invoke my authority. I gave my son freedom, and after he tried and tried, he finally looked up and said, "Daddy, you do it."

We are God's children and we cannot live without Him, but when we think we can live without God, what does God do? He does not bring fire down upon us. He says, "All right. Try to live without Me and see what happens." The result is unrighteousness.

America is moving in a direction of independence from God. It is about to reach the end of its resources, and God patiently allows this wonderful country to go the way it wants to go.

Paul was like that, himself. He was a Pharisee. He had become quite successful in life. Philippians 3:4-6 tells us he was a pure-blooded Jew. He was circumcised on the eighth day. He was zealous for God. He was blameless regarding the righteousness of the law, until God opened his eyes and revealed his sin problem.

The question is, "Have we lost confidence in ourselves?" This is why God allows man to live independently. He allows man to reach the end of his resources. The question is, "Have we reached the end of our resources? Have we realized that our only hope is in Jesus Christ and His righteousness?"

This is Paul's purpose in describing the sin problem. We do not have to learn about it the hard way. The Word of God makes it very clear, "Without Me," says Jesus, "you can do nothing" (John 15:4,5).

May each of us realize that God's wrath is against the ungodliness that leads to unrighteousness. God wants us to turn back to Him. He wants us to accept Him as the only source of the hope of salvation and righteousness. Whether in terms of our standing before God or of Christian living, the formula is always the same, "Not I, but Christ."

The "Not I" is the hardest part. This is why Paul spends so much time discussing the sin problem before he introduces the gospel. He wants the reader to be established in the gospel. But before that can happen, the lesson must be learned that without Christ mankind is hopelessly lost.

Only after a person recognizes that he or she is an absolute sinner in need of a Redeemer can they appreciate the incredible good news to come.

Chapter 3

The Sin of Self-righteousness

Romans 2:1-29

Imagine sitting in the church of Rome in Paul's day while the Epistle to the Romans is first being read. The elder, scribe, or messenger who brought the letter is reading Romans 1:18-32, the passage we covered last study.

Notice that as Paul describes the wrath of God revealed against men's ungodliness and unrighteousness, a group of Jewish Christians is sitting on one side of the room.

Indeed, in Paul's day many Jews live in Rome and significant numbers have accepted Jesus as their Savior. These Jewish Christians form a large section of the church at Rome, and as they listen to this passage, they nod their heads and whisper to one another: "This Paul certainly has it right. We have always known that these Gentiles are rebellious sinners."

But then the reader begins quoting from Romans 2, and the Jewish Christians hear the words in verses 1-4: "Therefore you are inexcusable, oh man, whoever you are who judge, for in whatever you judge another you condemn yourself, for you who judge practice the same things. But we know that the judgment of God is according to truth against those who practice such things. And do you think…that you will escape the judgment of God? Or do you despise the riches of His goodness, forbearance, and long-suffering, not knowing that the goodness of God leads you to repentance?"

"He seems to be talking about us. We who are Jews!" they begin to murmur. "How can he write about us like this? Surely he must mean somebody else."

But the reading continues, and in verse 17 these Jewish Christians hear the words: "Indeed you are called a Jew, and rest on the law, and make your boast in God."

In his first section, dealing with the sin problem (Romans 1:18-32), Paul describes a terrible picture of the Gentile world. The Gentiles are ungodly. They have deliberately suppressed the truth about God. They have made their own gods. They worship themselves and their own ideas. They live in sin.

The Jewish Dilemna

But he then changes the focus from the Gentiles to the Jews. Why does he distinguish between the two groups? Because the Jews are in a very special position. The Gentiles have knowledge of God, but it is an implicit knowledge revealed to them through nature and inner conviction. The Jews, on the other hand, have a direct revelation from God. Paul mentions in Romans 3:2 that God had given His oracles to the Jews. God had revealed Himself to them through His law, through Moses, and through other prophets in a very explicit way.

But, tragically, the Jews are relying for salvation on their knowledge of the law and the special position God has given them. They see themselves as God's covenant people. They look on the Gentiles as sinners. They feel that because God has given them a special position, that they are a special people; that because they have the law in explicit form, that they are better than the Gentiles. They believe that these things, in and of themselves, make them acceptable to God. But Paul is now saying the opposite—that these things do not make them special at all before God.

What is the Jews' problem? Where have they gone wrong? Their history has been recorded for our benefit and we must ask, "Can we learn lessons from their mistakes?" Indeed, we can.

We read in 1 Corinthians 10:11 where Paul says that whatsoever happened to them was recorded in Scripture for our benefit, upon whom the ends of the world are come.

So, what is the Jews' problem in Rome? Of what are they ignorant? Clearly there are three areas.

No Advantage

First, the Jews are ignorant that mere possession of the law—the truth—and mere knowledge of God's revealed will cannot make them righteous and acceptable. The fact that they know the law of God does not improve their situation.

Suppose in today's world we were to break a law and stand before a judge and demand, "Why are you accusing us? We know the law!"

More than likely, the judge would say, "The fact that you know the law puts you in a worse position, because you are better informed than the person who does not have knowledge of the law."

The Jews' knowledge of the law did not make them better than the Gentiles. Notice how Paul touches the heart of the problem in Romans

2:13: "For not the hearers of the law are just in the sight of God, but the doers of the law will be justified."

Mere knowledge of the law saves no one. The law says, "Only when you obey perfectly and continuously can you be saved." If we want to be saved by the law, it is not enough to say, "I know the law." We must perform the law in every detail, in thought, word, and deed.

Paul uses this argument when he discusses the Jewish problem in Romans 10:5. Moses had described the righteousness of the law by writing that those who do these things shall live by them.

The law comes to us and says in so many words, "If you want to live, you must obey me perfectly." A knowledge of the truth of the law does not save anyone. Unfortunately, the Jews thought that simply possessing the law made them better than the Gentiles. They would look at the Gentiles and say, "Oh, these Gentiles. Poor people! They do not know the law of God. They don't even know the true God. We have the truth and they are outside the covenant of God. They are hopelessly lost." This is how they boasted in Paul's day.

Paul reminds them of this in Romans 2:17-20: "Indeed, you are called a Jew, and rest on the law *(that is, in the knowledge of the law)*, and make your boast in God, and know His will, and approve the things that are excellent, being instructed out of the law, and are confident that you yourself are a guide to the blind, a light to those who are in darkness, an instructor of the foolish, a teacher of babes, having the form of knowledge and truth in the law."

But in verse 21 he chides them: "You, therefore, who teach another, do you not teach yourself? You who preach that a man should not steal, do you steal? You who say, 'Do not commit adultery,' do you commit adultery?"

Referring to Israel's apostasy as recorded in Ezekiel 16:23 onward, Paul says in Romans 2:24, "The name of God is blasphemed among the Gentiles because of you."

It is not enough to say we know the truth or that we know the gospel. The question is, "Has the truth set us free?" It is no use boasting about our knowledge of the law of God if, as Paul says, we are doing the same things as the Gentile believers.

The law cannot produce righteousness in sinners. The law only demands righteousness. The knowledge of the law will not make us righteous. We human beings are legalists by nature, and even those Jews, though they are not openly doing the terrible things Paul mentions in Romans 1:18-32, are doing them secretly, in their minds.

We read in Matthew 23:5 that all the things the Jews did in Jesus' day—especially the Pharisees and Scribes—were to show how good they were. But inside they were full of rotten bones. They were whitewashed sepulchers.

Outwardly the Jews looked like holy men, and the Pharisees tied little boxes on their foreheads, containing texts of Scripture. They paraded with those boxes dangling in front of their heads, like unicorns. They tried to show how holy they were. They prayed and gave alms publicly.

Paul is saying that it is not enough to simply know the truth. It is not enough to outwardly observe the law. There must be an inward solution.

The Best Is Not Enough

The second problem the Jews have is that they believe that keeping the law to the best of their ability is sufficient. They fail to heed what James 2:10 says, in effect: "If we have broken one of these commandments, we have broken them all because the law is a unit. If we fail in even one point, we come under condemnation of the whole law."

A church elder in Africa once told me, "Pastor, I have overcome by the grace of God most of my sins and I am living a good life. But I still cling to one or two sins. Surely God cannot bring His wrath against me for one or two sins, considering how much I have overcome and given up."

I replied, "Brother, if you are depending on the law for your salvation; if you are depending on your performance, on your good deeds, and what you have given up for your salvation, and break the law even in one small point, you have failed."

Matthew 19 illustrates this with the story of a young man who comes to Jesus and says, "Good Master (*notice he does not say Messiah, but Teacher*), what good thing must I do to earn eternal life?"

Jesus tells him that if he wants to go to heaven by his good deeds, he must observe the law. Jesus defines the law in terms of the last six commandments of the moral law, which deal with our relationship with our fellow men. Jesus summarizes the law, "Thou shalt love they neighbor as thyself."

The young man tells Jesus that he has kept the law from childhood. What more does he lack? He hopes Jesus will pat him on the back and say, "Keep up the good works."

But instead Jesus tests him to see if he really is obeying the law: He asks him to give his wealth to the poor. In exchange, he will receive the wealth of Christ. What a deal!

But the young man goes home sorrowful. Evidently he is not keeping the law, for he is not treating others as he treats himself. If we break the law in one point, we are lost, for the law is rigid and demands perfect obedience on every point—thought, word, and deed.

We need to be careful not to misunderstand Paul. Here he is discussing the law as a method of salvation, what he calls "the works of the law." When we study Romans 13, we will discover that Paul sees the law as a standard of Christian living. The fruit of justification by faith is holy living, and this holy living is in harmony with the law. But here in Romans 2, Paul is discussing the law as a means of salvation, and in other places, such as Galatians 3:10, he says, "Cursed is the one who does not keep the law to do all the things that the law requires."

The moment we use the law as a means of salvation, the law demands from us perfect obedience. The Jews went wrong because they were ignorant that they had to keep the law in every detail, continuously, if they were to be saved by keeping it.

Spiritual Renewal

This brings us to the Jews' third important point of failure. The Jews of Paul's day are correct in saying they are experts in the letter of the law. But they fail to see what the law demands in terms of the inward man—that is, the spirit of man. Unlike human laws, the law of God not only requires perfect performance, it requires perfect motives. Any act that is done by a man—even an outwardly good act, if motivated by egocentric concerns—is condemned by the law. This is the sin of self-righteousness.

The Pharisees would stand up and proclaim to all that they had never murdered anyone. But Jesus says in Matthew 5:21-24: "You may not have committed the act of murder, but if you hate somebody in your heart without a cause, you have murdered that person in the eyes of the law."

Bear in mind that at the time Jesus made this statement, the Jews were planning to kill Him. Keeping the law, then, is not only a question of outward performance—the letter of the law. Paul himself had been a victim of Judaism before his conversion.

In Romans 7:7 Paul says, "I had not known sin, but by the law." Paul was raised a Pharisee and learned to obey the rules his church had laid down. But now that his eyes are opened, he sees that the law demands more than perfect performance. Notice the commandment Paul quotes in Romans 7:7: "Thou shalt not covet." Coveting has nothing to do with overt acts. God does not only look at the act; He looks at the motives.

If we covet someone else's property or wife, even though we may never act out these desires, in the eyes of God's law we have sinned.

Those who plan to do something good so they may have a star in their crowns or show others how good they are, are sinning in God's eyes. The prophet, in Isaiah 64:6, says that all our righteousness is as filthy rags. God gave the Jews the law which is, in principle, a revelation of His character. To produce the character of God they needed to acquire a nature in the image of God. But because of the fall of Adam, they no longer possessed that nature.

The moment we try to keep the law of God in our own strength, we have to do what the Jews are doing in Romans 2. We have to take the law of God (which is as high as God Himself) and reduce it to rules of "do's" and "don'ts" that we can outwardly keep. Then, we must convince ourselves—in effect, fool ourselves—that in doing so we are keeping the law (Matthew 15:1-3).

Any act that is done outwardly with the wrong motive, no matter how good it is, is sin in God's eyes. If we sit in church, thinking of how we will transact business for ourselves, we may physically be in the church, but our minds are on business. We are far from God. This is why the key text for this study is Romans 2:28 and 29: "For he is not a Jew who is one outwardly, nor is that circumcision which is outward in the flesh; but he is a Jew who is one inwardly and circumcision is that of the heart (*a spiritual, not a literal matter*), in the Spirit, and not in the letter; whose praise is not from men but from God."

The Jews were doing many good things so that they would be praised by men. But the true Christian is one whose praise is not of men but of God. God reads the mind more than the act. The one who is truly keeping the law is the one who is loving his neighbor as himself. To do this, in and of ourselves, is impossible. We need the gift of God's love and the Holy Spirit to make this a reality. This gift comes only to those who are standing on the platform of justification by faith alone in Jesus Christ.

Paul says in Romans 7:6: "But now we (*the believers*) have been delivered from the law (*legalism*)." We have been delivered from that system by which we cannot save ourselves under the law, "having died to what we were held by, so that we should serve in the newness of the spirit and not in the oldness of the letter."

Paul is demolishing the platform on which the Jews were standing, depending on their law-keeping to reach heaven. The Jews were also depending on circumcision. Paul says in Romans 2:25, in effect, "For circumcision is indeed profitable if you keep the law; but if you are a breaker of the law, your circumcision has become uncircumcision."

In other words, if we have been circumcised and have failed to keep the law, circumcision does not help us. If we have made circumcision a way to heaven and want to be accepted by God, but are failing to keep the whole law (which is what "under law" means), our circumcision is of no value.

Useless Good Works

Paul would say much the same things to us, if we were depending for salvation on things we had done or were doing. For example, the act of baptism by water does not save us. Belonging to a church does not save us. Giving clothes to the poor and food to the hungry, in and of themselves does not save us. These are good things, if we have a right relationship with Christ. Without this relationship, however, they are useless (Matthew 7: 21-23).

Having our names in the books of a Christian church cannot qualify us for heaven. Having Christian parents does not guarantee salvation. Even if our grandparents were pillars of the church and pioneers of a missionary movement, their achievements cannot help us. The Bible makes it very clear that God has no grandchildren. Every believer must accept Jesus Christ personally. It matters not where we have come from or who we are. God is no respecter of persons (Acts 10:34).

Paul explains to the Jews, in Romans 2:14, that those Gentiles who do not know the law, but by nature do the things contained in the law, have the law in themselves. In other words, some Gentiles are closer to God than the Jews—a devastating thought. If Paul had read Romans 2:14-16 personally to the Jews, they would have stood up and killed him. We read that this is what they later tried to do. They laid their hands on him and said, "This is the man who is against our people" (Acts 21:28).

In Romans 2 Paul is destroying every confidence that men have in themselves, Jew or Gentile, for he cannot deliver the gospel to them unless he first destroys their self-righteousness. Those who are depending on good works and legal fulfillment of the law for salvation have no hope.

In our next study, Paul will summarize and conclude the study of the universal sin problem. What we have been covering is a dark, dismal, hopeless picture for both Jews and Gentiles. But Paul must do this to prepare us for the incredibly good news to come.

CHAPTER 4

The Universal Sin Problem

Romans 3:1-20

We have been examining the sin problem as explained by the apostle Paul in Romans 1:18 to Romans 2:29, where he clearly shows that both Gentiles and Jews are sinners.

Now we conclude this study by turning to Romans 3:9-20, as Paul finalizes his presentation of the sin problem and prepares to introduce us to the gospel.

Paul began in Romans 1:18 by telling us that the wrath of God is revealed from heaven against all ungodliness and unrighteousness of man. Then he proves that humanity by nature is anti-God. Though mankind knows about God, human beings by nature turn their backs to Him and try to live without Him. The result is increasing unrighteousness.

As Paul penned this first section on the sin problem, evaluating the Gentile world under sin, he could imagine the Jews in the congregation nodding their heads in agreement.

But in Romans 2, Paul turns his attention to the Jews—to his own kin—and tells them they are no better than the Gentiles, even though they have an advantage. In effect he chides them, "Yes, you have the oracles of God, but the fact that you have the knowledge of the law has not made you any better than the Gentiles" (Romans 3:1-8).

Now, having painted a dark, dismal, hopeless picture of both Jews and Gentiles, he brings the whole matter to a conclusion in Romans 3:9-20. In these last few verses about the sin problem, Paul describes an ancient truth that applies to us even today.

Goodness Without God

A few years back, a scientific survey on religious preferences was taken by a Christian denomination in three major cities in the United States— Pittsburgh, Des Moines, and Seattle.

In Seattle only one-third of those interviewed were affiliated with a church, and most believed that human beings could live good and proper lives without a formal religious structure. And what was true of Seattle was true only to a slightly lesser extent in the other two cities.

Oh! How they needed to read and understand what Paul is saying in Romans 1:18 to 3:1-20. These participants felt that through proper human interactions—through proper education—people could live full and morally upright lives. In other words they could live good lives without God.

If what these people said is true, the question we must ask them is "Why is crime rampant in our country? Why is lawlessness so pervasive, even among so-called 'decent' citizens?" Let us see what the Bible has to say in Romans 3:9-20.

We will first examine this passage in a general way and then in detail to understand what Paul is saying about our universal sin problem. Unless we learn what Paul is saying about man's total depravity, we can never appreciate what it truly means to go to God as we are. From head to foot there is nothing good in us. Salvation is entirely a gift from our Lord, Jesus Christ, and that gift is acceptable only when man recognizes his total sinfulness.

Paul is now concluding the subject he began discussing in Romans 1:18, "What then, are we better than they?" The "we" refers to the Jews; the "they" refers to the Gentiles. Paul is asking whether the Jews, discussed in Romans 2, are better than the Gentiles, discussed in Chapter 1:18-32.

Paul's answer, in Romans 3:9, is: "For we have previously proved or charged both Jews and Gentiles that they are all under sin." Then, to defend his conclusion, he puts together a stream of quotations from the Old Testament, mainly from Psalms but including Ecclesiastes, Proverbs, and Isaiah. All these quotations say basically the same thing—that all are unrighteous.

Romans 3:10 and 12 confirms that there is none righteous, not even one. There is none who does good, not even one. Mankind, in and of itself, is a slave to sin. This is what the phrase "under sin" means.

Once Paul has proven this point, he concludes in verse 19 and 20: "Now we know that whatsoever the law says, it says to those who are under the law that every mouth may be stopped and all the world may become guilty before God. Therefore (*in view of these facts*) by the deeds of the law (*by the works of the law*) no flesh (*no human being*) will be justified in his sight."

In other words, no one will ever make it to heaven on their own, whether Jew or Gentile. Every human being will reach heaven only because of Jesus Christ and Him crucified. By the works of the law, no flesh will be justified in God's sight.

All the law can do, says Paul in Romans 3:20, is give us the knowledge of sin and convince us that we are sinners.

Let us look at this passage in more detail, starting with Verse 9: "What then, are we Jews better than they (*the Gentiles*)?"

Paul has told us earlier that the Gentiles have a knowledge of the law but that this knowledge is not explicit, but implicit in their consciences. They know in their consciences what is right and what is wrong. But the Jews, over and above this natural knowledge, have the specific knowledge of the law given to them through Moses.

This extra, special knowledge, however, does not make the Jews any better than the Gentiles. Instead of the law convincing the Jews that they are sinners in need of a Savior, it has done the very opposite. It has made them proud, self-righteous people. So they have lost the blessings of the law, which was intended to lead them to Jesus Christ (Galatians 3:24).

Are we today any better than the Jews of Paul's day? Have we become a proud, self-righteous people? Many Christians look down upon unbelievers as lost sinners. But remember, all are sinners whose only hope is in the grace of our Lord, Jesus Christ. Paul is saying that, ultimately, there is no distinction between Jews and Gentiles, even though one has an advantage over the other. Both Jews and Gentiles are under sin.

This brings us to Paul's next point about the term "under sin." We no longer use this phrase in modern English, though it was common in the slave society in which Paul lived. The word "under" was a term used to define a slave's relationship to his master—that of being ruled, or dominated.

Paul is saying, then, that all mankind—whether Jew or Gentile—is dominated, or ruled, by sin. Paul says in Romans 7:14: "The law is spiritual; but I (*the "I" here is generic*) am unspiritual, sold as a slave to sin."

We are by nature slaves to sin. Paul has proven this without a shadow of doubt, pointing out that this is what God has clearly revealed in the Old Testament.

The Jews had knowledge of God, but they were doing precisely the same things the Gentiles were doing. When we look at Jewish history as recorded in the Old Testament, we find that though God revealed Himself to them in a most wonderful way, their history is one of turning their backs on God and worshipping idols.

Whether we are Jew or Gentile, in our fallen, sinful condition we have a tendency to turn away from God. As Romans 3:12 says, "They have all gone out of the way." Mankind, as in Paul's day, is today trying to live independently of God. They have become altogether unprofitable, Paul says. There is none who does good, not even one. They cannot understand their actual condition, so God has to open their eyes.

Then, in Romans 3:19, having given a list of quotations from the Old Testament proving our sinfulness, Paul says, "Now we know that whatever the law says, it says to those who are under the law, that every mouth may be stopped and all the world may become guilty before God."

Has the law stopped our mouths? Have we come to the knowledge of our total sinfulness? Paul is saying that the whole world is under the law, as well as under sin. So the whole world stands guilty before God.

We ask, then, once again, "Has the law silenced our mouths?" This is the main function of the law—to silence our self-righteousness. But it is not the only function, for the law was given by God as a standard of Christian living. Therefore, we must never read the law without reading its preamble. In Exodus 20, God says in effect to the Jews of the Exodus, "I am the Lord that delivered you from the house of bondage, therefore, this is how I want you to live."

Unless we are delivered from the bondage of sin, we cannot live a life in harmony with God's law, for we are by nature slaves to sin.

Paul has already clearly said that the gospel is not for good people—or even people who see themselves as half good, or three-quarters good, or as doing their best. The gospel is for men and women who realize their total sinfulness, their total depravity.

Has the law silenced our mouths, or are we still boasting about how good we are? This is the question. If it hasn't silenced our mouths—if we have not become undone by the law—it is useless for us to hear the good news of salvation, for it will only become a stumbling block to us.

Paul is very forthright. The law must silence our mouths. The Jew who stood up and said, "I thank God I am not like that publican," will never accept the gospel. It is a stumbling block to him. The gospel is an obstacle in the pathway of any who thinks he is good or says, "I thank God I am a good man. I pay my tithe. I go to church. I give alms to the poor. I help the needy. I am an honest Christian." No, all those good things are profitable only if we are standing in a right relationship to God.

Paul says that nobody has ever been able to keep the law. By this he means the spirit of the law. Therefore, by the deeds of the law, no human being will ever make it to heaven.

We need to pause here to ask, Why did God give the Jews the law over their conscience, convicting them of good and evil? Why did God sidetrack them on their journey to Canaan and lead them in a direction almost opposite to the one leading up the Sinai Peninsula? Why did He, through Moses, give them the law, if it was not to be an added requirement for salvation?

Paul's answer is that the law was given that they might recognize that they were sinners in need of grace. God never gave the law as a means of salvation. Nowhere in Scripture does God ever cite the law as a means of salvation. He gave the law that we human beings, Jews and Gentiles, might have knowledge of sin. Using the law as a means of salvation is a perverted gospel.

Some Christians today believe that from Moses to Christ God gave the law as a method of salvation. They say that because this failed, God did away with that system and introduced salvation by grace through Jesus Christ.

The problem with such reasoning is that the Bible only prescribes one way for mankind's salvation—the gospel of our Lord, Jesus Christ. The law was never given to save mankind. In Galatians 2:16, Paul reminds Peter, "By the works of the law, no flesh will be justified in God's sight" (see also Romans 3:20).

God never gave the law as a means of salvation. We must emphasize this, for too many today think that salvation is by faith *plus* works—grace *plus* law keeping. Yes, genuine justification by faith does produce works, but works contribute not one iota to salvation.

A second misconception about the law is that God gave it to retain our salvation in Christ. Some Christians believe that though they are justified by faith, to preserve that salvation they must obey the law. In other words, they believe God saved them, forgave them, and gave them the Holy Spirit. But now God says to them, "I want you to be good; otherwise I will punish you." No, from beginning to end, man is saved by faith alone (Romans 1:17).

In Galatians 3:17-25 Paul asks the Galatian Christians who had accepted a perverted gospel (salvation by faith, *plus* works), "Why did God give the law 430 years after He promised salvation as a gift to Abraham and to his seed?"

The answer is simple: The law was given that humanity might have knowledge of its sin and be convinced of its transgressions.

Jeremiah 17:9 says in effect, "Our hearts are deceitful, so God has to expose our sins." God has to show us that we have the nature of sin, and He does this by opening up the lid of our respectability, as mentioned in our last study, and showing us what we truly are inside.

Paul knows this through his own experience as a Jew. He was reared with the idea that he could save himself through the law. He brings this out in Romans 7:7-13. He had not fully understood the true function of the law, as a Pharisee, but in Romans 7:9, he says, "When the commandment came (*when I understood the true purpose of the law*), sin revived and I died."

He had been taught in Judaism that the law was to be the means of salvation, but after he discovered the true meaning of the law, it became the means of his death. The law was not responsible for his death, but the sin which the law condemns (1 Corinthians 15:56).

When we talk to people who have never known the law of God, they always define sin as an act. But the law brings out that sin is not only an act, it is a cherished desire.

Paul says in Romans 7:7: "For I would not have known covetousness unless the law had said, "You shall not covet." Coveting has nothing to do with an act. It is a cherished, sinful desire. When Paul realized that sin begins as a concept in the mind, he recognized that there was no way he could save himself.

Jesus clearly teaches this in Matthew 5 in the Sermon on the Mount. The Pharisee stands up and says, "I have never committed murder. I have never committed adultery." But Jesus answers, "If you look at a woman to lust, even though you may not commit the act, you have already sinned against the law of adultery." In Romans 5:20, Paul asks, "Why did the law enter the promise? It entered that sin may abound."

God gave the law to open the eyes of the human race to the reality that we, the children of Adam, are sinners. This is the third reason why God gave the law. It was to show us that sin is more than an act. It is a cherished desire.

Paul tells us in Romans 3:19 that every one of us, without exception, belongs on Death Row. The only way we can escape from the prison cell is through Jesus Christ.

In Romans 7:13-14, we now come to the fourth purpose of the law. God gave the law to remove sin from its hiding place. Sin is a deceiver and a liar, and the law opens our eyes to the fact that we are sinners, when before we deceived ourselves that we were righteous. The law exposes our exceeding sinfullness. If it hasn't yet, then we are still boasting, "I may be bad, but not that bad."

The law tells us that we are not just bad, but that we are totally sinful. Our only hope is Jesus Christ and Him crucified.

As we conclude this study of Romans 3:9-20, verse 19 tells us we are all under law. Verse 9 has already told us we are all under sin. Therefore, man is incapable of saving himself. Before Paul introduces the wonderful gospel, he convinces us that we need a Savior.

Paul has shown that we cannot save ourselves. We need to come to the point where we can say with Isaiah, as he saw God lifted up in His glory, "I am undone. I am a man of unclean lips" Isaiah 6:5.

Paul has shown that we are all sinners in need of a Savior. At last we are ready to begin studying the everlasting gospel of Jesus Christ, where we find the solution to our sin problem. For Jesus has told us, "You shall know the truth and the truth shall set you free" (John 8:32,36).

As we study the gospel in the next chapter, let us search with open minds, as we recognize that we are sinners, savable only by grace.

Chapter 5

The Gospel Introduced

Romans 3:21-23

We've studied Paul's explanation of the universal sin problem and in Romans 1:18 learned that the wrath of God is revealed from heaven against all men's ungodliness and unrighteousness. We then discovered the Gentile world's problem of ungodliness—of their natural desire to live without God.

In Romans 2:1 through 3:8 we turned our attention to the Jews, where Paul tells his countrymen that they are no better than the Gentiles. In Romans 3:9-20 he says that ultimately, before God, there is no difference between Jews and Gentiles. It makes no difference whether we have an explicit or implicit knowledge of the law, for both Jews and Gentiles are under sin. In verse 9 Paul says: "What then? Are we Jews better than they (*the Gentiles*)?" (KJV). The answer is, "No," there is none righteous, there is none that does good.

In Romans 3:19 and 20 Paul concludes that the whole world stands guilty, condemned before God under His law. By the works of the law, no flesh (person) will be justified. All the law can do is convince us—show us—that we are sinners.

Incredibly Good News

But now, from Romans 3:21 onward, Paul proclaims the incredibly good news of salvation.

He introduces the gospel with these words: "But now the righteousness of God apart from the law is revealed, being witnessed by the Law and the Prophets." The only way we can make it to heaven and attain to righteousness is by faith in the righteousness obtained for us by God in Jesus Christ.

In Galatians 3:17-26 Paul asks those who had accepted a perverted Gospel, "Why did God give the law 430 years after He promised salvation to Abraham and his seed as a gift?" God gave it, not as an added requirement for salvation, says Paul, but that man's confidence in himself might be totally destroyed. He mentions in Philippians 3:3 that a Christian is a person who rejoices in Christ and has no confidence in the flesh—that is, in his own human nature or ability.

The 11 verses in Romans 3:21-31 are crucial in this study, for here Paul reveals in a nutshell the plan of salvation. He tells how mankind is saved and how this salvation can become effective in our lives.

We will study this passage in two chapters, beginning with verses 21-23 here and verses 24-31 in Chapter 6 of this book.

"But Now"

Notice that Paul introduces the gospel with the words "But now," words we sometimes gloss over. There are at least three reasons, however, why these two words are important.

First, Paul uses these words "But now" to contrast the gospel message with the dark, dismal, hopeless picture he has painted of the human race under sin.

"But now," he is saying, there is good news. After the law has shut us up in the prison cell of Death Row with no escape, Paul says in so many words, "there is a righteousness that is available to you so that you may be set free."

The second reason the words "But now" are important are to denote a time factor. Paul wrote Romans only a few years after the birth, life, death, resurrection, and ascension of Christ. To understand what "time factor" means, notice in Romans 1:1 how Paul introduces himself and his epistle: "Paul, a servant of Jesus Christ, called to be an apostle, separated unto the gospel of God" (KJV).

In verse 2, then, he says: "Which (*that is, the gospel*) He promised before through His prophets in the Holy Scriptures."

Salvation is not an afterthought. God promised salvation to the human race the moment Adam sinned. It was a promise He repeated to Noah, Abraham, and throughout the Old Testament. Paul makes it very clear in Galatians and Romans that Abraham was saved by a promise—a promise that has now become a reality. Paul says in Romans 3:21, "But now the righteousness of God apart from the law is manifested (*or is revealed*)." Notice that he uses the past tense.

Christ makes the difference when it comes to dividing time between B.C. and A.D. This time factor is not only to be applied to the historical Christ but to each believer, for every Christian can divide his or her life into two periods—B.C. and A.D.

Before Christ, humanity stood condemned under God's law. There was no hope, peace, or assurance. It lived in fear and insecurity. "But now," that the Christians have accepted Christ, they are no longer living in that time period. They are living in the A.D. period. Christ has now become their Righteousness. He is their Surety, their Substitute, their Hope, their Peace, and their Salvation. As he pointed out to the Christians in Ephesus, they are already sitting in heavenly places in Christ Jesus (Ephesians 2:6).

The third reason these words "But now" are so important is as defenses against the fiery darts of the devil.

Suppose, for example, that the devil comes to a Christian—a believer—and by a powerful temptation causes him to fall. The devil then tempts the Christian with the thought, "You don't deserve salvation. You are not good enough." What should the Christian do? Does he remain on the ground, defeated, or does he stand up and say, "Yes, Satan. I am a sinner. I am not good enough to be saved. I don't feel righteous. I have let Christ down 'but now' it is the righteousness of God that justifies me" (1 Timothy 1:15).

Justification by faith is the most powerful weapon against the fiery darts of Satan. But more than that, justification by faith is the only pathway to victorious living. Mankind cannot make itself righteous or reach heaven by its own good works, for as we saw, it is a slave to sin, and a sinner cannot produce righteousness apart from the grace of the Lord, Jesus Christ. The gospel protects the Christian as a shield against the fiery darts of Satan.

The Righteousness of God

But now let us return to Romans 3:21 and finish the statement: "But now the righteousness of God." What does Paul mean by this? The righteousness of God was planned by God; it was promised by God; it was fulfilled by God; it is all of God. Before Adam was even created, God had already chosen us to be His children, to be righteous in His Son, from the foundation of the world (Ephesians 1:4).

In the Book of Revelation, Jesus is called the Lamb slain from the foundation of the world. God in His foreknowledge knew that Adam would sin. He knew that our first parents would fail to fulfill the command God gave them.

So, when Adam sinned and God came to visit him, Adam and Eve thought God was coming to punish them, to execute judgment. No, God did not come to punish Adam and Eve. He came to give them a promise, and He repeated this promise to Noah, to Abraham, and to all those living in Old Testament times. God fulfilled the promise in Jesus Christ so that salvation is now more than a promise. It is a reality. It is the righteousness of God, which He planned but now has fulfilled in Jesus Christ.

So let's complete the phrase with Paul: "But now the righteousness of God apart from the law is manifested."

Many Christians misinterpret the significance of the phrase "apart from the law." They believe that from Moses to Christ, God had placed mankind—especially the Jews—under the law as a method of salvation. This theology divides the Bible into dispensations, teaching that God dealt with the human race in different ways in different periods of time. It denies the fundamental unity of the Bible.

But as we read all of the Bible, we find that God offers only one means of salvation. From Adam to the last human being, all are saved the same way—by grace and faith in the righteousness of God obtained for us in Jesus Christ. The only difference is that in the Old Testament it is by faith in the promise, while in the New Testament it is by faith in the reality.

Whatever interpretation we give this phrase, "apart from the law," it must never conflict with verse 31, for Paul never contradicts himself.

Establishing the Law

Romans 3:31 says: "Do we then make void the law?" Paul is asking, "Do we do away with the law through this preaching of the doctrine of justification by faith?" The answer is a strong, "No." The King James Version of the English Bible reads, "God forbid." It is unthinkable. On the contrary, the doctrine of justification by faith establishes the law, as we shall see in the next chapter.

The following two statements give us even more help as we probe the meaning of the words "apart from the law."

The first is found in Romans 3:20. The statement "apart from the law" made in verse 21 is written in the context of verse 20, where Paul says, "Therefore by the deeds of the law no flesh will be justified in his sight."

The righteousness of God that saves us is entirely from God, and we human beings make no contribution whatever through law-keeping to that righteousness.

The second statement is found in Romans 3:28, where Paul concludes his definition of the gospel: "Therefore we conclude that a man is justified by faith apart from the deeds of the law."

The righteousness that saves us comes from God and is offered to man entirely as a free gift. It is a heavenly garment without a single thread of human devising. Romans 3:24 explains the phrase, "being justified freely." The word "freely" means without any contribution on our part.

But more than that, "freely" means given by grace. Here we see that the phrase "apart from the law" means that the righteousness of God that saves us is entirely a free gift. (Incidentally, the "being justified freely" of verse 23 applies to the "all" of verse 22—that is, both Jews and Gentiles, the entire human race).

What Is Faith?

We ask, "How can we have this righteousness? What must we do that this righteousness of God may become ours individually? Do we need to go on a pilgrimage to the Holy Land? Do we have to pay money? How do we receive this righteousness?"

The answers are found in Romans 3:22: "Even the righteousness of God which is through faith in Jesus Christ to all and on all who believe. For there is no difference."

Here Paul is saying that this righteousness of God comes through faith alone. Many Christians misunderstand and misuse the word "faith," so let's pause here to explain what the New Testament means by "faith."

There are three basic requirements—three elements—that make up genuine New Testament faith.

The first prerequisite for genuine faith is a knowledge of the gospel. In Romans 10:17 Paul says that faith comes by hearing and hearing by the Word of Christ preached. Jesus says in John 8:32: "You shall know the truth, and the truth shall make you free." By "truth" Jesus is referring to Himself (see verse 36).

Knowledge of the gospel does not come through our rationale, investigation, or the scientific method. It comes by the preaching of the Word—by the preaching of the gospel by Christians. Romans 10:15 says, "How beautiful are the feet of those who preach the gospel of peace, who bring glad tidings of good things."

Before Jesus left, having finished the redemption of the human race, He gave the disciples a great commission. We find it in Mark 16:15, 16, where He tells them, "Go into all the world and preach the gospel to every creature."

In Matthew 24:14 Jesus prophesies about His Second Coming and says, "This gospel of the kingdom shall be preached to all the world for a witness to every nation, kindred, tongue and people and then the end will come" (Revelation 14:6). God will not bring this sin-cursed world to an end nor send His Son a second time, until the world has had a chance to hear the gospel preached.

So, the first ingredient of true faith is to know the truth about the gospel. Point 2 is that we must believe this gospel. This may sound easy, until we realize that to believe the gospel is to believe God's word against our own rationale, against our own way of thinking.

Suppose a married woman passes the age of childbearing and the doctors tell her she simply can have no more children. But God tells her, "Next year you are going to have a son."

Abraham and Sarah faced this situation when Abraham was 99 years old. God told him that he was going to have a son, but his wife, Sarah, had passed the age of childbearing. The physicians had said "Impossible." But against all hope, Abraham believed (Romans 4:17). So, we have to believe, even though what God tells us seems impossible and makes no sense to us.

In 1961 I worked during my summer vacation in Kiruna, Sweden, 150 miles north of the Arctic Circle. For six weeks the sun never went below the horizon. The first night I was there, I waited till midnight to see how low the sun would go. Then I photographed the sun with my watch in the foreground. A few years later I showed this slide to some Africans on the equator, where the sun sets at approximately 6:30 all year round. One elderly man came to me and said, "Who are you fooling? I know what you did. You changed your watch to 12 o'clock and then photographed the sun at five o'clock in the afternoon, and you are telling us that it was midnight!"

If I had the money, I would have taken him to Sweden in the month of June and shown him for himself, and then he would have said he believed.

Remember Thomas. He would not believe that Jesus had risen from the dead until he actually saw and put his finger in the nail prints. Jesus said to him, "Thomas, because you have seen Me, you have believed. Blessed are those who have not seen and yet have believed" (John 20:29).

God tells us that we stand righteous in Christ. But do we believe what God is telling us?

The third requirement for genuine faith—one many Christians ignore—is obedience. In Romans 1 Paul introduces himself and his message. After introducing Jesus Christ as the Son of man, the seed of David, and the Son of God, he says that God called him unto the obedience of faith.

The word "obedience" in Romans 1:5 defines faith. In Romans 6:17, referring to the Roman Christians, Paul makes this statement: "But God be thanked that though you were the slaves of sin, yet you obeyed from the heart that form of doctrine to which you were delivered."

In Romans 10:16, addressing the Jews who have turned their backs on the gospel, Paul says that the reason they will be lost is not because God did not keep His promise, but because they did not obey the gospel. All through Paul's writings and the New Testament we find this concept—that faith includes obeying the gospel (see Galatians 5:7; 2 Thessalonians 1:6-8; 1 Peter 4:17).

But what does it mean to obey the gospel? Is it the same as obeying the law? The answer is "No." To obey the law we have to do something. But the gospel comes to us without a single "do this" or "don't do that." The gospel reaches us with the truth as it is in Jesus Christ.

To obey the gospel means to surrender our wills to God—to the truth as it is in Christ, because in Christ (as we will see later in our study of Romans 5) God rewrote our history. God put us into Christ in the incarnation and rewrote man's history in His life and death. In this new history we stand perfect, as if we had lived perfect lives. Paul tells us in 2 Corinthians 5:14 that when Christ died, all men died in Him. Obeying the gospel means accepting the death of Christ as our death.

Obeying the gospel means saying, as in Galatians 2:20, "I am crucified with Christ. Yet I am living. No, it is no longer I that I am living but it is Christ who lives in me and the life that I now live, I live by faith, by a faith obedience to the Son of God who loved me and gave Himself for me."

No Cheap Grace

When we understand the true meaning of faith, faith becomes more than simply a mental assent to truth and we will cease to find cheap grace in the Christian church. When we obey the gospel, we will live under the formula, "Not I, but Christ." And Christ is the same yesterday, today, and forever. The life He lived some 2,000 years ago He will live in us today through the indwelling of the Holy Spirit.

God's righteousness is made effective in our lives by faith alone. In Romans 3:22 and 10:12, Paul adds that "there is no distinction between Jew and Greek." This is because all have sinned and are coming short of the glory of God. Paul is making two statements, one in the past tense and one in the present continuous tense.

"All have sinned." Now, the word "sinned" means "missing the mark" of the glory of God. Paul is saying that all have sinned in the past, plus, all are sinning in the present continuous tense.

Paul will explain this in Romans 5. All sin in Adam, and this is our inheritance. But besides Adam's sin—which condemns us—we have our continual personal sins. So, whether we look at our inheritance or our performance, there is no difference between Jew and Gentile. We have no right to heaven, in terms of our performance, heritage, or standing before God. God has only one way of saving Jew and Gentile, and this is through the righteousness of Christ.

Paul says in Romans 3:22,23: "For there is no difference, for all have sinned and fall short of the glory of God."

Our hope is built on nothing less than Jesus Christ and His righteousness. When we accept this righteousness by faith, we pass from death to life, as Jesus declares in John 5:24. It is extremely important that we understand what Paul is saying in this wonderful message of the gospel.

We have been silenced by the law and are being led by Paul to accept the gift of God by faith, so that we may know that heaven is ours—not because of our performance, but because of the righteousness of God which He obtained for us in Jesus Christ.

Chapter 6
The Law and the Gospel
Romans 3:24-31

Having painted a dismal picture of the human race under sin in Romans 1:18 - 3:20, Paul introduces the glorious gospel of Jesus Christ in Romans 3:21-31 with two wonderful words, "But now."

"But now," in spite of its total sinfulness, God has obtained a righteousness for sinful man, both Jews and Gentiles, that fully qualifies them for heaven—a righteousness by faith alone.

In our last study we looked at Romans 3:20-23. Now we turn to the second part of this glorious passage, verses 24-31, where we discover some very important truths about the gospel of the Lord, Jesus Christ.

In Romans 3:24 Paul tells us three facts about the righteousness of God now available through His Son, contained in these words: "Being justified freely by his grace through the redemption which is in Christ Jesus."

The Word "Justified"

The first truth Paul shares in this verse is that the righteousness of God justifies us. The word "justified" is a key word in the New Testament and primarily has a legal connotation, used in courts by judges.

An Old Testament example is found in Deuteronomy 25:1, where God is giving counsel through Moses to Israel: "If there is a dispute or a controversy between men and they come to court that the judge may judge them, justifying the righteous and condemning the wicked." Notice, they come to court. It is a legal matter and, according to the law, the judge justifies those who have obeyed the law and condemns those who have disobeyed.

So the word "justified," like the word "condemned," is a legal term. With this in mind, in Romans 3:24 we read that the righteousness of God in Christ "justifies freely." Justifies whom? As mentioned last chapter, the word "justified" is linked with the word "all" of verse 23. The word "justified" in verse 24 is therefore an objective truth applying to both Jews and Gentiles—the whole human race. This is God's supreme gift to all mankind and is made effective individually by faith. The moment a person believes in Jesus Christ and accepts Him by faith, God declares that person righteous.

The believer may say, "But I do not feel righteous, and I know I am not righteous." But God declares believers righteous, not because of their performance or feelings of righteousness, but because of His righteousness. It is the righteousness of God that justifies them (Romans 4:5).

Remember Romans 3:19, where Paul tells us that according to the law the whole world stands guilty before God. This means that the law of God condemns everyone, both Jews and Gentiles.

But the moment a person believes in Jesus Christ, the righteousness of God, which He obtained for all men in Jesus Christ, is made effective and the believer stands justified by faith.

The word "justified" in Romans 3:24 refers to what Christ accomplished for the entire human race on the cross. This is God's free gift to all mankind. At the moment we believe we come subjectively under the umbrella of justification by faith. In John 5:24, Jesus, addressing His disciples, says: "Most assuredly (*'Verily, verily,' KJV*) I say to you, He who hears My word and believes in him who sent Me has everlasting life, and shall not come into judgment, but has passed from death into life (*in other words, from condemnation to justification*)."

Yes, in ourselves we stand condemned to death. But in Christ we have passed from condemnation to justification. This is the glorious message of justification by faith. The moment we believe, the righteousness of Christ becomes effective to us. We have passed from death to life, from condemnation to justification.

More Than Unmerited Favor

Second, in Romans 3:24, notice that this justification comes freely: "Being justified freely." It comes without cost. Isaiah says it is without money and without price (Isaiah 55:1). It is a free gift to the entire human race. For Paul tells us: "Being justified freely by his grace." What does he mean by the phrase "by his grace?" The word "grace" gives a very definite connotation to the word "free."

The primary meaning of the word "grace" is "unmerited or undeserved favor" (Ephesians 1:7). But grace as used here refers to the obedience of Christ, His life and death. When the word "grace" is used to mean unmerited favor, it actually implies more than simply undeserved rewards. When we give our children gifts on special occasions, it may be unmerited favor but it is not grace.

For example, suppose my neighbor is away from home I break into his house, smash his furniture, and beat up his wife.

He returns home later in the day and finds his wife on the floor, beaten and bloody, and his furniture smashed.

"What happened! Who did this!" he cries. She whispers in pain, pointing toward my house, "He did it. The neighbor man did it."

So the husband rushes from his house to confront me. I see him coming and I say to myself, "He's coming to get revenge." I notice he's hiding something behind his back, and I imagine he has a weapon—perhaps a gun. Shall I run or stand like a man?

I decide to confront him, confident I can disarm him before he injures me. He arrives at my door and I open it. But instead of trying to shoot me, he says with deep concern and love, "Why did you do this to us? I am your friend."

Then from behind his back he reveals, not a gun, but a check for $1,000: "Friend, here's a gift for you in spite of what you've done to my wife and my house." That check is far more than a simple, unmerited gift. That check is grace!

Grace is not only doing an undeserved favor. Grace is doing a special favor for an enemy—for somebody who hates you. We imagine the scene as Jesus is crucified and see that some are spitting on Him. But Jesus says, "Father, forgive them." This is grace!

When we come to Romans 5:10, we will discover that while we were still enemies of God, we were reconciled to Him by the death of His Son. This is grace! What incredibly good news! God does not come to us and say, "You need to straighten up your life first. Show Me evidence that you are trying to be good, then I will justify you." No! God justifies us freely by His grace.

Just Redemption

But now we move on to an extremely important third point. In Romans 3:24 we read that God not only justifies us freely and graciously, but that this justification comes through the redemption that is in Christ. It is here that redemption and creation part company. The New Testament clearly declares that Jesus created this world. He spoke and it happened (see John 1:3). Jesus did not have to depend on preexisting matter, according to Hebrews 11:3. We believe that the worlds were created without any preexisting matter, for God's breath is energy. He spoke and it happened. But God could not redeem us by simply speaking. God could not come to us and say, "Yes, I know you have rebelled against Me. I know you are my enemies, but I love you in spite of your rebellious attitude. I love you unconditionally, and since I am Sovereign, I will forgive your sins by excusing them."

God cannot do this, because the God we worship is also a holy God. He is a just God. Even though He loves us unconditionally, He cannot redeem us—He cannot justify us—by bypassing His law. His law tells us, as we find in Ezekiel 18:20, that the soul that sins, it must die.

But the same law says that without shedding of blood there can be no remission of sins (Hebrews 9:22). Suppose a policeman catches us speeding wildly down the highway but lets us go without writing us a ticket. The officer may indeed be doing us a good turn, but in the end he's being unjust, unless he himself volunteers to pay the fine for the ticket we deserve.

God, unlike the forgiving policeman, is a just God and cannot forgive us by simply excusing our sins. Yes, God's justification is free and gracious, but extremely costly to Him, for we are told that we are justified through the redemption that is in Christ.

If God were to give us each a million dollars, wonderful as that might be, it would cost Him nothing, for God can speak and turn stones into gold. But He cannot justify us by simply speaking. Some liberal theologians teach that God did not have to send His Son and that Jesus did not have to die on the cross to forgive us.

These theologians tell us that God is Sovereign; He is Love; He can forgive us by bypassing His law. They call it the Moral Influence Theory. They say that Jesus died only to influence us—that He really did not have to die to save us. This is not the teaching of the New Testament.

Since the days of the apostles, the Christian church has come up with many theories about the atonement. These include the Satisfaction Theory, the Ransom Theory, and the Moral Influence Theory. Each claims to have the correct understanding of the atonement. But the atonement is too big an event to be locked up by any one theory. We will spend eternity wrestling with the atonement. Each of these theories has an aspect of truth. They become wrong—they become heresy—only when they deny the others.

The truth is that God's love and justice both met at the cross. It was at the cross that God demonstrated His love. But it was likewise at the cross that God became legally empowered to justify the ungodly.

This is what Paul brings out in Romans 3:25 and 26: "Whom God displayed publicly as a propitiation in his blood through faith. This was to demonstrate his righteousness because in the forbearance of God, he passed over the sins previously committed for the demonstration, I say, of his righteousness at the present time that he might be just and the justifier of the one who has faith in Jesus" (NASB).

Propitiation—Its Meaning

These two verses are difficult, except as we recall that in Romans 3:24, Paul says we were justified freely through His grace, through the redemption that is in Jesus Christ. Now, in Romans 3:25-27, he tells us that this justification, which is freely and graciously bestowed, is also a propitiation. The word "propitiation," in the pagan culture, meant "appeasement" of an angry god. But in New Testament Christianity, "propitiation" is used in a different sense, in that it is not we who offer up a sacrifice to appease an angry God. We read, instead, that God was in Christ reconciling the world unto Himself. It is God who offers Himself as a sacrifice, in the person of Jesus Christ.

In the Old Testament the word "propitiation" refers to the mercy seat, placed on top of the ark of the covenant. In Leviticus 16:15,16 and Hebrews 9:5, we find that this word simply means a mercy seat that covers the condemnation of the tablets of the law that lie within the ark.

The Meaning of "Blood"

This brings us to the next point—the word "blood." It is through the blood of Christ that He becomes our propitiation. In other words, it is through the blood of Christ that our sins are expiated, canceled, or taken away.

What does the New Testament mean by the word "blood?" As in the Old Testament, it refers to life. It symbolizes life. Shed blood denotes life laid down in death.

In Leviticus 17:11, we read: "For the life of the flesh is in the blood and I have given it to you...to make an atonement for your sins." So shed blood means life that is laid down in death for the remission of sins. This is what Jesus did on the cross. When He introduced The Last Supper, He took the cup and said, "This is My blood" (or "This is My life") which is shed for the remission of sins, laid down in death for the remission of sins because the wages of sin is death.

Now let us look again at Romans 3:25 and notice that Paul says that the blood of Christ overlooks the sins that were previously committed. This is how the New American Standard Version puts it: "He says to us that in the past, out of forbearance, God passed over the sins that were previously committed."

Paul is not talking here of the believers' past sins, as some interpret this passage. Both New and Old Testaments tell us clearly that some men in the Old Testament were forgiven by God. Noah was forgiven by God, Abraham was forgiven by God, as was Moses. But was that forgiving legal? Actually, No. God forgave them out of forbearance—out of kindness—because the blood of bulls and goats, as brought out in Hebrews 9 and 10, could not forgive them.

God forgave them out of patience, out of kindness. But since the cross, God becomes legally empowered to forgive men, because the blood of Christ actually meets the wages of sin on behalf of mankind.

We read in Romans 3:26 that God's sacrifice through Jesus Christ demonstrates His justice so that He is both just and the justifier of those who believe.

No Legalism

In Romans 3:27 Paul reminds the believer that there is no boasting in justification by faith. Paul does say, in 1 Corinthians 1:31, that Christians can indeed boast, but only in Christ and for what He has done.

But here, in Romans 3:27, there is no human boasting, for salvation is entirely a gift through the grace of our Lord, Jesus Christ, received by faith.

Paul therefore concludes in Romans 3:28, "for we maintain that a man is justified by faith apart from the works of the law." We must pause here, because many misunderstand the phrase "works of the law." Our English word "legalism" (which means using the law as a method of salvation) has no equivalent in New Testament Greek.

But whenever we come across the phrase "works of the law," especially in Pauline writings, we can be assured that the author is referring to use of the law as a method, or means, of salvation—that is, legalism. Paul, however, upholds the law as a standard of Christian living (Romans 13:8-10).

But here Paul tells us that justification by faith comes entirely from God, with no contribution on our part. Our law-keeping contributes nothing whatever to our salvation. This, he says in Romans 3:29, 30, applies to both Jews and Gentiles.

Then in verse 31 he concludes with an important question: "Do we then nullify the law through faith?" The answer is, "May it never be," or, as the King James Version says, "God forbid. On the contrary, we establish the law."

Romans 3:31 has brought confusion to some Christians because of its use of the word "faith." Normally we use the word "faith" to refer to the believer's response to the gospel. But here the word "faith" is preceded in the original by the definite article "the." Paul is really asking, "Do we make void, or do we nullify, the law through the faith."

Here the word "faith" refers, not to the believer's faith, but to the doctrine of justification by faith which Paul has just explained.

Paul tells us in Romans 3:28 that we are justified by faith apart from our deeds of the law. Now he asks a question (for he is aware that some believers in Rome—especially Jewish believers—will accuse him of undermining the law or undermining justification by faith in terms of the legal aspect of the law). So he asks, "Does this doctrine of justification by faith bypass the law, do away with the law, or nullify the law?" The answer is, "…unthinkable. God forbid. It can never be so." Why? Because God is a just God. The gospel establishes the just requirements of the law of God.

Paul does not mean that our performance establishes the law, for our performance never measures up to the full demands of the law. The law, after all, demands two unattainable things from every sinner—perfect obedience and perfect justice. No human being born under sin can measure up to this standard.

If the doctrine of justification by faith establishes the law, the question is how? We will study this in detail when we reach Romans 5.

In Summary

But for now let us summarize. First, God had to qualify Jesus to be our Savior. He did this by uniting the divinity of Jesus to the human race that needed redeeming. At the incarnation, God the Son and humanity became one. They were joined together through the mystery of the incarnation. This did not save us, but it qualified Jesus to be our Savior, our Substitute, our Representative. He became the second Adam for mankind.

Then Jesus by His perfect life met all the positive demands of the law on behalf of the fallen human race. Having obtained this perfect obedience, He went to the cross and met the justice of the law. Thus, by His life (which met the positive demands of the law) and by His dying (which met the justice of the law) Jesus became our righteousness—the righteousness of God.

This righteousness fully satisfied the law, both in its positive demands and its call for justice.

Therefore, a believer stands perfectly righteous—perfectly just—before the law of God in Jesus Christ. This is the glorious gospel of our Lord, Jesus Christ.

What foolishness to reject such a gospel that allows us to stand justified before God, through faith alone in Jesus Christ.

Chapter 7

Justification by Faith Alone

Romans 4:1-25

The greatest joy in life is knowing the gospel of the Lord, Jesus Christ, which we began studying as we covered Romans 3:21-31 in our past two chapters.

We have seen, first of all, that the apostle defines the word "gospel" as "the righteousness of God." We should never forget this, because Paul means that the gospel is a righteousness that is all God's doing. He planned it and fulfilled it in Jesus Christ.

This righteousness, Paul says, is made effective in the life of every human being through faith alone. We cannot earn it by our good works. We cannot buy it with money. It is ours by faith alone. It doesn't matter whether we are rich or poor, educated or uneducated, good sinners or bad sinners. The righteousness of God that qualifies us for heaven, now and in the judgment comes by faith alone. This is why it is called justification by faith; when Luther made this great discovery, he was delivered from the bondage of legalism (Romans 3:22).

In Romans 3:24 Paul explains to us that this righteousness that justifies is given freely and graciously. We do not deserve it. In fact, we deserve the very opposite, but it comes as a gift, at no cost to us. Yet, it cost God a tremendous price—the death of His Son.

Finally, in Romans 3:31, Paul shows us that God who justifies us is right—He is legal; He is lawful in doing it. The righteousness of God is for Jews and Gentiles alike. It matters not who we are, for it is the life and death of Jesus Christ, the Son of God, that legally qualifies us for heaven.

Justification, Paul concludes in Romans 3:31, establishes the law. There is no cause for us to boast, since it is entirely God's gift—His righteousness in Christ that fully met the demands of the law.

Now, in Romans 4, Paul defends justification by faith against the threefold opposition that he faced throughout his ministry.

Opposition to Grace

This opposition came from the Judaizers—Jewish Christians—who dogged his footsteps and opposed his message of salvation by grace alone. Paul addresses the first point of opposition in Romans 4:1-8—the disagreement concerning works. The Jewish Christians insisted that works were essential for justification. They taught that God requires us to do good to be saved. Justification is not by faith alone but by faith plus good works. Paul meets this objection by saying that we are justified without works. Justification comes to us only by faith in Jesus Christ.

The second point of opposition concerns circumcision. Today Christians do not circumcise believers, but they do baptize—which Paul in Colossians 2:11 and 12 equates with circumcision. The Jews insisted, however, that salvation was impossible without circumcision.

In Acts 15 Luke describes the first Jerusalem Council, where the fundamental issue was the demand of Judaizers that Gentile believers be circumcised. Paul too is dealing with this problem in Romans 4:9-12.

Finally, in Romans 4:13-17 Paul deals with a third element of opposition—the keeping of the law. The Jewish Christians were saying, "Yes, Jesus does save us, but it is not enough for us to believe. We must by His help also keep the law, besides good works and circumcision."

Works are essential for justification, they said; circumcision is required for believers; and the law must be kept to ensure salvation.

To all three points Paul says "No." Clearly Paul is not against good works—he clearly says so. He is not against circumcision either, for he circumcised Timothy. And he definitely is not against the keeping of the law, for in Romans 13 he brings up the law as a standard of Christian living (verses 8-10).

Then what is Paul against? He is against using these practices as a means, or method, to obtain salvation or maintain the believers' salvation. Paul here is not addressing works as the fruit of justification; he is not discussing law-keeping as a standard of Christian living. He is showing that works, circumcision, and law-keeping contribute nothing to salvation, and he makes it clear that believers are not justified by faith plus works, or anything else.

Yes, Christians are justified by faith *that* works, but never by faith *plus* works. His discussion in Romans 4 is entirely related to justification, not sanctification. Paul will lay the foundation for sanctification in Romans 6-8 and explain it more fully still in Romans 12-15.

The Model of Abraham

Since Paul is dealing primarily with Jewish believers, he uses Abraham as the model of justification by faith. For the Jews Abraham was more than just a father. He was the example; he was the prototype; he was the one on whom they based their religion.

In taking Abraham as a model, Paul asks the question in Romans 4:1: "What shall we say then concerning Abraham our father according to the flesh?" The New American Standard Bible puts it this way: "What shall we say that Abraham, our forefather according to the flesh, has found?"

The word "flesh" can be confusing. In English, the word "flesh" means the soft exterior of the human body. But Paul is not referring to Abraham's "flesh," in that sense. To explain what Paul means by the word "flesh," we turn to Philippians 3:3. There we see that Christians are the ones who rejoice in Jesus Christ. We are the ones who are truly circumcised, not in the flesh but in the Spirit. We are the ones who rejoice in Christ and have no confidence in the flesh.

In Philippians 3:4-6, Paul explains to the Phillipian believers what he means by the word "flesh," "although I myself might have confidence even in the flesh. If anyone else has a mind to put confidence in the flesh, I far more: circumcised the eighth day, of the nation of Israel, of the tribe of Benjamin, a Hebrew of Hebrews; as to the law, a Pharisee, as to zeal (for God), a persecutor of the church; as to the righteousness which is in the law, found blameless" (NASB).

Obviously, by the word "flesh," Paul means anything that pertains to our birth, lineage, inheritance, or performance—anything we either depend on wholly or partially for our right standing before God. As a Jewish Pharisee, Paul once depended on those things for his justification. But in Philippians 3:7 onward Paul says that all these things that were a benefit to him according to Judaism, when he discovered Christ were of no value. He gave them up.

In fact he counted them as dung—as rubbish—that he might win Christ and have His righteousness, which is by faith and not by works of the law. So the word "flesh" here refers to anything that is true of us that we may be tempted to depend on, either wholly or partially, for our right standing before God.

"How about Abraham?" Paul is asking. "What did his works or his circumcision, or even his law-keeping contribute to his salvation?" In Romans 4:1-8 Paul is concerned with works, but we must be very careful. Paul is not opposed to works as the fruits of salvation. In fact, Abraham did many good and wonderful works. But did these works contribute to his justification?

Romans 4:2 says: "For if Abraham was justified by works, he has something to boast about; but not before God. For what does the Scripture say?"

What are the facts according to the Word of God? Paul then quotes Genesis 15:6: "Abraham believed God, and it was reckoned (*counted*) to him as righteousness."

Romans 4:4 says, "Now to the one who works, his wage is not reckoned as a favor, but as what is due." If a man at the end of the month goes to his employer to collect his salary and the employer hands him a check and says, "This is a gift," how will the employee respond? He will say, "No, I earned this." That's exactly what Paul means in verse 4.

Verse 5 continues, "But to the one who does not work, but believes in Him who justifies the ungodly (*Greek wicked*), his faith is reckoned as righteousness" (NASB). Righteousness is by faith, not by works. It is not a wage, but a gift.

Then in verses 6-8, Paul adds another name very special to the Jews. "David also speaks about the blessings that we receive whom God reckons righteous apart from works." Then he quotes Psalms 32: "Blessed are those whose lawless deeds have been forgiven and whose sins have been covered. Blessed is the man whose sin the Lord will not take into account."

Then Paul adds in verse 9: "Is this blessing then upon the circumcised, or upon the uncircumcised also (*meaning Jews or Gentiles*)? For we say, 'faith was reckoned to Abraham as righteousness?'" (NASB).

Just as Abraham is justified by faith, so are we. Then, in verses 9 and 10, Paul addresses circumcision: "Is this blessing upon the circumcised or upon the uncircumcised, for we see that Abraham was justified by faith. He was reckoned righteous and not by circumcision, because he was justified by faith before he was circumcised."

Why Circumcision? Why Baptism?

If Abraham was justified before he was circumcised, then why did God give circumcision?

The answer, Paul says, is that Abraham received the sign of circumcision as a seal of the righteousness of the faith which he had while uncircumcised. He becomes, then, the spiritual father of all who believe without being circumcised. Abraham is the prototype of all those who believe in Jesus Christ. Circumcision was merely a sign—a seal.

To better understand this, let us move quickly into Abraham's life story. God comes to Abraham when he is 75 years old (Genesis 12:4) and says to him, "Leave your country and your people and go to the land I will give you, and I will make of you a great nation."

Abraham believes God, though he has no son. That faith is reckoned to him for righteousness. Eight years go by, but still no son comes. So Abraham's faith begins to dwindle. God comes to him and says, in effect (Genesis 15), "Why are you doubtful? Why are you fearful?"

As we read between the lines, we can hear Abraham saying, "Because you have not kept Your promise. It takes nine months for human beings to produce a child. How long does it take You, God? It is eight years now."

Then God takes Abraham out and shows him the stars. "Abraham,' he says, "this is how many children you will have. Do you believe Me?" Genesis 15 contains the statement Paul loves to quote: Abraham believed God and "He accounted it to him for righteousness" (verse 6). At that moment Abraham's doubts are removed.

But two more years go by, and finally Sarah comes to Abraham and says, "Yes, God promised a child out of your loins, but I do not think He is capable of giving a child to me. Why don't you go to Hagar, my slave maid, and let her be a surrogate mother to help God keep His promise?"

Abraham thinks this is a wonderful idea and he and Hagar produce Ishmael. Abraham brings Ishmael to God and says, in effect, "God, You promised a son and I have helped you to fulfill the promise. You, plus me."

God says "Nothing doing" to Abraham but waits another 13 to 14 years until Abraham and Sarah are exhausted and their resources depleted, for Sarah has passed the age of childbearing. Then God comes to Abraham and says, "Do you still believe, in spite of medical science and human experience telling you 'Impossible,' that I can give you a son?"

Abraham says, "Yes." God says, "I will seal that faith. I want no more doubt." So that faith is sealed by the covenant of circumcision.

In Deuteronomy 10:16 and Jeremiah 4:4, we are told that circumcision is the removal of unbelief. This is why Moses said to the rebellious Jews, "Circumcise your heart and not your flesh." It is the sign—the seal—of righteousness by faith. When Abraham was about 117 years of age, between 17 and 20 years after he and Sarah had Isaac, God tested that faith (Hebrews 11:17-19). God said to Abraham, "Take this child and sacrifice him—that is, kill him."

A Seal of Faith

Abraham passed the test because his faith had already been sealed. Circumcision did not justify Abraham; it only sealed something he already had.

Finally, in Romans 4:13 Paul discusses the third problem: "For the promise to Abraham or to his descendants that he would be heir of the world was not through the Law, but through the righteousness of faith. For if those who are of the law are heirs, faith is made void and the promise is nullified" (NASB).

God gave Abraham the promise of salvation by faith long before He gave the law; in fact, 430 years before the law was given.

Opposing Systems

In verse 14 Paul says clearly that righteousness through the law and righteousness through faith are two opposing systems. The two cannot be married, for they are opposites.

In Romans 4:15 Paul adds: "For the Law brings about wrath, but where there is no law, neither is there violation" (NASB). When God gave the law and the Jews tried to use the law as a method of salvation, they could no longer be saved by faith, because the law does not save by faith. It saves by performance—by perfect obedience.

Abraham was the prototype, not of his blood descendants, but of those who had faith like his. Irrespective of race, if we lack the faith of Abraham, we are not really his children. Paul brings this out clearly in Romans 9-11, as well as in Galatians 3:6-9. If we have the faith of Abraham, then we are part of spiritual Israel.

The Working of Faith

Now we turn to the important concluding verses. After defending justification by faith against the threefold opposition of the Judaizers—that is, works, circumcision, and keeping of the law—Paul in Romans 4:17 and to the end of the chapter explains how faith works.

How did it work in Abraham's life? In Romans 4:18 we read: "Who, contrary to hope, in hope believed, so that he became the father of many nations, according to what was spoken, 'So shall your descendants be.'" Abraham is the father of all who have faith like his.

Then we read in verses 19 and 20: "Not being weak in faith, he did not consider his own body, already dead (*that is, unable to produce children through Sarai*) and the deadness of Sarai's womb. He did not waver (*or doubt*) at the promise of God (*that is, after he was circumcised*) through unbelief, but was strengthened in faith, giving glory to God."

Continuing on in verse 21, we read: "And being fully convinced that what He had promised, He was also able to perform." Faith is taking God at His word, irrespective of our feelings, our human rationale, or the scientific method. Faith is saying "Yes" to God, in spite of our environment and everything else that says "No."

We cannot use the scientific method when it comes to salvation by faith. The scientific method does not accept anything that is outside of human experience. It rejects everything that cannot be demonstrated. Therefore, the scientific method rejects miracles. It rejects all supernatural acts. But Paul tells us that Abraham believed God, in spite of what medical science told him about Sarah. Against hope, he believed.

Romans 4:22 says: "And therefore 'it was accounted to him for righteousness.'" It was not written for his sake alone, but for ours too. This is the way we must live. Salvation by faith means we depend totally on God and totally accept what God says, irrespective of everything else. This is how faith works!

God tells us he created this world in six days. This completely contradicts the scientific method, so scientists challenge, "Give us scientific evidence that God created the world in six days. Give us scientific evidence that God did not depend on pre-existing matter to create this world." We cannot give any scientific proof, but God says it in His Word. We believe that Genesis 1 and 2 is history, not a fable. What God says is true.

God says to us, "I have justified you in Christ. I have obtained a righteousness that fully qualifies you for heaven, now and in the judgment." We may not feel it. We may not experience it. But that is not how faith works. Faith simply takes God at His word.

Abraham's history has been recorded for our benefit. Verse 23 says, "Now not for his sake only was it written, that it was reckoned to him (*verse 24*) but for our sake also, to whom it will be reckoned, as those who believe in Him who raised Jesus our Lord from the dead" (NASB).

Scientists do not believe in the resurrection of the dead. Do we believe that Jesus actually rose from the dead, or do we think that the disciples invented the story to cover their embarrassment, as some liberal theologians teach? No!

God declares that He raised His Son from the dead. This is the greatest proof that Jesus Christ is God's power over sin, for the ultimate power of sin is to put us in the grave. Through His resurrection, Jesus proved that His power is greater than the combined sins of the entire human race (Romans 8:11,12).

Paul ends Romans 4 with these words: "He (*Jesus*) who was delivered up because of our transgressions and was raised because of our justification." He was delivered up to the wages of sin on the cross, but was resurrected as evidence of our justification.

There is only one way to be justified before God. It is by faith in Jesus Christ. Works, important as they may be in witnessing for Christ; law-keeping, important as that may be as evidence of rebirth; and the fruits of salvation by faith contribute not one iota toward salvation. Justification is by faith alone. Let us stand on this platform of the Reformation.

CHAPTER 8

Fruits of Justification by Faith

Romans 5:1-5

We now turn our attention to Romans 5, the most important chapter in the whole Epistle to the Romans. It is full of tremendous significance, so we will spend several studies here, beginning now with verses 1-5.

In these verses Paul describes the fruits of justification by faith. But to understand his trend of thought, we must go back to Romans 3:21-31. There Paul defines justification by faith. We saw in two former chapters that justification by faith is the righteousness of God, obtained for us in the holy history of Jesus Christ and made effective in our lives through faith alone.

Many Problems

This message, unfortunately, caused Paul many problems, mainly with the Judaizers who opposed his message of grace alone. So in Romans 4 Paul defends the doctrine of justification by faith against the Jewish Christians' three arguments.

These Jewish Christians insisted that works, circumcision, and keeping of the law were all essential for justification. Paul spends the whole of Romans 4 discussing this issue, making clear that works, circumcision (or baptism), and keeping the law contribute nothing to salvation.

Paul is not opposed to works. In passages such as Ephesians 2:10 and Titus 3:8 Paul says that genuine justification by faith produces good works. He is not opposed to circumcision and definitely supports the keeping of the law, as a fruit of justification by faith (Romans 13:8-10; Galatians 5: 13,14).

But the moment these external acts are claimed as a means of salvation, he strongly rejects them. He then concludes Romans 4 with the wonderful definition of how faith works. Using Abraham as an example, he explains that faith transforms the life of believers as God performs great things in their lives.

Fruits of Justification

Now we turn to Romans 5:1-3, where Paul discusses the threefold fruits of justification by faith. These fruits follow an important progression and must be kept in sequence, as Paul expresses them in these three verses. The first fruit is immediate; the second fruit is continuous; the third fruit is final. If we try to reach the last fruit without experiencing the first two, we waste our time.

Now, what are these three fruits? We find them in Romans 5:1-3. Paul defines the first fruit in verse 1: "Therefore being justified by faith, we have peace with God through our Lord, Jesus Christ" (KJV). The second fruit is found in verse 2: "By whom also we have access by faith into this grace wherein we stand, and rejoice in hope of the glory of God" (KJV). The third fruit is to arrive at the glory of God, as described in the second part of verse 2.

Let us consider them one by one: (1) The first fruit is immediate peace with God; (2) The second fruit is the believer's standing under grace; (3) The third—and ultimate—fruit is to arrive at the glory of God.

We now can examine each in some detail, remembering that at the foundation of these three fruits is justification by faith. Hebrews 11:6 tells us that without faith it is impossible to please God. So these fruits—whether peace with God, standing in grace, or arriving at the glory of God—are each the result of justification by faith, experienced only by faith in the righteousness of God, obtained for mankind in Jesus Christ.

"Therefore," Paul says, "being justified by faith, we have peace." But Paul does not stop here. He doesn't say that justification by faith brings us total peace, for there are many areas in which we will have no peace. We may not have peace with our enemies. We may not have peace in our country. But here Paul is dealing with a specific peace, "Being justified by faith, we have peace with God." If we have peace with God, then nothing else matters. If we have peace with God, we are able to face all the pressures of life.

The first phrase Paul uses is "having been justified" or "being justified," written originally in Greek, in the historical past tense. Justification, Paul says, becomes a historical reality the moment we believe.

In a previous chapter we quoted John 5:24, where Jesus says that the moment we believe in His Father who sent Him, we have already passed from death to life, from condemnation to justification. So the phrase "being justified" is something that takes place the moment we believe.

Yes, it is true that Jesus obtained justification for all men by His doing and dying. But the moment we believe, this justification becomes effective; it becomes ours.

When Paul talks about peace with God, however, he does not use the past or future tenses, but the present continuous tense. In other words, the moment we step under the umbrella of justification by faith, we have peace with God continually, regardless of our up-and-down performance.

Paul told us that the whole human race stands under the wrath of God. In Adam we all die, Paul says in 1 Corinthians 15:22. We stand under the death sentence of God apart from grace. In Ephesians 2:3 Paul tells us that we are by nature the children of wrath, but the moment we believe and accept Christ, we have peace with God.

But before that, as Paul brings out in Romans 2:8, 9, we were full of indignation and wrath, tribulation and anguish. Medical science tells us, in fact, that 90 percent of our disease is the result of guilt and anguish.

Since this world does not know what peace is, when believers discover the gospel and accept it by faith, they experience peace that passes understanding. Our experience may be up and down, but our relationship with God is peace. We can come to Him every time with a clear conscience through the righteousness of Jesus Christ (Hebrews 10:22).

How tragic to meet Christians who still have no peace. Too many try to reach the glory of God in order to achieve peace, when all the time peace is the prerequisite for arriving at the glory of God.

Believers do not arrive at the glory of God by performance. They reach the glory of God after realizing a right relationship with God, through faith in Christ. Anyone who serves God, whether out of fear of punishment or desire for reward, must know that such religion is paganism and worth nothing.

Good Works

In true Christianity all our good works are the fruit of salvation. In paganism, good works are the means of salvation. Though on the surface, the good works in both may appear similar, the motivation is altogether different in true Christianity. The Christian is saved by grace. In every other religion, good works are the means of salvation.

This bears repeating, for many Christians fall into the trap of Galatianism—a belief that they are saved partly by grace and partly by what they do. No, Christians are saved by grace alone, and the immediate fruit of justification by faith is peace with God.

Notice, Paul does not say simply "peace with God" but adds in

Romans 5:1 it is "through our Lord, Jesus Christ." This means that we receive this peace because of the performance of Jesus Christ in redeeming us—His doing and dying. Christ—not we—brings peace into our hearts! That is why He came. "Peace I leave with you," He said to His disciples, "not as the world gives it *(the world cannot give us this vertical peace with God; only Jesus Christ can)* give I unto you" (John 14:27).

In view of this, we must never depend on our performance to bring us peace with God. And we must never allow our own striving attitude or anyone else to rob us of that peace. As long as we are under the umbrella of justification by faith, we have peace. As long as we are walking by faith, we have peace.

True, only those whose faith endures unto the end will be justified, in terms of going to heaven (Matthew 10:22; Hebrews 10:38,39). But as long as we believe and are justified by faith, we have peace with God, unless we decide to remove ourselves from that position. Peace with God is possible only for those who are justified by faith. As long as our faith remains, our justification and peace remains.

Standing in Grace

Now, then, let us consider the second fruit of justification. The immediate fruit is peace with God; the second fruit is to stand in grace. The word "grace" has three primary meanings in the New Testament. The first is God's loving disposition toward sinful man, by which He through Jesus Christ redeemed us and gave us hope. Paul defines this in Ephesians 2:8, 9: "By grace are we saved through faith; it is not by works lest any man should boast. It is a gift of God." In Ephesians 1:7 Paul refers to it as the "exceeding riches of His grace."

Then, when we come to Romans 5:15-21 we will find that Paul uses the word "grace" in reference to the perfect obedience of Christ, in contrast to the disobedience of Adam.

Finally, the New Testament also uses "grace" to refer to the power of God made available to those who are standing under the umbrella of justification by faith. This is how he uses it in Romans 5:1 (second half).

Our first example of this grace is found in 1 Corinthians 15:9, where Paul says: "For I am the least of the apostles, that am not meet *(worthy)* to be called an apostle, because I persecuted the church of God" (KJV). Paul feels that he has no right to be an apostle, since he was one of the greatest persecutors of the Christian church before his conversion. He adds in verse 10, however: "But by the grace of God I am what I am." Then he says:

"And His grace which was bestowed upon me was not in vain; but I labored (*worked*) more abundantly than they all." By the phrase "they all" he means the other apostles, because in verse 9 he says, "I am the least of the apostles" (KJV).

So, on the one hand in verse 9, he says "I am the least of the apostles," and on the other he says in verse 10, "I have worked more than all the apostles put together."

This does sound like bragging, but in the last part of verse 10 he corrects any misunderstanding, saying "But, I want you to know it is 'not I, but the grace of God which was with me'" (KJV). All the works he had done were accomplished, not by him, but by the grace of God in him.

In Matthew 5:16, Jesus says, "Let your light so shine before men, that they may see your good works, and glorify your Father." The construction of this statement is very interesting. The word "light" is in the singular; the word "you" is in the plural. We Christians are many, but there is but one light, and that light is Jesus Christ (John 8:12).

A second example of the word "grace" used to refer to the power of God is found in 2 Corinthians 12. Paul here tells us that there was a problem in his life. It came from Satan but was allowed by God to keep him humble. He does not tell us what the problem is. Some scholars speculate that it was an eye problem. Some say that he had a cleft lip, but Paul tells us only that it was from Satan, allowed by God for a purpose.

Paul says: "And lest (*unless*) I should be exalted above measure through the abundance of the revelations, there was given to me a thorn in the flesh, the messenger of Satan to buffet me, lest I should be exalted" (KJV).

Paul was a human being. God had given him some tremendous revelations and was aware that, as a human being, Paul could become a victim of pride. He could become a boaster. So, to keep him humble, God allowed Satan to buffet him with a thorn in the flesh.

In verses 8 and 9, we discover that Paul prayed three times about this problem. He asked that it be taken from him. He said, "Lord, if You could remove this thorn in the flesh, I will do greater works for you." But God's answer was "No." "My grace is sufficient for you," God replies, "for my strength is made perfect in weakness."

Notice that God defines His grace as His strength. "My grace is sufficient for you," is synonymous with "My strength." Paul responds: "Therefore most gladly I will rather boast in my infirmities (*that is, in my weakness, in my inability*) that the power of Christ may rest upon me." The grace of God is the strength of God, the power of Christ. The Christian who stands under this umbrella of grace not only has peace with God but has power and strength available to him through the indwelling Spirit, that he may fulfill God's purpose.

There are many other passages, such as Ephesians 3:7 and 1 Timothy 1:14. Grace is the power of God, made available to believers, that God's purpose in their lives may be realized. It is in this sense that Paul uses the word "grace" in Romans 5:2.

The moment a person believes and comes under the umbrella of justification by faith, they achieve immediate peace with God. But justification does not stop there! It goes on and gives them power from God through the indwelling Spirit. They gain access to the power of the Holy Spirit in their lives (Romans 8:11).

Hope

This brings us to the third fruit. Because the power of God is available to believers, they have a hope—the ultimate fruit of the doctrine of justification by faith. The ultimate fruit is the hope of the glory of God, as expressed in the last part of verse 2.

What does Paul mean by the phrase "Glory of God"? Does he mean some bright light around us? In studying the New Testament, we find that the glory of God is His self-sacrificing love. In John 1:14, we are told that "the word became flesh, and dwelt among us, and we beheld His glory,... full of grace and truth." God's glory is His self-sacrificing love, revealed on the cross when Jesus was willing to pay the full price for our sins and set us free. This is the glory of God. It is the unconditional, self-emptying *agape* love of God first revealed in Jesus Christ and now manifested in the lives of believers.

A very interesting statement is found in Colossians 1:27, where Paul tells the believers that he wants them to experience the glory of God. Speaking to the Gentiles, he says: "Christ in you, the hope of glory." In 2 Corinthians 3:17, Paul explains how this glory is experienced: "Now the Lord is that Spirit: and where the Spirit of the Lord is, there is liberty." This is liberty from the selfish flesh that we were born with, liberty from the slavery of sin. Then he adds in verse 18: "We all, with unveiled face, beholding as in a mirror the glory of the Lord, (*the glory of Jesus Christ*) are being transformed (*changed*) into the same image from glory to glory, just as by the Spirit of the Lord."

Jesus Christ does not only give us peace, He gives us the Holy Spirit to transform our lives that we may reflect the character of God. Jesus says in John 13:35: "By this shall all men know that you are my disciples when you reflect My love for each other."

For the Holy Spirit to do this, however, we have to go through a process. That process is described in Romans 5:3-4: "And not only this, but we also exult in our tribulations, knowing that tribulation brings about perseverance; and perseverance, proven character; and proven character, (*brings that*) hope" (NASB). When the Holy Spirit works in us, it goes against the grain of our selfish flesh. The love of God has no self in it. In 1 Corinthians 13:5, the special, unconditional love of God is described: *Agape* "seeketh not her own" (KJV).

When the Holy Spirit produces this unselfish love in us, the flesh may suffer persecution, rejection, and opposition. But we hold on, and this suffering produces perseverance. Jesus says in Matthew 10:22 that the person's faith that endures unto the end will be saved. This is what the word remnant means—those who hold on to God and justification by faith, though their fellowmen may apostatize—even in persecution, they hold on.

The ultimate goal of justification by faith is that the believer may reflect the glory of God. We read in Romans 5:5: "And hope does not disappoint, because the love of God has been poured out within our hearts through the Holy Spirit who was given to us" (NASB).

What a wonderful gospel this is! God takes the initiative. He comes to us, sinners and enemies, and says in Romans 5:8-10, "I have reconciled you to Myself by the death of My Son." He comes to us with the unconditional good news of salvation through the gospel of the Lord, Jesus Christ. Then He says to us, "Please accept this."

So we respond by faith.

God first comes with the gospel. The believer responds by faith, which brings peace, hope, and assurance. Then the Holy Spirit is sent to dwell in their hearts, and with the Holy Spirit comes His supreme gift, the love of God. God gives the believer this gift of *agape* love (1 Corinthians 13). It comes vertically from God, through the Holy Spirit, that it may go out horizontally to the world.

When the world sees this reflection of Christ's love—this unconditional love of God—they are convinced that the gospel is the power of God unto salvation.

This is the ultimate goal of the gospel. First it gives peace and assurance; second it gives power; and ultimately it reproduces in every Christian the power of the gospel—which is the love of God.

Chapter 9

God's Unconditional Love

Romans 5:6-10

We have now discovered that justification by faith—the theme of Paul's great Epistle to the Romans—is not just a theory or philosophy. It is a truth that must be experienced. We have also found that the experience of justification by faith produces threefold fruits in our lives.

Justification by faith first brings us peace with God. In Romans 5:1 Paul says, "Therefore, being justified by faith, we have peace with God." We have this peace because our status has changed from condemnation to justification. The moment we accept Jesus Christ as our Savior, we pass from death to life, which brings us peace with God—peace that passes understanding.

God does not only forgive us when we accept Christ as our Savior. Not only does He reconcile us through Christ, he looks upon us as if we had never sinned, just as He looks at His Son, Jesus Christ.

Remember what God announced to the world at Jesus' baptism, recorded in Matthew 3:17: "Here is my beloved Son in whom I am well pleased." This is exactly what He says about those who, by faith, have received Christ and are now standing on the platform, under the umbrella of justification by faith.

Second, justification by faith brings us the experience of power. Paul tells us in Romans 5:2 that those who have peace through justification by faith also have access to the grace of God. Here the word "grace" means the power of God given to the believers to fulfill God's purpose in each of their lives. It is the power to withstand temptation and behave as children of God. The believer stands in grace, not only before God's law—which is righteousness—but with God's power to transform lives.

Finally, the third experience is that of possessing the love of God in the heart. This third and ultimate fruit of justification by faith is so radical, so revolutionary, so unlike any human experience, that Paul devotes verses 6-10 of Romans 5 to talking about it. This is the love that the world needs to see—the love that totally contradicts human love.

Agape *Love*

Paul explains this love by contrasting it, rather than comparing it, with human love. The two loves—God's *agape* (ah-GAH-pay) love, which every believer should experience, and human love, which we have by nature—are absolute opposites.

When New Testament writers describe this love, they choose a unique word, in the noun form, rarely found in secular Greek. This word is so revolutionary that the enemies of the gospel accused the disciples of turning the world upside down (Acts 17:6). The word is *agape*, for which there is no English equivalent. The English word "love," with all its noble characteristics, not only does a tremendous injustice to the Greek noun *agape* but totally contradicts it. Paul's concern in this passage is that the believers understand this *agape* love of God.

There are two reasons for his concern: First, when the believer has the love of God, then, and only then, can he or she fully understand justification by faith and experience, in the fullest sense, the peace of God. The basis for peace with God and salvation is God's *agape* love. It is only as Christians are grounded in God's love, as Paul explains it in Ephesians 3:17, that they will be settled in the truth of the gospel and truly experience peace. They will be able to withstand the pressures of this wicked world, because once they have peace with God, nothing else matters.

The second reason Paul wants Christians to understand the love of God is so that they can shed it abroad to their neighbors. The greatest demonstration in a Christian's life that they are justified by faith is that their fellow men see the love of God in their interaction among human beings. In order for that love to be manifested in a Christian's life, he or she needs to understand the love of God.

Human and Divine Love

With this background, notice in Romans 5:6-10 that verses 6, 8, 9, and 10 describe the love of God in contrast to verse 7, which describes human love.

We need to study the difference to understand the true meaning of God's love. One problem some Christians have is that they project human ideals of love onto God. When they do this, they distort God's character as well as the gospel of Jesus Christ. In this passage, four words deal especially with the love of God, in terms of salvation.

Two of these are found in verse 6: "For when we were still without strength...." The Greek here means when we were still helpless, incapable of saving ourselves. "In due time (*that is, in the appointed time*), Christ died for the ungodly." The two are "helpless (*without strength*) and ungodly (*while we were unlike God, while we were contrary to God's character*)." Paul is saying that while humanity was in this condition, Jesus died for them. He died while we were helpless. So, immediately we find that the love of God is unconditional. This is such a radical and revolutionary concept of God's love that Paul wants to show us this love, not by comparing, but by contrasting it to human love.

In verse 7 Paul says of human love: "For scarcely for a righteous man will one die, yet perhaps (*maybe*) for a good man someone would even dare to die." People do not usually give their lives for an evil man, Paul says. Human beings have been known to lay down their lives for a good man, for their loved ones, or even for their country. But even this is rare.

But when it comes to God's *agape* love, the very opposite occurs. It is likely that verse 7 is alluding to a Greek myth familiar to the people of Paul's day. The story is told of two young people, one a good citizen who for some reason is falsely accused and sentenced to death. His girlfriend knows he is innocent and does not deserve to die. So she goes to the judge, tells him the young man does not deserve to die, but since the sentence cannot be changed under Greek law, she offers to die in his place. The judge accepts this, and the story ends with this conclusion, "This is the epitome of genuine love. Here is a woman who is willing to die for a good man."

Love for the Unlovely

In verse 8 Paul says that while it is possible for human beings to die for good causes and good people (though this is uncommon), God's love is completely different. Jesus did not die on the cross for good people. But God "commended (*demonstrated*) his own love towards us in that while we were still sinners, Christ died for us."

So, first we were helpless; second, we were ungodly (that is, wicked); and now, in verse 8, Paul tells us that while we were sinners, Christ died for us.

God does not say, "If you are good, I will send My Son to die for your sins." No! While we were yet sinners—while we were helpless, while we were still ungodly—Christ died for us.

Paul says that God's love for us is unconditional, in complete contrast to conditional human love. In Romans 5:9—the next verse—Paul says, "Much more then, having now been justified by His blood (*that is, by His death*), we shall be saved from wrath through him." This text is dealing with believers—those who have accepted Jesus Christ and are standing under the umbrella of justification by faith.

Paul is saying, "If God loves us and died for us, while we were still ungodly, helpless sinners, how can you Christians doubt the love of God? Why are you doubting your justification? Don't you realize that if God loved you when you were sinners, He loves you even more now that you have accepted Him and stand in favor with Him? How much more do you have to be sure that God will save you, now that you have accepted justification by faith? Why are you doubting, Christians?"

Insecure Christians

How tragic that some Christians doubt their salvation, unconvinced they will make it to heaven. When we project human love onto God, these kinds of doubts creep in. We become unsure about our salvation, because human love is conditional. It has to be aroused. It depends on goodness. It is reciprocal: "You have to be good to me if I have to be good to you."

Because of this false idea about God's love, some still imagine that they have to be good before God accepts us. As humans, we are accustomed to gaining the love of others through incentives—by doing good acts. This is the human way.

But thank God, He loves us in spite of what we are. He loves us unconditionally. He loves us because He is *agape* Love, not because we deserve it.

Paul says "Much more," now that we have accepted justification by faith, through His blood (His sacrifice), we can be sure that our salvation is secure in Christ. Why? Because He who died for us will defend us and vindicate us until He takes us to heaven. This is true as long as we are justified by faith and are not depending on ourselves.

Paul then continues in Romans 5:10, using the fourth noteworthy word. He has mentioned that we were helpless, ungodly, and sinners. Now Paul says in verse 10: "For if when we were enemies (*that is, enemies of God*) we were reconciled." Note the verb: Not, "we will be reconciled" but "we were reconciled" to God through the death of His Son. "Much more, having been justified (*reconciled*), we shall be saved by His life."

God is on our side! He was on our side before we ever turned to Him. While we were enemies, God sent His Son to this world to save it. God said to His Son, "I want you to go down and save the world, even though they deserve condemnation."

We read in John 3:17 that God sent His Son, not to condemn the world, but that the world through Him might be saved.

Now, having studied through this passage, we must look at its context. Why does Paul explain the love of God? He explains God's unique *agape* love in Romans 5:6-10 because this is his explanation of verse 5. We need to keep in mind what Paul says to us in Romans 5: 5: "Now hope does not disappoint, because the love of God has been poured out in our hearts by the Holy Spirit who was given to us." What does this mean to us? How does it affect us?

It should affect us in at least two ways: First, we have a God who loves us unconditionally—a God whose love is unchangeable. Human love differs from God's love in at least three ways: *First,* human love is conditional. It is a reciprocal "I love you if you will love me" situation. In contrast, God's love is unconditional and there will never come a time when He will stop loving us (Romans 8:35-39); *Second,* human love is changeable. Human beings do love, but their love is not everlasting—note our high divorce rate. But God's love is eternal. "The fact that you love me today is no guarantee that you will love me tomorrow," we say as humans. But God's love never changes. We read in Jeremiah 31:3 what God told the rebellious Israelites: "I have loved you with an everlasting love." In 1 Corinthians 13: 8, Paul defines the beautiful word *agape*. He says *agape* never fails. In John 13:1, we read that, having loved them, Jesus loved them to the very end.

Finally, human love is self-seeking. At the heart of all human love is self. This is because of our inborn, egocentric nature, the result of the fall of Adam and Eve. We have sinful natures that do not know how to love others unconditionally.

Self-giving Love

But God's love is self-giving, the very opposite of human love. God's love empties itself of self. In Philippians 2:6-8 we read about the self-emptying love of God. Jesus was equal with God but He did not hold on to that equality. He emptied Himself and stepped down, down, down until He became obedient, even to the death of the cross. On the cross, Christ had two choices. He could choose between Himself or the world. In reading Luke 23:35-39 we discover that the devil came to Christ three times while He hung on the cross—once through the soldiers, once through the priests, and once through the thief on the cross to his left. Three times the devil came with his fiercest temptation: "Come down from the cross and save Yourself."

We know Jesus could have done that. He could have grasped hold of His divine power, independent of the Father, and come down. But, had He done that, the world would have been lost, for Christ could not save the world and Himself at the same time. He had to make a choice: "Shall I save the world and accept the wages of sin—God-abandonment, good-bye to life forever—or shall I come down from the cross and let the rebellious world that has crucified Me die forever?"

His choice was to die that we might live. This is the demonstration Paul mentions in Romans 5:8: "While we were still sinners, God demonstrated His own unconditional love for us that Jesus laid down His life for us."

Sharing Love

The second way the love of God affects us is that it is the kind of love God wants us to shed abroad to our neighbors. The world needs to see the love of God. We have seen this love in the face of Jesus Christ. But Christ is no longer in this world. He is in heaven, where nobody can see Him. But His body—the church—is here on earth. God wants the world to see a demonstration of this unconditional, unchanging, self-emptying love through His people, the believers.

In Romans 5:6-10 Paul simply says what Jesus taught in the Sermon on the Mount; in Matthew 5:43-48 Jesus says exactly what Paul is saying here. Jesus contrasts human love with God's love. He says that divine love is the kind of love that Christians should reflect in their Christian living.

In Matthew 5:14-16 Jesus says that we believers are the light of the world. In verse 16 He says to let this light shine. Let this love of God in us, which represents Christ, shine that men may see our good works and glorify God in heaven.

In Matthew 5:43 Jesus describes the love taught by the Pharisees and the Scribes of His day. Jesus says, "You have heard that it was said, You shall love your neighbor and hate your enemies." This is typical human love. But Jesus says in contrast, "I say to you, love your enemies, bless those that curse you, do good to them that hate you, and pray for them which do spitefully use and persecute you" (KJV). In other words, the love we Christians must reflect in our lives is God's love.

We cannot do this naturally. Man cannot, using his own willpower and effort, love his enemies. But the love of God is made available to the believer because he has the Holy Spirit dwelling in him. This Spirit brings with Him the *agape* love of God.

In Matthew 5:45 Jesus explains that when we love our enemies, we are behaving like the children of God and become the sons of our Father in heaven. The Father makes the sun rise on both the evil and the good. He sends rain on the just and the unjust.

God's love is unconditional—as our love must be. We find an example in Exodus, where God delivers His people in a miraculous way. As they travel through that great Sinai Peninsula desert, it is hot in the daytime and cold at night. So, in the nighttime He warms them with a pillar of fire. In the daytime He keeps them cool with a cloud canopy.

But what does Hebrews 3 and 4 say about God's evaluation of the Jews of the Exodus? Was He pleased with them? No. He was not pleased with them, yet He blessed them. Why? Because God's love is unconditional.

Jesus says in Matthew 5 that if we love our neighbors—if we love our friends—we are no different than the tax collectors. Here the tax collectors refer to sinners. Even the atheist loves his own friends. But Jesus says in Matthew 5:48: "Be ye therefore perfect." In other words, "Let your love be without discrimination. Let it be unconditional like your Father's love toward you, that the world may see that you are My disciples."

This is what Jesus says in John 13:34, 35. He tells His disciples that they must love each other, as He loved them. Then in John 13:35, Jesus makes this statement: "By this shall all men know that you are my disciples, if you have love one for another" (NASB).

This *agape* love, reproduced in the believer, is the greatest demonstration of true Christianity. Jesus says through John in 1 John 4:7 and 12 that this love comes from God, and when we love as God loves, it proves that God is dwelling in us and we in Him.

As we conclude this wonderful passage, it is clear that God gives this *agape* love through the Holy Spirit, that it may be shed horizontally to our neighbors. When the world sees this love, we will be known as His disciples. This is true law-keeping (Romans 13:8-10).

"If you Christians expect me to believe in your Redeemer, you will have to look a lot more redeemed," writes Friedrich Nietzsche, a modern pagan philosopher who left a mainline Christian church and became an atheist. What a challenge!

Then, there is Mahatma Ghandi. While he was fighting the apartheid system in South Africa, he said to the Dutch Reformed Church: "When you Christians live the life of your Master—when you love each other unconditionally—then all India will bow down to Christianity."

We have peace with God through justification by faith, and we will reflect the love of God as we allow Jesus to live in us and reflect His love through us. This is what justification is all about.

Chapter 10

Adam—A Type of Christ

Romans 5:11-18

In the next three studies, we turn our attention to the most important passage in the Epistle to the Romans—and, for that matter, in the whole Bible. It lays the foundation of our understanding of righteousness by faith, and we will be blessed as we study Romans 5:11-21.

Anders Nygren, a great theologian and Bible scholar, has referred to this passage as the high point of Romans and writes in his *Commentary on Romans*: "The place to begin for an inclusive view of the meaning of Romans is the fifth chapter's comparison of Adam and Christ. This gives us the key to the whole epistle. When we attain to its height, all that precedes and all that follows spread out before us in one inclusive view, we see how part fits directly into part, how Paul's thoughts move from step to step under its inherent compulsion. With this passage as our point of orientation, we can with surer understanding pursue the epistle from beginning to end" (p. 27).

If we can understand this passage, we are assured that we will truly understand the gospel of our Lord, Jesus Christ.

Western Thinking

For the Western mind the passage is at first very difficult to understand, for Paul's thoughts seem to contradict our way of thinking. His audience's mindset was far different from ours, so we will have to put on Jewish, or Eastern, caps as we look at this passage.

Compounding the difficulty of Romans 5:11-21 is the controversy that surrounds it. Throughout the history of the Christian church, this passage has attracted more scholarly ink than any other part of the New Testament. Today we rarely hear a sermon on this passage, because many pastors claim it is too difficult to preach. But avoidance is no solution, for without understanding this passage, we can never understand Paul's message of the gospel.

So let us wrestle with this passage, as Jacob wrestled with the angel until he obtained a blessing. First, we must follow Paul's logic in Romans

5:11: "And not only that, but we also rejoice in God through our Lord, Jesus Christ, through whom we have now received the reconciliation." By "not only that," Paul is referring to God's unconditional love, by which we were justified while we were still helpless, ungodly sinners and enemies of God.

In verse 11 Paul says that not only do we believers rejoice in the unconditional, changeless, self-emptying love of God, but that through our Lord, Jesus Christ we have already been reconciled to God, or received the atonement (KJV).

Paul then plunges into our sin problem in Adam. Why does he spend verses 12, 13, and 14 describing Adam and mankind's situation in Adam? What has Adam to do with our reconciliation? The answer is, "Nothing."

Adam and Christ

In the last part of Romans 5:14, however, Paul tells us why he is concerned about our situation in Adam: Adam is a type of "him who was to come." Of course, the One to come is Jesus Christ. Paul is telling us that there is a similarity between Adam and Christ, so he wants to use Adam as a pattern—a type or figure—of Christ.

"This is impossible," we might well say, for when we compare Adam and Christ—especially in verses 15-18—we discover that Adam and Christ are absolute opposites. Adam is the source of our sin problem. In contrast, Christ is the Source of our salvation. It is in Christ that we stand justified. So, how can Paul use Adam as a type of Christ?

In one point—in one area, alone—Adam and Christ are similar, and because of this similarity Paul can use Adam as a type of Christ.

What is this similarity? Simply put, what Adam did affected the whole human race. Likewise, what Christ did affects everyone. This is true only of Adam and of Christ; therefore, Paul can use Adam as a type of Christ. That is why Paul refers to Christ as the "last Adam" (1 Corinthians 15:45). "Adam" in Hebrew means "Mankind."

Now we turn to verse 12, where Paul tells us three things: "Therefore, just as through one man sin entered the world, and death through sin, and thus death spread to all men, because all sinned." What are the three facts of which Paul informs his readers in this verse?

Through One Man

First, Paul tells us that through one man sin entered the world. The words "one man" refer to Adam.

What, then, does Paul mean by the word "world"? The Greek word used here has at least six meanings in the New Testament. But the context supplies the meaning—here the word "world" has the same meaning as in John 3:16, where Jesus tells Nicodemus, "God so loved the world." The word "world" refers here to the entire human race. Paul tells us that sin entered (past tense) the human race through one man.

The second fact Paul brings out in verse 12 is that sin brought death to Adam. When God created Adam and placed him in the Garden of Eden, He told Adam and Eve in Genesis 2:16 and 17 that "The day you eat of the forbidden fruit (*he could eat from every other tree in the garden*) you shall surely die." Adam did eat of that fruit, and the moment he did he came under condemnation of death.

The third fact Paul brings out in verse 12 is that this death, which came upon Adam, spread to the whole human race—death became universal. Now, Paul is aware that this third fact will create problems, because he knows that his readers—especially the Jewish readers—are familiar with statements found in Deuteronomy and Ezekiel which say that the soul that sins will die; the father cannot die for the son, and so on. In other words, no law will allow guilt and punishment to be transferred from the guilty to the innocent or for an innocent man to die in place of a guilty one (see Deuteronomy 24:16 and Ezekiel 18:20).

Here Paul tells us that Adam's sin brought death to all men. We immediately shout, "Unfair! Why should I die because of the sins of somebody else?" Paul tells us why in the last part of Romans 5:12: "Because all sinned."

Incomplete Phrase

Unfortunately, this is an incomplete phrase and has caused major controversy in the history of the Christian church. There are two ways we can finish the sentence: We can say, "All die because all sinned *like* Adam," or, "All die because all sinned *in* Adam." Which one does Paul mean?

First, let us examine the differences in these two statements. If we say that we all die because we sinned *like* Adam, then we make Adam our example. We are saying that Adam's sin is our example and that his example leads us to sin and come under the sentence of death.

On the other hand, if we say that we all die because we sinned in Adam, then we are making Adam the cause of our condemnation, our debt. Depending on the way we interpret the phrase, "For all sinned" or "Inasmuch all sinned," we come to two different conclusions.

The Only Conclusion

The only conclusion we can come to is that we all die because we all sinned in Adam. Here are five reasons for this conclusion.

(1) History: Not everybody dies because they sin like Adam. For example, babies die, even though they have not sinned like Adam. Therefore, those who believe that we die because we sin like Adam have a problem with those who die who have not sinned like Adam.

(2) Verb Tense: The second reason is that the verb Paul uses in the phrase, "For all have sinned" or "because all sinned," is in the past tense, which here in the Greek means something that took place once and for all, in the past. If Paul means that our personal sins bring us the death sentence, he would use the present continuous tense. But he uses the past historic tense.

(3) Context: The third argument is based in Romans 5:13, 14, which is the immediate context of this statement in Romans 5:12. Paul says in verses 13 and 14 that the people who lived from Adam to Moses—that is, the human race before God gave the law—died or were dying, even though their sins were unlike Adam's deliberate transgression. Paul is saying that the people from Adam to Moses were not sinning legally, because God had not spelled out the Ten Commandments until Moses' time, at Mount Sinai. But these people, from Adam to Moses, while they were sinning (missing the mark, which is what the word *sin* means), their sins were unlike Adam's transgression. Paul is very careful in his use of terms. The people from Adam to Moses were sinning (missing the mark), but Adam transgressed. The word *transgressed* means a deliberate violation of the law. So, Paul says, even though these people were sinning and their sins were unlike the deliberate act of disobedience that Adam committed, they were still dying.

Why were they dying? It could not be for their personal sins, because verse 13 says the sin is not counted where there is no law. God did not post His law until Moses at Mount Sinai. And yet, while these people were sinning, God could not condemn them for breaking His law, because He had not yet revealed the law in its explicit form.

(4) Repetition: Now, the fourth piece of evidence, found in verses 16-18 and still part of the context, includes at least four statements—that humanity is judged, condemned, and sentenced to death, not because of its personal sins, but because of Adam's sin.

(5) Use of Adam: The fifth reason we believe that the apostle is saying that we all die because we sinned in Adam and not like Adam is that Paul

uses Adam and our situation in Adam so that he can use Adam as a pattern of Christ.

If we insist that we all die because we sin *like* Adam, Adam becomes only an example; if we say we die because we sin like Adam did, then, for this analogy to fit Christ, we would have to teach that we are all justified because we obey like Christ. But nobody obeys like Christ. Remember in Romans 3:9-12, Paul tells us that all have sinned—that all have come under the dominion of sin. There is none good; there is not even one who is righteous. There is only one Man who has lived a perfect, righteous life. This is Jesus Christ. No other human being has fully obeyed the law as Christ has—in thought, word, and deed.

If we teach that we die because we sin like Adam, then we must teach (to be fair with Paul's analogy) that we are justified because we obey like Christ. This is far from Paul's teaching. In fact, it totally contradicts Paul's teaching. All through his life he condemns justification by the works of the law (see Galatians 2:16).

Therefore, Paul must be saying that humanity all dies because it sinned in Adam. And since Adam is a pattern of Christ, we all live (we are all justified) because we obeyed in Christ.

All Created in Adam

This may be difficult to grasp, but Paul's argument is based on the biblical truth that God created all men in one man, Adam. We were not created when our mothers conceived us. And, likewise, God incorporated the whole human race in one man—Jesus Christ. Acts 17:26 tells us that God created all men in one man at creation. Out of one person God created the whole human race that dwells upon this earth. Likewise, God united His Son to the corporate human race that needed redeeming. Thus, Christ became the second Adam, the second mankind. God did this so that the history of Christ might become our history.

Missing the Mark

Romans 5: 13,14 explains Romans 5:12. Paul tells us in verse 13 that, until the law—and by that he means until God spelled out the law through Moses—sin was in the world. The human race that lived before Moses was sinning—missing the mark. Nevertheless, sin is not counted—it is not imputed, it is not reckoned—where there is no law.

Paul is not saying that the law did not exist before Moses. We saw in

Romans 1 and 2 that the law was in the consciences of the Gentiles. These people were sinning, Paul says, but God had not yet posted the law. And since He did not post the law until Moses, legally, He had no right to condemn them for their sins.

Yet, in verse 14 Paul says, "Nevertheless, death reigned from Adam to Moses." These people were dying, and since God is a just God, Paul's implication here is that they were not dying for their personal sins. They were dying because in Adam they had already transgressed. When Adam sinned, we were implicated in that sin. We did not choose to sin in Adam, so we are not guilty of Adam's sin. The doctrine of original guilt is not taught in the Bible. But we were in Adam when he sinned. We are implicated in his sin; therefore, the condemnation of death that came to Adam is passed on to us. The life we receive at birth has been passed down to us from Adam and is a life condemned to death.

As Paul brings out in 1 Corinthians 15:22: "In Adam all die," we, because of Adam's Fall, are born on Death Row. We say, "This is unfair!" Yes, it is unfair in the sense that at the moment Adam sinned he should have died. And if he had died, where would we be?

If my great-great-grandfather had died at the age of three, where would I be? I could not exist, because I would have died in him. Likewise, had Adam died the moment he sinned (as he deserved), the whole human race would have died in him. But God allowed Adam to live, and because Adam lived, he had children and his children had children, until here we are today.

But why did God allow the human race to live, if it deserved death? Because He had a plan to save it. He chose to save it in Jesus Christ (Ephesians 1:4). He chose to do so in Christ from the foundation of the world, that humanity might become holy and blameless before him through his Son, Jesus Christ.

"If Christ took our nature upon Him, as we believe, by an act of love, it was not that of one but of all. He was not one man only among many men, but in him all humanity was gathered up. And thus now, as at all time, mankind is, so to speak organically united to Him. His acts are in a true sense our acts, so far as we realize the union. His death is our death, His resurrection our resurrection," writes Brook Foss Westcott in his book *The Gospel of the Resurrection*, p. 39.

Theologian H.P. Liddon says, "As human nature was present in Adam, when by his representative sin he ruined his posterity; so was human nature present in Christ our Lord. Our nature is his own. He carried it with him through life to death. He made it do and bear that which as utterly beyond its native strength," *University Sermons*, p. 225, p. 226.

Dietrich Bonhoeffer adds, "...when God's Son took on flesh, He truly and bodily took on, out of pure grace, our being, our nature, ourselves. This was the eternal counsel of the triune God. Now we are in Him. Where He is, there we are too, in the incarnation, on the cross, and in His resurrection. We belong to him because we are in Him" *Life Together*, p. 35.

Paul is describing in Romans 5:12-14 humanity's hopeless situation in Adam. We are not born neutral. We are born under the death sentence, because we are the children of Adam and there is nothing we can do to change that death sentence. We are born on Death Row. Galatians 3: 23,24 tells us that God gave the law to lead us to Christ. The law puts us in the prison cell of death, until Christ came and set us free. This is why in John 8:32 Jesus tells the Jews: "You shall know the truth, and the truth shall make you free." By the word "truth" Jesus means Himself. In John 8:36 Jesus says: "If the Son shall make you free, you shall be free indeed."

Romans 5:12-14 tells us we are born sinners, condemned to death in this world with only one hope—Jesus Christ.

Sin is not something that we have produced—we are born under the sin problem. Sin is something we inherit. As we look at Romans 5:19 in a future study, we will see that Adam's sin made us sinners—it constituted us as sinners. So a baby, while it is born innocent in the sense of experience, is not born innocent under the law of God. A baby is born under the condemnation of the law. Because of this, every human being needs a Savior.

As Paul said to the jailer, "If you believe, you and your household will be saved," so our only hope is in Christ.

We realize that we are born under condemnation and that only through Jesus Christ we have hope. There is only one righteousness that qualifies us for heaven. It is the righteousness of Jesus. When we know this truth, the truth will set us free—free from guilt and insecurity.

CHAPTER 11

The Two Adams

Romans 5:11-18 (Continued)

We continue our study of the crucial biblical passage—Romans 5: 11-18, described by Swedish theologian Anders Nygren as the high point of Romans.

As we learned last study in verses 12-14, Paul points to Adam as the one who introduced sin and death to the human race.

In this study we turn to the next part of this crucial passage, verses 15-18. This part is the most neglected passage in all of Christendom—yet the doctrine here is crucial. When this doctrine is clearly understood and applied by God's people, it does three things.

First, it cures the Christian of legalism in all its forms—an age-long problem.

Second, this message, clearly understood and applied, cures us of the opposite of legalism—antinomianism, or "cheap grace." Cheap grace says that "since Christ did it all, a Christian can live and do as he or she pleases." When we really understand this passage, we find that the gospel gives no such liberty.

And finally, this doctrine, once understood and applied, can bring revival and reformation and light the earth with the glory of God. These are three reasons why it is important to understand this passage.

As we learned last study, this is a difficult passage, and for us to understand it, we must put aside our preconceived ideas and prejudices. Our great concern in looking at this passage is to ask ourselves exactly what Paul is saying here—for he is the inspired writer. We are not to put into this text what we think Paul is saying. Rather, we are to pull out of this passage exactly what Paul means.

A great preacher from California, Brian Morgan, said in one of his sermons: "In all of Romans, I find this text (Romans 5:12-21) the most difficult to teach. In fact, I was dreading it. For years, I taught this material without discovering a clear outline or an understanding of Paul's argument. But, as I meditated on this truth, I realized that our difficulty lies in the fact that we do not approach this passage with the mind of Paul, because we do not think as he does. We cannot fully comprehend the thoughts of

God. But, by changing my way of thinking, the magnitude and the glory of the work of Christ revealed in the passage, became greater than ever before. I pray that this might happen for you as well."

Let us put aside our preconceived ideas—put off our Western way of thinking—and let us study this passage as Paul meant it to be seen.

A Brief Look Back

But first, let us review what we have covered already in our study of Romans 5:12-14. Here Paul discusses mankind's situation in Adam and shows that Adam is a type—a figure and pattern—of Christ. Adam and Christ are parallels, in the sense that what they did affected all of humanity.

But as we turn to Romans 5:15-18, we discover that they are also opposites. Adam sinned; Christ did the very opposite—He obeyed. The effects, therefore, are opposite. The effect of Adam's sin brought condemnation and death to all mankind, while Christ's obedience brought justification unto life to all mankind.

Adam and Christ are the representatives of the human race. This, as we saw last chapter, is based on the Bible truth that all human beings are in one man. In other words, the reason Adam's sin brought the death sentence on all mankind is not that God transferred Adam's guilt and punishment to us. If God had done that, God would have broken His own law, which clearly declares that guilt and punishment cannot be legally transferred (Deuteronomy 24:16).

For example, if while Ted Bundy, the infamous serial killer, was on Death Row, his mother had gone to the judge and said to him, "I love my son. I know he has murdered many young women, but I want him to live. I want to take his place in the electric chair." Could the judge legally reply, "Yes"? No.

In the law of the land and the law of God, guilt cannot be legally transferred. This is a fundamental truth of all law.

Then why do we die because of Adam's sin? The answer, we've learned, is not that Adam's guilt is transferred to us, but that we are implicated—we participated in his sin because we were genetically "in" Adam when he transgressed.

We must remember that God did not create us when our mothers conceived us. God created all mankind—billions and billions of people—in one individual man. In Genesis 2:7, we read that after God formed Adam out of the dust of the ground, He breathed into him the breath of life. The word "life" is the English translation. But when we look at the Hebrew text, the original language, we find that the word "life" here is in the plural. "He breathed into Adam, the breath of lives." In Hebrew the plural can indeed mean singular, but the Hebrew word "Adam" has a plural connotation. It means "Mankind" (see Genesis 5:2, where the word "Mankind" is "Adam" in the original).

The truth is confirmed in Acts 17:26, which tells us that out of one—that is, out of Adam's life— God created all men to dwell upon this earth. The human race is simply the multiplication of Adam's life and the life Adam passed on to his posterity—to his children—is a life that (1) has already sinned, (2) is a life condemned, and finally, (3) is a life sentenced to death.

Because of our position in Adam, we all belong on Death Row because we, in him, participated in his sin. Paul tells us in 1 Corinthians 15:22, "In Adam, all die."

By uniting Christ's divinity with the corporate humanity of the human race in need of redemption, Christ became the last Adam (1 Corinthians 15:45). Since we are, by the incarnation, in Christ by God's act, His obedience can legally be credited to us. It can be lawfully ours because all mankind was implicated in His obedience.

As quoted last chapter, Greek scholar Brook Foss Westcott says that Christ's humanity was not the humanity of one person. In Him all humanity was gathered together so that when He obeyed the law and when He died on the cross, it was not one man obeying and dying instead of all men, but all men obeying and dying in one Man. The obedience and death of Christ was both a corporate obedience and a corporate death. Hence, the gospel is not legal fiction, as alleged by those who opposed the Reformation. Second Corinthians 5:14 makes it clear that when one died, all died.

On the cross, it was not one Man dying instead of all men—though the Bible does use the phrase "in place of." But when we interpret that statement in the context of Paul's theology, we discover that Christ could die in place of all men because all men were in him.

This may be hard for us to understand, but it represents good Hebrew logic. In 1 Corinthians 1:30 we read that God put us—all mankind—into Christ. God made Christ to be our wisdom, our righteousness, our redemption, our everything. As we turn to this passage in Romans 5:15-18, we lay the very foundation for Christ our Righteousness.

Many scholars today, like John R.W. Stott and Clark H. Pinnock, admit that the "In Christ" motif brought out in this passage is the central theme of Paul's theology. It is the core of the message of righteousness by faith.

God's Free Gift

With this foundation, let us turn to Romans 5:15-18. After reading it through, we will discuss it: "But the free gift is not like the offense. For if by the one man's offense many died, much more the grace of God and the gift by the grace of the one man, Jesus Christ, abounded to many. And the gift is not like that which came through the one who sinned. For the judgment which came from one offense resulted in condemnation, but the free gift which came from many offenses resulted in justification. For if by one man's offense death reigned through the one, much more those who receive abundance of grace and of the gift of righteousness will reign in life through the One, Jesus Christ. Therefore, as through one man's offense, judgment came to all men, resulting in condemnation, even so through one Man's righteous act the free gift came to all men, resulting in justification of life."

What a tremendous passage! Now, let us study it in some detail.

The first things we should notice are two major differences between our situation in Christ and our condition in Adam.

First, when Paul refers to the obedience of Christ that justifies us, he calls it a free gift. This term applies to Christ but never to Adam. It is very important to notice this, for like any gift, we cannot enjoy it if we reject it.

What is true of us in Adam is not a gift. It belongs to us by native right. We inherit it by birth. We are by creation—by nature—in Adam. Therefore, what he passed on to the human race—sin, condemnation, and death—is ours by inheritance. As Paul brings out in Ephesians 2:3, this means that we are by nature the children of wrath.

But when it comes to Christ, what we receive through Him and in Him is a gift—we can either accept it or reject it.

Second, Paul applies a distinctive phrase to Christ but not to Adam. This phrase is "much more." Paul directs this phrase to our situation in Christ several times in this passage. The phrase simply means that we receive in Christ much more than what we lost in Adam. Remember these two points as we analyze this passage.

Now let us read Romans 5:15: "But the free gift is not like the offense. For if by the one man's offense, many died, much more the grace of God and the gift by that grace of the one Man, Jesus Christ abounded to many."

First, Paul is telling us that when one man sinned, many died. The word "many" in the original is proceeded by the definite article "the." Paul is really saying that when one man sinned, the many died. There's a very important difference between "many" by itself and "the many." In English, the word "many" can be a large number out of a greater number. But here "the many" refers to a specific group, mentioned in verse 18, "all men."

Paul is telling us in verse 15 that what Adam did affected all mankind. But the second half of verse 15 says the very same thing about Christ and His obedience: "Much more the grace of God and the gift by the grace of the one Man, Jesus Christ, abounded to the many."

In other words, what Adam did affected the many. Likewise, what Christ did affected the many and the effect is much more than the damage of Adam's one sin.

We continue reading in verse 16: "And the gift is not like that which came through the one who sinned for the judgment which came from one offense resulted in condemnation. But the free gift, which came from many offenses, resulted in justification." (The words "free gift" in the King James Version is actually translated from the word "grace" in the original and refers to the obedience of Christ, in contrast to the offense of Adam).

All Obey in Jesus

Paul is saying that when Adam sinned, the judgment of condemnation unto death came to all mankind. When Christ obeyed, He did much more than cancel Adam's sin. Notice the phrase "many offenses." The free gift (obedience of Christ) that came from many offenses resulted in justification.

Here Paul is simply saying that if all that Christ did on the cross was to cancel Adam's sin—if all that Christ did was to die for Adam's sin, which condemns us—we still would have a problem. Besides Adam's sin, which condemns us, we have also added our own personal sins, which are many.

Therefore it was not enough for Christ to die for Adam's sin only, to save humanity. He also had to pay the price for our sins.

On the cross Christ did "much more" than die for Adam's sin. He died for Adam's sin, plus our personal sins which are many. Hence the phrase "many offenses."

Do you see the "much more"—the superabundance of the grace of God? God took care of Adam's sin, plus our sins past, present, and future. What wonderful, beautiful grace!

Now let us continue in Romans 5:17: "For if by the one man's offense death reigned through the one, much more those who receive abundance of grace and of the gift of righteousness will reign in life through the one, Jesus Christ."

Here Paul is saying that when Adam sinned, not only did we come under the death sentence, but death came as a conqueror. The phrase "death reigned" means death came to rule over every human being, however morally strong. No one except Jesus Christ has been able to conquer death. So Adam's sin brought death to rule over all humanity. This is our natural situation. It is our inheritance—the "Grim Reaper."

Receiving the Gift

But, thank God, Paul continues, "Much more those who receive abundance of grace and of the gift of righteousness, will reign in life through the one, Jesus Christ."

Jesus came not only to cancel the death sentence that reigns over us, but to give much more to those who receive Him as their righteousness. The word "receive" is used, because what God did to us in Christ is a gift. And like any gift, it has to be received—or accepted—to be enjoyed.

Paul says that those who accept the gift of righteousness by faith will reign. They are not reigning now, but in the future when Christ comes, they will reign through the One, Jesus Christ. This is overflowing abundance!

Mankind, as created by God in Adam even before the Fall, was still a third-class citizenry. God is always first. The angels are second. The book of Hebrews tells us that human beings were created a little lower than the angels (Hebrews 2:6-8). When Adam sinned, he brought us down to the bottom of the pit.

Ruling the Universe

Did Christ, by His act of obedience and His righteousness, restore us to the position we lost? The answer is "No." He did "much more." He took us to where He is so that in Him we are above the angels and shall reign and rule over them. We shall rule the universe with Him.

In Romans 8:16 and 17, the apostle Paul tells us that we are joint heirs with Christ—that we have equal rights with Him. In Revelation 20:6, John tells us that those who have part in the first resurrection—the believers—not only conquer the second death but reign with Christ for 1,000 years.

Then in Revelation 22:5, when Christ restores this earth to its original perfection, the saved shall reign with Him forever and ever.

How can we refuse this gift of righteousness? It is a gift that not only liberates us from the reign of death but takes us to the very place where God Himself reigns. We shall reign with Him; we will be joint heirs with Him.

Moving on to Romans 5:18, we read: "As through one man's offense (*notice offense is in the singular, referring to Adam's one sin*) judgment came (*past historical tense*) to all men, resulting in condemnation, even so through one man's righteous act (*not our performance but His performance; not your righteousness but His righteousness, through the act of Jesus Christ, His doing and dying*) the free gift came (*past historical tense*) to all men."

This gift came not only to the believers but to all mankind. But unfortunately not all mankind will be saved, because this justification unto life is a gift for all men. Sad to say, all men will not accept this gift.

Jesus said to Nicodemus in John 3:16: "God so loved the world, that he gave his only begotten Son that whosoever believeth in him shall not perish, but have everlasting life" (KJV).

John continues in John 3:36, saying that he who rejects the Son shall not see life, but the wrath of God still abides on him.

In Summary

So, what have we learned from Romans 5:15-18? First, we've discovered that Adam's sin deprived humanity of life and brought on all mankind the sentence of eternal death. Because we are children of Adam we are disqualified to live. The only reason we are living today is because God has given us a probationary time in which to accept His gift (Ephesians 1:4; 2 Corinthians 5:19).

Second, we have discovered that Christ's obedience—His doing and dying—did three things for all mankind: (a) It saved all humanity from the condemnation of eternal death, (b) It brought the verdict of justification to eternal life upon all men, and (c) Whether we qualify for life or for death depends on the segment of humanity to which we belong. We are by nature in Adam. But if by faith we have accepted the righteousness of Christ—God's gift to humanity—the death sentence is removed and we are justified unto life (John 5:24).

We should not reject this gift, for it is our only hope. There is no other way we can ever make it to heaven. There is no other way we can ever escape eternal death (the wages of sin), except by receiving by faith the gift of our Lord, Jesus Christ—the gift of righteousness that He obtained for the entire human race.

Chapter 12

The Reign of Sin and Grace

Romans 5:19-21

In Romans 5:15-18, that tremendous passage we covered last study, we discovered that because of Adam's sin, we received the sentence of eternal death. Through Christ's obedience, however, we receive the verdict of justification unto eternal life. We also discovered that Christ not only canceled Adam's sin (which condemns us), He canceled all of our sins by His life and death. He restored to us justification unto life.

God's supreme gift is Jesus Christ. No one will ever be in heaven because of their own righteousness. There is only one way mankind can make it to heaven—through the righteousness of Christ. This is what we saw in our last study. By one Man's obedience and righteousness, justification unto life came to all mankind.

Now we shall turn to our final study of this tremendous passage—Romans 5:19-21.

Here we discover that we inherit another problem from Adam and another blessing from Christ: "For as by one man's disobedience, many were made sinners, so also by one Man's obedience, many will be made righteous. Moreover, the law entered that the offense might abound. But where sin abounded, grace abounded much more, so that as sin reigned in death, even so grace might reign through righteousness to eternal life through Jesus Christ, our Lord."

This wonderful passage states our predicament—our sin problem. According to Romans 5:19, Adam's one sin made us sinners. In other words, we were born sinners because of Adam's fall. Paul is not saying that we are guilty of Adam's sin. Original guilt is not biblical. But the Bible does teach that Adam's sin makes us sinners.

Now, if we reverse that, we find that the opposite is true of Christ. It is by the righteousness of Christ that the believer is made righteous. The reason we sin is not that we are sinners by choice, but sinners by nature. Sins that we commit are simply the fruit of what we are by nature.

In the same sense, we must apply this to Christ and our situation in Him. Is it our own goodness that makes us righteous, or is our righteous living evidence that we are already righteous in Christ? Only the latter.

We have no ability to produce righteousness, in and of ourselves. Paul clearly tells us in Romans 3:10: "There is none righteous, no not one," and in verse 12: "They have all gone out of the way." But thank God, in Jesus Christ we have hope and all believers, according to Paul, are saints. We are not saints only when we have reached 100 percent righteousness. We are already saints in Jesus Christ.

Look, for example, at 1 Corinthians, where Paul writes to a church whose members are living far from holy lives. This church had many problems. Members were taking each other to court. There were sexual problems of the worst kind which even the Gentiles—the unbelievers—did not practice. And yet, Paul calls these Corinthian Christians saints. They were saints not because of their performance, but because they were in Christ. They were anything but saintly in their behavior. Paul tells us in Romans 5:19: "For as by one man's disobedience, many were made sinners." We were made—or constituted—sinners by the fall of Adam. "So also by one Man's obedience many will be made righteous."

Sinners By Nature

Paul uses the past tense when he talks about Adam—a one-time happening. When he talks about Christ and our situation in Christ, he uses the future tense. All of us are already born sinners, but we are not yet righteous by nature. We will be made righteous by nature at the Second Coming of Christ, when this corruption puts on incorruption. This is what Paul tells us in 1 Corinthians 15:53. Only then will those who have accepted Christ be made righteous.

Whenever Paul uses the past tense regarding our situation in Christ, he is talking about an objective truth which took place in Jesus Christ and which applies to all men. When he uses the future tense, as in Romans 5:17, "We shall reign with Him" and in verse 19, "We shall be made righteous," he is referring only to those who have received, accepted, and believed the gospel. We must remember this—otherwise we may become confused.

In Romans 5:19 Paul says that the moment we are born, Adam's sin makes us unrighteous. We are born sinners—not guilty sinners, but sinners by nature. Therefore the condemnation of the law rested on us. The opposite occurs through Jesus Christ. Believers will be made righteous in nature at the Second Coming of Christ but are righteous today only through faith in Christ.

Paul says that both Adam and we are made of dust. We all bear the image of Adam because of his fall. This is found in 1 Corinthians 15: 48-49: "As was the man of dust (*Adam*), so also are those who are made of dust (*his children*). And as is the heavenly Man (*Christ*), so also are those who are heavenly (*those who believe in Christ*). And as we have borne the image of the man of dust (*Adam*), we shall (*future tense*) also bear the image of the heavenly."

Faith, Not Reality

A believer is now declared righteous. He is justified by faith, not by reality. It is only at the Second Coming of Christ that Christians will experience the reality and be made righteous in the fullest sense of the word. This does not mean that they cannot live righteous lives now, while they are waiting for Christ to come. It is possible, by the grace of God. We see this in Romans 5:1-3. A Christian, saved by grace and justified by faith, stands under the umbrella of grace. In the power of God through the Holy Spirit, he or she can lead a righteous life. It is possible indeed for a Christian to live a righteous life and have victory over sin. But this righteous living—this victory over sin—does not change human nature one iota. That nature remains 100 percent sinful and will not change until the Second Coming of Christ, when this corruption puts on incorruption. Only then will the Christian be made righteous.

Those believers who feel they are still sinners are correct, for their sinful natures declare them to be sinners. In fact, if we claim that we are not sinners, then the apostle John tells us in 1 John 1:8 and 10 that we are liars and the truth does not abide in us. Christians are sinners, saved by grace. As Luther put it, Christians are 100 percent sinners and 100 percent righteous at the same time—sinners in themselves but righteous in Christ.

In 1 Timothy 1:15 Paul makes a statement that he says is a "true saying, worthy of all acceptation, that Jesus Christ came to save sinners." Then he adds, not in the past tense but in the present continuous tense, "of whom I am chief (*foremost*)." Thank God it is by the grace of God that Christians are saved. Yes, they want to live righteous lives so they can reflect to the world the character of God—the character of Jesus Christ, who dwells in them through the Holy Spirit. But Christians need to understand that it is not their performance that gives them the assurance of salvation, but the righteousness of Christ.

Offense Abounds

Now let us move to verse 20, for this verse amplifies what Paul has already told us in verse 19. Let us read them together: "For as by one man's disobedience, many were made sinners, so also by one Man's obedience many will be made righteous. Moreover, the law entered that the offense might abound. But where sin abounded, grace abounded much more."

Verse 20 says, "Moreover, the law entered." Where did the law enter? Paul uses the word "entered" in the way we use the word "promised." God promised Abraham salvation as a gift, not only to him, but to all who accept the Messiah as Abraham did, by faith. Did God, 430 years after Abraham, give the law as an added requirement? No. Then why did God give the law—why did the law enter, after He had promised grace and salvation as a gift?

Paul tells us in verse 20 that one of the reasons God gave the law is that offense might abound. God gave the law first to the Jews and through the Jews to the human race, not to make them righteous—not to save them—but that they might recognize that sin has abounded in their lives.

Look at the word "offense." Some translations use the word "trespass." Note that this word is in the singular. It is not referring to personal sins. It is referring to Adam's offense—Adam's sin. This is why it is in the singular. Moreover, the law entered that Adam's sin might abound. Where did Adam's sin abound? It abounded in the lives of his children. In verse 19 Paul tells us that Adam's sin made us sinners. Therefore, since you and I are sinners by nature, the only fruits we can bear are sinful acts. But how do we know that our fruits are sin? How do we know that we are sinners? How do we know that Adam's sin has produced a whole human race of sinners? The law gives us the knowledge of sin (Romans 3:20).

In other words, God gave the law, not to solve the sin problem, but to expose the sin problem to the human race. He gave us the law to remove the lid of our self-respectability. He gave the law to remove the deception of self-righteousness and show us what we really are like inside. We are rotten from head to foot. We are sinners. This is why Paul can say in Romans 7:7-9: "I did not know sin until I understood the law. When I understood the law, sin revived. I discovered I was a sinner worthy of death."

Judaism had taught Paul that he could be saved by keeping the law. Paul, at one time a Pharisee, believed this. He brings this out in Philippians 3:4-6. But when he discovered the true meaning of the law, he found that the law could not save him and simply condemned him as a sinner. God gave the law, not as an added requirement, but that the promise might become desirable. God gave the law to expose us as sinners. Adam's sin made us sinners (verse 19) and the law simply proved it.

But now, in the second half of Romans 5:20 we read: "But where sin abounded, grace did much more abound (or *"grace abounded much more."*) Oh, what a wonderful truth!

So now, let us list what Paul is saying here: (1) Adam's sin made us sinners. Because of this, we have borne many sins as fruits. In other words, besides Adam's sin, we have committed many, many personal sins. So we have a dual problem. We have Adam's sin, which condemns us, plus our sins revealed by the law. There is nothing we can do to escape this problem except to receive the gift of God, Jesus Christ.

(2) The second half of verse 20 says that even though we have a dual problem—Adam's sin plus our sins—the grace of God abounded much more. Paul means two things by this: (a) First, that the grace of God—the life and death of Jesus Christ—has not only liberated us (saved us from Adam's sin, plus ours). It also gives us positive righteousness. The fact that the grace of God cancels Adam's sin; the fact that the blood of Christ forgives me of all my personal sins, wonderful as forgiveness may be, still leaves a negative thing. I am still not qualified for heaven. What Jesus did is much more than cancel or pay the price of Adam's sin. He did much more than simply pay the price for our personal sins, past, present and future. He also brought to us positive righteousness so that, in Jesus Christ, we have not only forgiveness but righteousness—a righteousness that fully satisfies the positive demands of the law. This is what Paul means by the phrase "much more."

We can see why Paul could say to the Christians in Corinth, "I want to know nothing among you except Jesus Christ and Him crucified." Paul says in Galatians 6, "I want to glory in nothing else but Jesus Christ and His cross."

May we, like Paul, boast only in Him who loved us and gave Himself for us. It is the righteousness of Christ, His obedience, and His life and death that take away all our sins and give us in exchange a righteousness that fully qualifies us for heaven. How can anyone be so foolish as to reject this gift?

From Bikes to Motorcycles

One day I was talking to a group of children and asked them, "How many of you have bicycles?" All their hands went up. "Then, how would you like to give away these bicycles to those who have no bicycles? Would that be a sacrifice?" The children said, "Yes, it would be a sacrifice."

"Now, let me change the offer," I continued. "If I say to you to give your bicycles and, in exchange, I will give you each a Honda motorcycle with all the gas you need as long as you have it, would it still be a sacrifice to give up that bicycle?"

"No way!" came the response.

"Then, what would you say to a person who rejects giving up his bicycle in exchange for a motorcycle?" I asked.

One boy shouted, "He is a fool. He needs to have his head examined."

Anyone who rejects the gift of Jesus Christ is a fool, for if we think we can make ourselves righteous—if we think we can reach heaven by our own efforts—we make a great mistake. The Bible is clear that there is none righteous; there is none who does good (Romans 3:10 and 12). Yes, we may do many good things. But none of them are good enough to satisfy the law of God, for the law of God demands not only perfect acts but perfect motives. Since we are born egocentric, all our righteousness is polluted with self. Isaiah 64:6 says, "All our righteousness (*not our sins, but all our righteousness*) is filthy rags."

Born on Death Row

With this in mind, let us turn to the final verse, Romans 5:21, which begins: "So that as sin reigned in death...." The moment we were born into this world, sin reigned over us. Paul is using the past historical tense. We were born on Death Row. You may have been the most beautiful baby in the world; you may have been an innocent baby in the eyes of your parents. But as far as the law of God is concerned, you were born on Death Row. You were born to die in Adam!

The moment we were born, sin and death reigned over us. Paul is saying that we are born sinners and that sin rules over us until it takes us to the grave. This is what happens if we do not accept Jesus Christ. True, Christians also die. But, according to Jesus in John 11 and Paul in 1 Thessalonians 4:13-18, the death Christians die is only sleep. The hope of the believer is the resurrection. The unbeliever has no hope. When he dies, he is saying good-bye to life forever. The Christian who dies is only going to sleep. This is why Paul can say in Philippians 1:21: "For me to live is Christ and if I have to die in the process, it is gain."

Paul says we are born under the reign of sin. If we allow it to reign over us we will die eternally. Talking to Christians, Paul says in Romans 5: 21 "Even so grace might reign." Again he is using the past historical tense. The moment we believe, we come under the reign of grace. When we live under grace, righteousness is seen by God as He looks upon us. Righteousness is ours in Christ.

Paul says in Romans 5:21, "Even so, grace might reign through righteousness (*of Christ*) to eternal life through Jesus Christ our Lord." Christians live under the umbrella of Christ's righteousness, God's grace, and justification by faith. As long as they remain by faith under that umbrella, the law does not condemn them.

We as Christians stand righteous and have a hope. That hope is eternal life when Christ comes—when this mortal shall put on immortality and this corruption puts on incorruption (1 Corinthians 15:51-54).

What a wonderful message this is to the world! "For God so loved the world that He gave His only begotten Son, that whosoever believeth in Him should not perish… (John 3:16)."

We read in Ephesians 2:8- 9, "It is by grace that you and I are saved. It is through faith and not of ourselves; it is the gift of God." The word "it" in Ephesians 2:8 refers to grace. Grace is a gift; therefore, there is no boasting in righteousness by faith. All we can boast in is Jesus Christ and Him crucified.

Let us accept the gift of Christ so that we will pass from death to life and, as we wait for His Second Coming, reflect His righteousness in our lives.

CHAPTER 13

Dead to Sin, Alive to God

Romans 6:1-13

In Paul's Epistle to the Romans, God gives a complete picture of the wonderful message of salvation by grace. The Epistle's key passage is Romans 5:12-21.

We have spent three chapters examining this passage in detail, for it lays the foundation for understanding all of Romans. The parallel in Romans between Adam and Christ undergirds the biblical truth that all mankind is represented in both Adam and Christ.

In the great majority of the 510 times the word "Adam" appears in the Hebrew Old Testament, it possesses a collective significance. In the same sense, Christ in the New Testament is referred to as the last, or second, Adam. Just as Adam's sin affected the whole human race, Christ's obedience affects us all. As Adam's sin brings the judgment of condemnation and the sentence of death to all men, we have discovered that by one Man's obedience, Jesus Christ's, justification unto life came to all men. But this justification becomes effective individually only when the believer accepts it by the faith. This is the glorious truth of the gospel!

Having examined Romans 5:12-21 in some depth, we now prepare to turn to Romans 6, where Paul deals with the great danger of the gospel. In Romans 4, Paul dealt with the great enemy of the gospel—legalism, or salvation by self-dependence, or self-righteousness.

Cheap Grace

Now, in Romans 6, Paul looks at the danger that we face as Christians. The famous German martyr who died under Hitler, Dietrich Bonhoeffer, defines this danger as "cheap grace." What do we mean by "cheap grace?"

Let me illustrate with a personal experience. While I was a Christian missionary in Western Uganda, a young man came to me, believing me to be a Hindu (since I am of Asian Indian descent). The young Christian wanted to share his faith with me, so he asked me a question, "Are you saved?"

"Saved from what?" I asked, warming to the conversation.

"Are you saved from sin?"

"Can you be more specific?" I prodded. "Are you referring to the guilt and punishment of sin, the power and slavery of sin, or the nature and presence of sin? Which one are you talking about?"

He looked at me and said, "You sound like a pastor."

"Yes, I am a pastor," I acknowledged, "and I would like to ask you the same question, 'Are you saved?'"

With great enthusiasm he raised his arms and cried, "Brother, I was saved three months ago."

"Really! How come?" I responded, concern in my voice.

"I believed in Jesus Christ," he exulted.

"May I correct you?" I interjected. "You were not saved three months ago. You were saved some 2,000 years ago. You accepted that salvation three months ago. Please do not give any credit to your faith. The Bible does not teach that we are saved because of our faith. But we are saved through faith, or by faith. Faith is only a channel—an instrument—by which we receive the righteousness of Christ that saves us. And if you are saved, how come I smell beer on your breath?" I probed.

He looked at me in amazement: "Brother, you know that we are saved by grace, not by works."

"Then please explain to me what you mean by salvation by grace," I urged.

"It is very simple. Christ did it all for me," he answered.

"Really!" I responded. "You mean Christ lived a perfect life instead of you?"

"Yes!" he said.

"And He died instead of you?" I continued.

"Now you have it!" he cried.

"One more step, then," I answered. "There is a third step, if I take your argument to its logical conclusion."

"What step is that?" he asked.

"He also went to heaven, instead of you."

"No way!" he cried. "I plan to go to heaven!" He had a small New Testament Bible in his pocket, so I asked him to read 2 Timothy 2:11. He turned to it and read: "This is a faithful saying: For if we died with Him, We shall also live with Him."

This young Christian had turned the wonderful message of salvation by grace into "cheap grace," or antinomianism. He believed that "Christ did it all, so I can live as I please."

But the gospel of grace does not give liberty for believers to live as they please. This issue Paul deals with in Romans 6.

Bent to Sin

The gospel is incredibly good news—the New Testament and, especially, Paul's epistle to the Romans make this clear. We've seen in Romans 5: 6-10 that while we were helpless, ungodly enemies of God, we were reconciled to Him by the death of His Son. The gospel is incredibly good news! Praise the Lord for that!

But because we possess sinful natures—natures that are not only bent to sin, but that enjoy sin—it is easy for us to take this message of salvation by grace alone and pervert it into license to sin.

In Romans 5:20 Paul makes a wonderful statement about the gospel of Jesus Christ in the last part of the verse: "But where sin abounded, grace abounded much more."

It doesn't matter how terribly we have fallen as sinners; grace is able to save the worst of us, because grace is greater than all our sins put together. But we can take that statement and twist it—exactly as the Judaizing, legalistic Christians accused Paul of doing in his day. They said he was turning the gospel into a license to sin.

License to Sin?

"If you tell men and women that salvation is entirely a free gift—obtained by the holy history of Christ—you are opening the door for sinful living," they argued. "Our performance *does* make a contribution toward salvation!"

But Paul responds, "One moment, please. That is not what I am teaching." Paul deals with it from two different angles, one of which appears in Romans 6:1-13. Then, in our next study, we will look at the second half of Romans 6, which covers the same problem from a different angle.

In light of what Paul has been saying in Romans 5:20, he begins Romans 6 with a question. "What shall we say then? Shall we continue (*keep on*) in sin that grace may abound?" Is this what I am teaching? Is this what I mean when I say that where sin abounded, grace did much more abound?

In verse 2 he replies, "Certainly not!" or "God forbid!" Paul finds it unthinkable that any Christian should come to such a conclusion. "How shall we, who died to sin, live any longer in it?"

Dying to Sin

Paul is not discussing falling into sin out of weakness; he's talking here about an attitude toward sin. Can a Christian condone sinning, in view of the fact that he is saved by grace alone? The answer is, "Certainly not!" It is not because the believer has promised God to be good, but because he or she has died to sin. How can anyone who is dead to sin say it is all right to sin?

The phrase, "dead to sin," appears three times in the first half of Romans 6. It appears for the first time in verse 2, where it refers to the justified believer—the person who has accepted by faith the righteousness of Christ.

It appears the second time in verse 10 and refers to Christ: "For the death that He (*Christ*) died, He died to sin once for all." On the cross Jesus Christ brought sin to an end—humanity's sin.

The third time we find this statement is in verse 11: "Likewise (*in the same way*), you also, reckon (*consider*) yourselves to be dead indeed to sin but alive to God in Christ Jesus our Lord."

Why should a believer reckon himself dead to sin and alive to God? It is because true Christianity offers more than a merely transformed life. The gospel never offers transformation, or reformation, of the old life. Paul is offering a new life—the life and history of Christ in exchange for the old life and its history.

As we covered in Romans 5:12 to 21, for Jesus to be our Savior and redeemer from sin, He had to identify Himself with the humanity that needed redeeming. In the incarnation, God united Jesus Christ—the second Person of the Godhead, the Son of God—with the corporate human race that needed redeeming. Thus, by uniting Jesus with the corporate human race, Jesus Christ became the second, or last, Adam. He became legally qualified to be our Substitute and our Representative. So whatever took place in His history becomes our history, because we were in Him through the incarnation.

Jesus was not merely one man among many men. All humanity was gathered up in Him. The Bible teaches that Jesus' death was a corporate death. When He died on the cross, all men died in Him (2 Corinthians 5:14).

When God comes to us with the gospel, He brings the message, "I took you, a sinner, and I united you to My Son, Jesus Christ. In His perfect life—His perfect obedience—and His death on the cross, I rewrote your history. I did it out of love, but My love will not coerce. I will not force this history upon you, so I need your acceptance."

Our positive response to this gospel is faith. As we found in an earlier chapter, faith is a thankful obedience to the truth as it is in Christ. Just as Christ had to identify Himself with us in order to become our Savior, we must identify ourselves with Him and His holy history for this salvation to be made effective. Faith is more than a mental assent to truth. Faith is obeying the gospel. Faith is saying, "Yes, God, I accept my history in Your Son, Jesus Christ." The moment we do this, we are accepting His death as our death, His life as our life. If we accept His death as our death, then we need to be buried.

Buried in Baptism

Jesus in Mark 16:15 and 16 commissions his disciples, "Go into all the world and preach the gospel to every creature," and adds, "He who believes and is baptized shall be saved."

Why did Jesus add baptism as an element for salvation? Did He mean that the act of baptism saves us? No. It is the *truth* of baptism that makes salvation effective, because the truth of baptism is the public confession that a believer has obeyed the gospel. The truth of baptism is found in Romans 6:3-6: "Or do you not know (*Paul says to the believer*) that as many of us as were baptized into Christ Jesus were baptized into His death? Therefore, we were buried with Him through baptism into death that just as Christ was raised from the dead by the glory of the Father, even so we also should walk in newness of life. For if we have been united together in the likeness of his death, certainly we also shall be in the likeness of his resurrection, knowing this that our old man (*self-life*) was crucified with Him that the body of sin might be done away with, that we should no longer be slaves of sin."

Notice the various things Paul is saying here: First, that baptism is always into Christ. In Galatians 3:27 we discover what Paul means by "baptism into Christ": "For as many of you as were baptized into Christ have put on Christ." Baptism means identifying by faith with Jesus Christ and Him crucified, buried, and resurrected. It means abiding in Christ.

Going back to Romans 6, Paul says that when believers are baptized into Christ, they accept the death of Christ as their death. And just as Christ was buried after He died, so the believer must be buried in the waters of baptism. This is why, in the New Testament, baptism is always by immersion, for baptism by immersion is a beautiful symbol of death and burial in Jesus Christ.

Rising to New Life

But Paul says that Christians do not remain in the grave, for Christ did not remain in the grave. He left sin in the grave, but He rose up and with Him raised the human race.

So, when the Christian rises out of the waters of baptism, Paul says in the last part of verse 4 that he or she rises up to walk in newness of life.

This is how Christianity differs from every other religion, for in all others, the converts must change their lifestyles, reform their lives, and improve their living to be saved. But Christianity is not a reformation of the old life. Christianity involves exchanging the old life for the life of Jesus Christ. The old life inherited from Adam is a slave to sin. It cannot be transformed. That is why it was put to death on Christ's cross (Romans 7:4; Galatians 5:24). God saves His followers by giving them new lives in exchange for their old, buried lives.

As Jesus said to Nicodemus, that which is born of the flesh is flesh. We cannot change that. So, when a believer accepts Christ and is baptized into Christ, he accepts Jesus' life in exchange for his old, Adamic life. Or, as Paul says in Galatians 2:20, a believer is a person who confesses from the heart, "I have been crucified with Christ; it is no longer I who live but Christ lives in me; and the life which I now live in the flesh I live by faith in the Son of God who loved me and gave Himself for me."

Christ is the same yesterday, today, and forever. The life He lived 2,000 years ago—the life of unconditional love, going about doing good—is the life He will reproduce in the baptized believer. Christians cannot condone sin without contradicting their faith and baptism. Faith and baptism means that they have put on Christ; they have identified themselves with Christ crucified; His death becomes their death, and His death was to sin.

The believer dies to sin in Jesus Christ. Romans 6:6 reads: "Knowing this, that our old man was crucified with Him...." Here the "old man" means the old self-life—the life that comes through Adam, after he sinned. That life died on the cross. It met the wages of sin in Jesus Christ so the old life should no longer control the body.

The body, in and of itself, is not sin. This concept comes from Greek philosophy and is not biblical. The real problem is with the old self-life, which has been done away with on the cross. In exchange the believer receives the life of Christ, through the new-birth experience and indwelling Holy Spirit. This new life now has—or should have—control.

Paul continues in verse 7: "For he who has died has been freed from sin." The word "freed" appears three times in Romans 6—in verses 7, 18, and 22. In verses 18 and 22 he uses the same Greek word, but in verse 7 he uses an entirely different word. The word he uses in Romans 6:7 is the same word we find in Acts 13:39, translated there as "justified." The word Paul used in Romans 6:7 is indeed "justified."

The word "free" is a correct translation of that word, because when a person dies to sin in Christ, he is acquitted from the law. The law cannot condemn after the believer has died to sin in Christ, for the law (as Paul says in Romans 7:1) has dominion only as long as we are living. But death in Christ saves the believers and sets them free from sin.

In Romans 7:14 Paul says all have been sold as slaves to sin because of Adam's fall. Through the gospel, not only can the believers go to heaven—not only do they have peace with God, not only do they stand justified before the law of God—but they have been freed from the dominion of sin.

Living in Jesus

Paul continues speaking to the believers in Romans 6:8: "Now if we died with Christ, we believe we shall also live with Him." In the world we begin by living— being born with life—and end up with death, since all are born with condemned lives. But in the gospel it is the other way around. We begin with death and end up with life. Paul is saying that unless we first die with Christ, we cannot live with Him. And if we have died with Christ, we can no longer condone sin, for sin has no more dominion over us.

In verses 9-13, then, Paul says in effect: "In view of this, do not let sin rule over you." Do not let it control you. Do not let it manipulate you, because you are no longer under law but under grace (verse 14). Present your bodies as instruments from death to life, instruments to righteousness that Christ may be revealed in you.

Justification by faith produces fruits, and the fruits of justification by faith are lives that reflect the love and good works of Jesus Christ. Jesus says, "And you shall know the truth, and the truth shall make you free" (John 8:32). The gospel must not be perverted into cheap grace. The world desperately needs to see Christ in us, the hope of glory. It is only as we understand the full gospel as explained by Paul that we will know how this can happen.

Chapter 14

From Law to Grace

Romans 6:14-23

In our study of Romans we have discovered that the gospel is incredibly good news and that salvation is by grace alone.

In Romans 6 we also find that the gospel is dangerous good news—dangerous because sinful natures can pervert it into cheap grace and license to sin.

In our study of Romans 6:1-13, Paul makes it extremely clear that believers are saved by grace alone and that this gives them no license to continue sinning. No follower of Jesus can adopt the attitude that it is all right to sin—to live as one pleases because salvation is by grace alone. Grace gives no such liberty. Jesus did not come to save believers in their sins. He came to save them from sin. He came to save them not only from the guilt and punishment of sin, but from the slavery and dominion of sin. Paul brings this out in Romans 6.

A Christian is a person who has identified himself with Jesus Christ—crucified, buried, and resurrected. Since Christ's death was unto sin (verse 10), Paul says that baptized believers must likewise consider themselves dead to sin but alive to God (verse 11). A Christian is a person who has died to sin in Christ. Just as Christ brought sin to an end on the cross, His followers must say good-bye to sin as they accept Him as their Savior.

Just as sin separated God from His Son on the cross, leading Jesus to cry in agony, "Father, Father, why hast Thou forsaken Me," sin also separates us from God, according to Isaiah 59:2.

But when a man or woman, boy or girl, dies to sin in Christ, separation from God ends. They become one with God and now live unto God, by the indwelling Spirit. The reconciliation obtained by Christ for all mankind on the cross, becomes effective in the believer by faith and baptism.

Sin's Dominion

One benefit of being saved by grace is expressed in Romans 6:14: "For sin shall not have dominion over you, for you are not under law but under grace."

Some say this means that before sinners become Christians, they sin all the time. But now that they have accepted Christ, sin no longer has dominion over them—that is, they only sin occasionally. This is a far cry from what Paul meant.

What does Paul mean, then, when he says that sin shall not have dominion over the believer? He means that Christians are delivered from the rulership of sin. In what sense? We find a help in 1 Corinthians 15: 56, where Paul says: "The sting of death is sin, and the strength of sin is the law." Sin is what kills us. The wages of sin is death (Romans 6: 23). Sin brings death, but sin cannot kill us or destroy us without the authority of the law. It is the law that gives sin this deadly authority.

But sin cannot cause us to perish forever, because a Christian is no longer under law but under grace. The believer now has diplomatic immunity. This is wonderfully good news!

Romans 5:20 says that where sin abounds, grace did much more abound, and Romans 6:14 tells the believer that he is not under law but under grace. Both statements are dangerous news, however, because believers may feel that since sin cannot destroy or kill them (*because they are under grace and not under law*), they are free to keep on sinning.

But Paul anticipates this excuse and writes in verse 15: "What then? Shall we sin because we are not under law but under grace?" He answers emphatically, "Certainly not!"

What Paul Truly Means

The reasoning behind Paul's emphatic answer is found in verses 16 and onward, and we'll explore that reasoning in our next study. But clearly Paul understands that verse 14 is dangerous, if misused. It can be perverted. It can be twisted. We must understand what Paul truly means when he says believers are not under law but under grace.

First we must make clear what Paul does not mean. Some Christians believe and teach that from Moses to Christ, men and women were saved under the law. They call it the Old Covenant. But when Christ came, they say He did away with the law; He did away with the Old Covenant and placed humanity under grace.

Such a teaching, however, contradicts the unity of the Bible. Nowhere does Scripture ever teach that mankind can be saved through the law. From Adam to the last man, men and women are saved by grace alone.

When Paul says that by the works of the law no flesh will be justified (Romans 3:20, Galatians 2:16), he applies the umbrella to all men, in both the Old and the New Testament. Scripture clearly teaches that mankind can be saved through grace alone. The only difference is that in the Old Testament, men and women were saved by faith in the promised Messiah, while in the New Testament they are saved by faith in the fulfillment of the promise, Jesus Christ.

Paul brings this out very clearly in Romans 4, where Abraham is said to be saved by faith alone in Jesus Christ. To him, Christ was a promise. To us, Christ is a reality—this is the only difference. But ultimate salvation comes only through faith in the redeeming grace of Jesus Christ.

Law Doesn't Save

We have also seen that God never intended the law as a means of salvation. He gave the law so humankind would recognize the depths of its sin. We have discovered in Romans 5:20 that Paul says, "Moreover the law entered that the offense might abound." God never gave the law as a means of salvation. That was the perversion of Judaism.

Paul will bring out in Romans 10 that the Jews had a zeal for God, but not according to a right knowledge. They tried to make it to heaven by the works of the law. Romans 9:30-33 says they failed because they rejected the gift of righteousness in Christ.

What does Paul mean, then, when he says believers are no longer under law but under grace? First, we must understand the term "under." The term comes from slaveholding societies. It means "to be ruled by" or "to be dominated by."

In Romans 3:9-20 we dealt with the conclusion of the universal sin problem. Paul makes two statements in that passage: In Romans 3:9 Paul tells us that both Jews and Gentiles are under sin—that is, ruled by sin. Then, in verse 19, Paul cites a second problem. All mankind, under the law, stands condemned. To be ruled by sin and the law results in condemnation, because the law gives sin the authority to condemn and execute the sinner (1 Corinthians 15:56).

But the good news of the gospel—to the believer who has accepted the gospel—is that he is no longer under law.

In Romans 7 Paul will explain how and why we have to be delivered from "under law." He will make it clear that we were not delivered from under law by Christ doing away with the law. It was not the law that died on the cross. It was we who died on the cross, in Jesus Christ. A believer is a person who accepts the death of Christ for his or her death, and since Christ died to sin, they also die to sin. The law has dominion only so long as they are living, but when Christ saved them from under the law, He did not leave them. He placed them under grace. To be under grace means to be ruled and dominated by grace.

When grace comes to us, it does not say what the law says. The law says, "Obey and you will live; if you disobey, you will die" (Deuteronomy 11:27). Grace does not do this. Grace says to you, "Abide in Me and I in you." This is what Jesus told His disciples in the gospel of John. This is what it means to live under grace. We find in John 15:1-5 these words: "I am the true vine and my Father is the vine dresser. Every branch in me that does not bear fruit he takes away. And every branch that bears fruit he prunes that it may bear more fruit. You are already clean because of the Word which I have spoken to you."

In John 15:3 Jesus is saying that a believer stands justified before God. He adds in verse 4: "Abide in me and I in you. As the branch cannot bear fruit of itself unless it abides in the vine, neither can you unless you abide in Me. I am the vine, you are the branches, He who abides in Me and I in him bears much fruit; for without Me you can do nothing." To live under grace means that we allow Christ, dwelling in us through the Holy Spirit, to control every impulse, every desire, every member of our body. This is what it means to live under grace. No longer is a Christian under the umbrella of the law. This is not true of the unbeliever, who has not yet died with Christ by faith. But the believer is freed from under the law. No longer can the law come to him and say, "Obey and you will live; disobey and you will die." No longer does a Christian live under that system. Christians live under grace and to live under grace means that they abide in Christ and He in them, and now they must allow Christ dwelling in them to control them and live in them.

Paul says in Galatians 2:20: "I have been crucified with Christ; it is no longer I who live, but Christ lives in me; and the life which I now live in the flesh I live by faith in the Son of God, who loved me and gave Himself for me."

This can be explained by quoting two texts that show what Paul means to live under grace. Living under grace does not give us the freedom to condone sin. In 2 Corinthians 12:7 Paul reminds us that because of the many revelations he was given through Jesus Christ, God allowed him to have a thorn in the flesh to keep him humble. Three times he prayed to Jesus to remove this thorn in the flesh. The answer to this prayer is found in 2 Corinthians 12:9: "My grace is sufficient for you, for My strength is made perfect in weakness." Paul responds, "Therefore most gladly I will rather boast in my infirmities that the power of Christ may rest upon me."

Grace is God's power, and when we live under grace, the power is made available to us.

Living Under Peace

In 1 Corinthians 15:9 Paul makes a statement about himself: "For I am the least of the apostles, who am not worthy to be called an apostle because I persecuted the church of God." In verse 10 he adds, "But by the grace of God, I am what I am. And His grace toward me was not in vain; but I labored more abundantly than they all, yet not I, but the grace of God which was with me."

To live under grace means to live under peace, on the one hand, but also under the umbrella of God's power. Under grace, every time we sin or fall, the law cannot condemn us. This is good news! But that must not allow a Christian to condone sin. The fact that the law has no more authority over us to condemn us must not be perverted into cheap grace. Grace gives us no such license. Grace gives us the privilege of living the life of Christ and the power to do God's will, for without that grace we are incapable of reflecting the character of God's love (Read Philippians 3:12-16).

But there is yet another question to answer: What does it mean to live under grace? While grace gives us peace, assurance, and the power to live holy lives, some Christians teach that once we come under this umbrella of grace, we can never be lost. But the Bible teaches no such thing.

As long as we are living by faith in Jesus Christ, under the umbrella of grace which is by faith alone, we can never be lost. We have the full assurance of salvation. Our eternal destiny is guaranteed. But it is possible for us to fall away from grace. Paul teaches this. In Galatians 5, Paul writes to the Galatian Christians who had accepted Christ by faith—who were living under the umbrella of grace—and then accepted the false teaching of the Judaizers. They turned from salvation by grace alone to salvation through circumcision and keeping of the law. Galatians 5:4 says: "You have become estranged from Christ, you who attempt to be justified by law; you have fallen from grace."

The righteousness that qualifies us for heaven, now and in the judgment day, is always in Christ. As we saw in Romans 5:12-21, it is the obedience of Christ; it is His doing and dying that justifies us. We make no contribution to our salvation. We are saved by grace alone, through faith apart from any works we do or that God does in us. For the works that God does in us through the Holy Spirit (which is revealing the character of Jesus Christ) are the fruits of salvation. These demonstrate and witness to our justification but never contribute to it. Nowhere in the Bible is the Holy Spirit referred to as a co-redeemer. His work in the plan of salvation is to communicate to us the righteousness of Christ.

Falling from Grace

Having said this, Paul makes it clear that it is possible to fall away from grace. The righteousness that saves us and qualifies us for heaven, now and in the judgment, is always in Christ. Nobody can destroy that. Satan cannot touch that righteousness—that much is true. But the faith by which that righteousness becomes ours and makes the righteousness of Christ effective in our life is not in Christ. This is in us. This Satan can touch. The book of Hebrews was written to Jewish Christians who were saved by grace but in constant danger of giving up Christ and reverting to Judaism. The writer of Hebrews makes it very clear to these Jewish Christians that the day they turn their backs to Christ, they fall from grace.

Let us read Galatians 5:4 again: "You have become estranged from Christ, you who attempt to be justified by law; you have fallen from grace." A Christian believer who turns his back on Christ and goes back to the world is no longer under grace. He has fallen from grace.

A clear text that cannot be perverted (though some try) is Hebrews 6:4 onward: "For it is impossible for those who were once enlightened, and have tasted the heavenly gift (*which is justification by faith*), and have become partakers of the Holy Spirit (*they have experienced the new birth; these are born again Christians*), and have tasted the good word of God and the powers of the age to come (*they have the blessed hope*), if they fall away (*fall away from grace*), to renew them again to repentance, since they crucify again for themselves the Son of God and put him to open shame." It is indeed possible for us to fall from grace.

But in Hebrews 10:38 and 39 we read: "Now the just shall live by faith; But if anyone draws back (*if anyone says good-bye to his faith*), My soul has no pleasure in him. But we are not of those who draw back to perdition but of those who believe to the saving of the soul." Or as Jesus says in Matthew 10:22: "But he who endures unto the end will be saved."

We are saved by grace, and as long as we live under the umbrella of grace, justification by faith is ours, salvation is ours, and heaven is ours. There is no condemnation for those who are in Christ (Romans 8:1). The believer is to hold onto that faith, not give up that faith. The Christian must remain under the umbrella of grace by faith at all cost, until that day when Christ will take His children to heaven. May this be your experience.

Chapter 15

Slaves of God

Romans 6:14-23 (Concluded)

The greatest enemy of the gospel is Satan. Since the birth of the Christian church, Satan has done his level best to pervert the gospel and blind the eyes of men, that they may not see the glorious truth of the gospel (2 Corinthians 4:3,4).

Even within the Christian church Satan has produced two major counterfeits that outwardly resemble—to some degree—the gospel of our Lord, Jesus Christ. But actually they are enemies of the gospel. Satan's purpose is to sidetrack Christians from the truth as it is in Christ.

The first counterfeit, which Paul deals with in Romans 4, is legalism—or, salvation by works. The second is antinomianism or, as Dietrich Bonhoeffer calls it, "cheap grace." Paul explains this in Romans chapter 6.

In the introduction to Romans 6, we were reminded that the gospel is not only incredibly good news but dangerous news. When Paul makes a statement like the one found in Romans 5:20, "Where sin abounded, grace abounded much more," it sounds wonderful. But that same statement may be perverted to say "The more I sin, the more grace will cover my sins. Praise the Lord. Let us keep on sinning, that grace may abound."

But we've seen in Romans 6:1-13 Paul's response to such perversion: "It is unthinkable! God forbid! How can we who have died to sin live any longer therein." A Christian, by faith and baptism, has died to sin in Christ Jesus and therefore cannot condone sin.

But another dangerous statement Paul makes about the gospel is the one we covered in the last study. This is found in Romans 6:14: "For sin shall not have dominion over you, for you are not under law but under grace." As long as we are under law, every time we sin, or fall, the law condemns us, because the law is the one that gives sin the authority to pass judgment (1 Corinthians 15:56).

But the good news of the gospel is that the gospel has liberated believers from under the law. A Christian is no longer under law but under grace, which means that the law can no longer condemn a Christian who falls. Grace does not condemn; grace saves.

But this is dangerous news, as Paul says in Romans 6:15: "What then? Shall we sin because we are not under law but under grace?" Paul's question in Romans 6:15 is similar to his question in Romans 6:1. Can a Christian who is not under law but under grace condone sin in view of the fact that the law can no longer condemn him?

Paul's response to the question is found in Romans 6:15: "God forbid," or "Certainly not."

A Christian under grace cannot allow his position to condone sin. Why not? The answer comes in Romans 6:16 and 17: "Do you not know that to whom you present yourselves slaves to obey, you are the one's slaves whom you obey, whether of sin to death, or of obedience to righteousness? But God be thanked that though you were slaves of sin, yet you obeyed from the heart that form of doctrine to which you were delivered." Then, in verse 18, he concludes: "And having been set free from sin, you become slaves of righteousness."

Slaves to Sin

First, he tells us that we are slaves of sin. Because of the fall of Adam (Romans 5:12-21), not only do we stand condemned before the Lord God, but we are born slaves to sin. Paul brings this out in Romans 7:14, where he says "the law is spiritual but I am carnal, sold (*as a slave*) under sin."

Because we are born slaves to sin, it is impossible for us to save ourselves. A slave needs a liberator, just as the Jews in the Exodus needed a deliverer. This deliverer is Jesus Christ. He has saved us, not only from the guilt and punishment of sin, but from the slavery of sin itself.

So Paul is saying that when a person becomes a Christian, not only does he or she stand justified before God, the Christian is also liberated from slavery to sin. In view of this, how can a Christian condone sin? In Romans 6:16 Paul tells us that we obey the one to whom we have surrendered. Those still enslaved by sin obey sin. Those who persist in obeying sin will suffer the fate the law requires—eternal death.

Faith is more than a mental assent to truth. Faith means accepting deliverance from our slavery to sin. In effect we accept a new slavery—in Jesus Christ.

Paul says in Romans 6:17 that true Christians obey from the heart. Faith is a heart-obedience to the gospel. They obey from the heart that form of doctrine to which they were delivered, the gospel of our Lord, Jesus Christ. Christians obey the gospel and the gospel sets them free from sin, its slavery, its condemnation, its curse (verse 18).

But having set the Christian free from sin, that obedience to the gospel also has made him obedient to Jesus Christ. Having been set free from sin, he or she becomes a slave of righteousness.

Two Kinds of Slaves

The Old Testament describes two kinds of slaves. The purchased slave is one who has been bought to be used by the master. This slave has no freedom. He has to do exactly as his master demands. He has no choice—his position is similar to ours under sin. According to the Old Testament law, a slave's master is not allowed to have a slave for more than seven years. After he has made full use of the slave for seven years, he is required by Old Testament law to set him free.

If the slave's master is a kind, benevolent man or woman and, after seven years, the slave realizes that he or she is better off under the master than being set free, the slave can go to the slavemaster and ask to be made a slave forever. Then the slavemaster pierces the slave's ears as the outward sign of the choice to remain a slave. From that day forward, the slave is a slave by choice rather than by purchase. The slave has chosen to remain a slave because of the kindness of the master.

Paul applies this illustration to the gospel. The Romans practiced slavery in Paul's day, and slaves made up approximately 40 percent of the inhabitants of Rome.

Christians, Paul says, are liberated from their compulsive slavery to sin and, by their own choice, have accepted being slaves of their benevolent Master, Jesus Christ. Paul says that Jesus is the author of righteousness. How can those who become slaves of Jesus Christ by choice ever think that it is all right to sin? The logic is crystal clear.

In Romans 6:19 Paul says: "I speak in human terms." In other words, "I am using slavery as an example—a metaphor, a model—because of the way you have difficulty in understanding the gospel." Paul uses the illustration, not to entertain but to make a point.

In other words, Paul says, "I am using this illustration of slavery that you may understand that when you obey the gospel, you have chosen from the heart to be a slave of Jesus Christ." In the great majority of his epistles, Paul introduces himself as a slave of Jesus Christ.

With this in mind, we look at Romans 6:20: "For when you were slaves of sin, you were free in regard to righteousness." This verse refers to the Roman Christians' previous slavery—the slavery under which we are all born when we had no choice—no freedom to do righteousness.

When the believer is a slave to sin, Sin, the master, gives no freedom to do righteousness. This is what Paul means when he says the non-Christian is free in regard to righteousness. Such people are incapable of producing genuine righteousness. They may do good things. But their goodness is selfishly motivated—as an investment in their own future success. It is impossible for an unbeliever—for a person who is not living under grace—to do genuine righteousness. All of us are born slaves to self—egocentric. This is our slavery to sin, for at the very heart of every sin is self (Isaiah 53:6). Because of our slavery to sin, it is impossible for us to do right things without an unselfish motive.

Very often that selfish motive is hidden from our own consciences, but the Bible makes it clear that all our righteousness is filthy rags (Isaiah 64:6). In Zechariah 3 we are told that filthy rags are synonymous with iniquity, and iniquity in Hebrew means a bent toward self, or selfishness.

Paul tells us that before we were converted, all that we did—good and bad things—were polluted with self. Paul says in verse 21 that the fruits of our slavery to sin is the fruit unto death. The wages of sin is death. Sin, our slavemaster, gives us no peace, no joy, but a curse and death. When we were under sin before our conversion, all we produced were sins and the fruits of that sin. The ultimate end of those sins was death. But now that we have accepted Jesus Christ—now that we have obeyed the gospel from the heart—no longer do we condone sin. In fact, we are ashamed of those things that we did.

Slaves of God

In verse 22 Paul says, "But now." Those believers who have accepted the gospel and have come under the umbrella of justification by faith and the grace of God are in a condition of "having been set free from sin."

Notice the word "sin" here is in the singular. He is not referring to the acts of sin. The gospel saves us from the condemnation of the acts of sin, but here Paul is not dealing with the acts of sin but sin as a principle, sin as a slavemaster.

Paul continues, "and have become slaves of God." Notice that the gospel exchanges one slavery for another. There is no such thing, in the spiritual realm, as genuine freedom. Either we are a slave of sin or we are a slave of Jesus Christ. Slaves we have to be, but being slaves of Christ is not something negative. It is something wonderful, because Jesus is a benevolent Master. He is not out to use us but to bless us. Our Master's greatest concern is our joy, our peace, and our happiness. To be a slave of Jesus Christ is something wonderful (Hebrews 12:2).

Paul says, "and having become slaves of God, you have your fruit to holiness." Living under the slavery to God—living under grace, abiding in Christ—means that He, through His Spirit, lives in us and produces fruits, as we saw in our previous study, "If you will abide in Me and I in you, you will bear much fruit" (John 15:5).

Now, having been set free from sin and having become slaves of God, we bear fruit to holiness and in the end everlasting life. The gospel saves us totally from the tyranny of sin. Many Christians think the gospel only saves us from the guilt and punishment. But, no, the gospel saves us not only from the guilt and punishment of sin, it delivers us from the power and slavery to sin, as well as sin's nature and presence. This third part of salvation will not be ours as a tangible reality, until Christ comes. But while we are living in this sinful world—while we still have sinful bodies but are living under grace—it is possible for Christians to live holy lives, because their slavemaster does not demand righteousness from them, but is able to produce righteousness in them. All that God demands from us under grace is that we abide in Christ, and the Holy Spirit will do the rest (Galatians 5:22-26).

The law does not lift one finger to help those under its condemnation. Jesus says in John 15:5, "Without Me you can do nothing." Jesus, our benevolent Master and Lord and Savior, can sympathize with our weakness, because He was tempted in all points like we are (Hebrews 4:15). But He is also able to help us. Paul could say, "I can do all things through Christ who strengthens me" (Philippians 4:13). This is the privilege of being a Christian.

In Summary

Now, let us sum up what Romans 6 is saying, as it deals with the great danger of the gospel. The danger of the gospel is that because the gospel saves us unconditionally, it is easy for a Christian to take advantage of that wonderful salvation and use it as an excuse to enjoy sin.

But Paul makes it very clear in Romans 6 that while it is true that Christians do fall and stand forgiven, a true Christian cannot adopt the attitude that he is free to sin. That we are saved by grace alone apart from anything we do gives us no license to live as we please. To be saved by grace—which is through faith—means that we have died to sin.

Justification by faith means that we have identified ourselves, through faith and baptism, with Jesus Christ and Him crucified, buried, and resurrected. Since the death of Jesus is a death to sin (Romans 6:10), in the same way Christians must consider themselves dead to sin and alive unto God (Romans 6:11).

The second reason Christians cannot condone sin is that they have, by their own choice and obedience to the gospel, chosen to be slaves of God. God is the Author of righteousness and not sin—therefore, if we have chosen to be a slave of God and God is the Source and Author of righteousness, then He requires from us not sin but righteousness. How can we who have become slaves of God by choice therefore condone sin? It is unthinkable, Paul says.

While the gospel is incredibly good news, a Christian must have the attitude "For me to live is Christ." A Christian cannot condone sin or say to himself, "It does not matter if I sin; it doesn't matter how I live, for I am saved by grace." We must never forget that while salvation is free to us, it came at infinite cost to Christ.

No, a Christian is not at liberty to condone sin. It is important that we understand the gospel of Jesus Christ. Jesus came to save us from sin—its condemnation as well as its slavery.

In John 8 Jesus talks to the Jews who are trapped in legalism, deceived by the devil, but sure they are going to heaven because of their good works. Verse 32 says: "You shall know the truth, and the truth shall make you free." To this the Jews respond: "We are Abraham's descendants, and have never been in bondage to anyone. How can you say, "You will be made free?"

How deceived these Jews were! At the very time they made this statement, they were in bondage to Rome. But Jesus was not talking about political bondage. Jesus responds in verse 34: "Most assuredly I say to you, whoever commits sin is a slave of sin." We sin because we are slaves to sin but the good news is, in verse 36, "Therefore if the son makes you free, you shall be free indeed."

Jesus said to Mary, after He forgave her, "Go and sin no more," for He, the Son of God, had set her free from the slavery of sin. In heartfelt response, she became one of his great disciples.

Chapter 16

Liberated from Under Law

Romans 7:1-6

When Paul deals with the universal sin problem (Romans 1:18-3:20), he concludes by pointing out two terrible predicaments every human being faces. In Romans 3:9 he tells us that both Jews and Gentiles are under sin. Then, in Romans 3:19 he says that because of this the whole human race stands guilty before God under the law. This is the terrible predicament human beings face because of Adam's fall.

The good news is that a Christian who accepts the redeeming salvation act of God in Jesus Christ is no longer under law and no longer under sin. In Romans 6:22 Paul tells us that the gospel has set us free from sin. But the gospel also has set us free from being under the law.

Paul explains in Romans 6:14: "For sin shall not have dominion over you, for you are not under law but under grace."

Romans 7 Overview

Paul knows that as soon as this statement is read in the church at Rome that the Jewish Christians will oppose him. An accusation the Jews traditionally make against Paul is that he undermines the law. Some accuse him of doing away with the law completely (Acts 21:27,28). Paul is certain his statement in Romans 6:14 will come under fire. So he devotes a whole chapter (Romans 7) to how and why believers must be delivered from under the law. First we will review Romans 7 and then study the first six verses in detail.

Like Romans 5, Romans 7 is a very difficult passage for Western readers, so we must study it carefully to understand Paul's reasoning.

Romans 7, in a nutshell, deals with deliverance from under the law. In the first six verses Paul tells Christians how they are no longer under the law. He points out in verses 4 and 6 that this is accomplished by their death in the body of Jesus Christ.

Then, in verses 7-12, Paul says the problem is not the law, for the law is good, holy, righteous and even spiritual (verse 12). The problem is humanity. Human beings are slaves to sin—which means human nature is incompatible with God's holy law. Paul brings out in Romans 8:7 that the carnal mind—the mind controlled by our sinful nature—is not only at enmity with God, but is not subject to the law of God, nor indeed can be. This applies to believers too, since no change has taken place in their sinful natures.

In verse 13 to the end of Romans 7, then, Paul explains slavery to sin. He proves what he says in Romans 7:7-12—that mankind is by nature enslaved to sin and, therefore, in and of itself is incapable of living good and holy lives, apart from the power of the indwelling Holy Spirit.

With this background and introduction, we now turn to an in-depth look at Romans 7:1-6.

A Message to the Jews

Paul makes his Romans 7:1 statement primarily with the Jewish believers in mind: "Or do you not know, brethren (*for I speak to those who know the law*)." Paul is saying, "In a special sense, I am addressing this passage to you Jewish Christians who know the law (*the Torah, or first five books of the Old Testament*)...that the law has dominion over a man as long as he lives?"

This is a fundamental principle of any law. For example, as long as we are living in a country, we come under the laws of that country. But the moment we die, the law of the country has no hold on us. When we were born, we were born under law, because when God created this world and the human race, He put Adam and Eve under law and the whole human race under it, in Adam.

All of creation, in fact, was placed under law. This is why scientists can help us reach the moon, by calculating exactly at what speed and in what direction to fire a rocket. The whole universe is under what we call natural law. Mankind was placed under law, but because we were created with the freedom of choice, we can decide to obey or disobey that law.

Adam disobeyed the law under which God had placed him. This law, found in Genesis 2:16 and 17, said that neither Adam nor Eve, his wife, were to eat of the one forbidden tree. If they ate they would surely die. Adam and Eve, unfortunately, ate of that fruit and came under the death sentence. Since all human beings were in Adam when he sinned, we were all implicated in his act and, therefore, were born under the curse of the law. That law has dominion over us as long as we live.

Two Men, One Woman

Paul then offers an illustration (Romans 7:2, 3) from the law (or Torah, the first five books of Moses which the Jews refer to as the book of the law). This statement, found in Genesis 3, tells us that when a man and woman marry, they are bound together for life. God says that the husband—because of the fall—will rule over the wife. This is not what God originally intended but came as a result of Adam's and Eve's disobedience. God originally intended Eve to be a partner—a helpmate—to Adam. But because of sin, man now rules over the woman (Genesis 3:16).

"For the woman who has a husband is bound by the law of marriage to her husband as long as he lives," Paul continues. "But if the husband dies, she is released from the law of her husband. So then if, while her husband lives, she marries another man, she will be called an adulteress; but if her husband dies, she is free from that law, so that she is no adulteress, though she has married another man" (Romans 7:2,3). Remember, this illustration is based on the book of the law, the Torah—not the customs of any country.

According to the Torah, a husband and a wife are linked together in marriage for life. But if the husband dies, the woman is free from the law of marriage to marry another man. But if she marries another man while her husband is still alive, the Torah accuses her of adultery. We must keep in mind that Paul is not addressing Christian marriage here, but is using the law of marriage to explain why and how we had to be delivered from under the law to be saved.

In this illustration there are two men and one woman. The woman is unhappy with her first husband and wants to marry the second man. But she cannot lawfully marry the second man until her first husband dies.

According to Romans 7:1 and the context of Romans 7: 1-6, the first husband is the law, to which the wife is bound. The second husband is Jesus Christ. The wife, of course, represents humanity.

In this illustration, in the first marriage the wife wants to be free from her first husband (the law) so she may marry the second man (Jesus Christ). We must clearly understand that the problem is not the husband, for Romans 7:12 says the law is holy, good, and just.

But there are two problems with the first marriage: Number one, the first husband is incapable of sympathizing with our weakness. The law comes to us and says, "Do this or don't do that and you shall live." We want to do what the law says, but because we are slaves to sin, we are incapable of obeying the law. But the law is not capable of sympathizing with our sinfulness. The law is a set of rules with no feelings. So we are married to a husband who is not capable of sympathizing with our sinfulness, our weakness, and our inability to obey.

Problem two is that the law, our first husband, is not capable of helping us. Suppose we go to the law and say, "Yes, husband, I want to obey you. I want to do what you want me to do, but I cannot do it. Can you please help me?"

The first husband is incapable of offering any assistance. All he can do is keep commanding us and condemning us when we fail to do what he has told us to do. This is our problem under the law. The law is incapable of sympathizing with our weakness and incapable of helping us meet its demands. The law and sinful human nature are incompatible.

But then we find a second Man, called Jesus Christ, and we discover two things. This second Man also wants us to live a righteous life, but He offers two things the first husband cannot give: (1) He is able to sympathize with our weakness (Hebrews 4:15), and, (2) He is able to help us do what we are incapable of doing (Hebrews 2:17, 18).

We say to ourselves, "Oh, I wish I could marry You," but we cannot marry the second Man until the first marriage is brought to a legal end. The only way the Torah allows the first marriage to end is at the death of the first husband—in this illustration, the law.

Law Is Eternal

Now, even if we lace his food and drink with arsenic, our first husband will refuse to die. Jesus Himself made it clear in Matthew 5:18 in the Sermon on the Mount, "till heaven and earth pass away, one jot or one tittle will by no means pass from the law." The law is immortal. It cannot die. So, we are in a predicament. We are incapable of saving ourselves from the first marriage because our first husband refuses to die.

So, humanity has no solution under the law. But Jesus says, "I can liberate you from under the law." "Really?" we reply. "Can You put an end to the law?"

Jesus answers, "No. I will not put an end to the law." The problem is not between Christ and the law. Many Christians have come to believe that law and grace are antagonistic to each other. This is a perversion of the truth. Who gave the law to Moses? God did! Who is the Source of grace? God! God is both the Author of the law and the Source of grace. If law and grace are antagonistic, then God is against Himself, and that is blasphemy.

No, the law and God are not antagonistic toward one another. Grace and law are totally compatible. The problem is between the law and sinful nature, neither of which has changed one iota since conversion.

How, then, does Christ liberate us from being under the law? In the illustration, the woman wants her husband to die so she can remarry. This is the human solution to her problem. But the solution that God gives in Jesus Christ is that she (we!) must die to the law. The marriage holds as long as both partners are alive. If the wife dies, the marriage ends, too.

In verse 4 we notice how Jesus liberates us from under the law. He does not free us from the law by doing away with the law. He does not nail the law to the cross, but He nails us, in Him, to the cross: "Therefore, my brethren, you (*that is, the wife*) also have become dead to the law through the body of Christ." It is not the law that died on the cross. It is us. The whole human race died in the second Adam, Jesus Christ.

Divinity and Humanity Combine

When Jesus came to this world, He gathered unto Himself the whole human race. At the incarnation, divinity and corporate humanity were joined together in one Person, Jesus Christ—the second Adam. When He died on the cross, mankind died with Him. Second Corinthians 5:14 makes this very clear: "When one died, all died."

By death in Christ the first marriage is brought to an end. In Romans 3:19 Paul says that the whole world stands guilty before God, under the law. In Romans 6:14 we read that the believer who has obeyed the gospel is no longer under the law, but under grace.

How does the gospel deliver humanity from under the law? Did Jesus do away with the law? "God forbid!" It is the human race that died to the law in Jesus Christ, and Him crucified (Galatians 2:19,20). Mankind is set free from that law by that death. But Jesus did not remain in the grave. He rose from the dead, and His followers rise with Him with new life. Now they are married to Christ, the second husband. Romans 7:4 sums it up, "Therefore, my brethren (*the believers*), you also have become dead to the law through the body of Christ, that you may be married to another, even to him who was raised from the dead, that we should bear fruit to God." The gospel is wonderful! It not only saves us, liberates us, redeems us from the guilt and punishment of sin, but it saves us from our predicament under the law. Bear in mind that on the cross the corporate sinful life of humanity died forever in Christ. Then in the resurrection, God gave the human race in Christ the eternal life of His Son. This is the great exchange that takes place at conversion (1 John 5:11, 12).

When we die in Christ—when we accept our death in Christ through faith and baptism—not only are we liberated from sin and its slavery (as Romans 6:22 brings out), but we are saved from under the law. The law no longer has dominion over us who have died in Christ and are raised in newness of life.

Bearing Fruit

The gospel does not only save us from being under law (the predicament in which we cannot save ourselves), but the gospel marries us to Jesus Christ. This is what it means to be under grace. And because we are under grace, we can now bear fruit. What we were incapable of doing under the law we can now do under grace. This is because, under grace, we have a husband who not only can sympathize with our sinfulness, weakness, and inability to be good, but He is able to produce righteousness in us. Paul says, "I can do all things through Jesus Christ who strengthens me" (Philippians 4:13).

The fruit, under grace, is a life of righteousness—a life of holiness. This is the privilege of being under grace (Galatians 5:22-24)

In Romans 7:5 Paul now reminds his readers of their situation under the first marriage—under the law, "For when we were in the flesh, (*before we accepted our death in Jesus Christ, when we were still under the law*), the passions of sins which were aroused by the law were at work in our members to bear fruit to death."

Before they accepted the gospel—while they were under the law in our sinful state—not only were we incompatible with the law but were anti-law. The law says to us, "Do this," and the sinful flesh says, "No, I will not do this."

Signs in some parks read, "Keep off the grass." When we see those signs, something in us rebels against such rules and regulations and we say, "We want to walk on the grass, anyway!" This is one reason the world has so many problems. Sinful man hates to live under law. This is why many young people oppose the establishment and its rules, regulations, and laws. Why? Humanity has rebellious streaks in it, because it was born under sin.

In Romans 7:5, in the first marriage, instead of obeying her husband, the wife did the very opposite. The law arouses in us desires to do the very opposite of what it requires. So we produce sinful fruit, the wages of which is death, because when we sin under the law, it condemns us; it curses us unto death.

In verse 6 we find part of the good news of salvation—of being "under grace." "But now we have been delivered from the law." A Christian has been delivered from under the law, not by Christ doing away with the law, but by death in Christ. The believers die. The law held them prisoners with no escape until they obeyed the gospel and were set free by death in Christ (Galatians 3:24,25).

The end result of the new marriage is "so that we may serve in the newness of the Spirit and not in the oldness of the letter." The believers now serve God. Under law they lived under fear, for every time they failed to obey the law, the law cursed them and condemned them to death.

Under the law, every attempt made to obey was motivated by egocentric concerns—fear of judgment or desire for reward—and every time the believers failed, they became more and more fearful. They were serving the letter of the law. The word "letter" simply means rules and regulations to obey. But now under grace, in this second marriage, the believers serve in newness of spirit. They worship Him out of deep gratitude for the gospel. They serve because the love of Christ compels them (2 Corinthians 5:14,15), and now they look at the requirements of the law under grace, not as the price of salvation, but as the standard of Christian living.

When Jesus says, "Please live this way through My grace," they choose to live that way, not because He will punish them, but because they love Him. Jesus said, "If you love me, keep my commandments (John 14:15). Their hearts are filled with gratitude so that with Paul they say, "For to me, to live is Christ" (Philippians 1:21).

The gospel not only gives peace with God but transforms their minds so that they want to live lives that are well-pleasing to God. This is true repentance—a changed mind (Romans 2:4). This is the truth in which Christ sets His followers free—free from fear, free from condemnation, free to serve God in love and gratitude. "You shall know this truth and this truth will set you free."

Chapter 17

Our Utter Sinfulness

Romans 7:7-13

Two of the great privileges Christians have, says Paul in Romans 6:14, is liberation from under the law and being covered by grace. In Romans 7:1-6, Paul explains how believers are delivered from under the law.

According to Romans 3:19 where Paul deals with the universal sin problem, the whole world—Jews and Gentiles alike—are all guilty before God under His law. This means that the human race, because of the entrance of sin, stands under the curse of God and has no way of escape except through the gospel of the Lord, Jesus Christ.

When God redeemed the believer from the curse of the law, He redeemed him or her from under the law. By this, Paul means that no longer does the law have jurisdiction over the believer. No longer can the law of God say to the believer, "Obey and you will live. Disobey and you will die" (Job 36:11,12).

This applies to those who are still under the law—to those who have not yet accepted the grace of God. But the believer has passed from under law to under grace. In our last study, we saw that God delivers believers from the law in the same way He delivers them from sin—by the Christian's death in the Lord, Jesus Christ.

Likewise, when believers die in Christ and accept this death through faith and baptism, they also die to the jurisdiction of the law. Paul tells us in Romans 7:1 that the law has dominion, authority, and rulership over a person only while he is alive.

In other words, the human race was born and placed under the law because it is Adam's lineage, but when we die in Christ, no longer are we under the law. The law is finished with us and we stand under grace.

Paul is aware that many believers in the church at Rome—especially Jewish believers—will accuse him (as we read in the Book of Acts) of undermining the law of God. So, as we study Romans 7:7-13, Paul will explain what the problem is and why it is essential for human beings to be liberated from under law.

The Problem is Humanity

The first thing Paul does in Romans 7:7 is to point out that the problem under the law is not with the law but with sinful human beings. "What shall we say then? Is the law sin?" he asks. Why does he pose this question? Paul has already told us in Romans 6:18 and 22 that through the cross of Christ we were liberated from sin. In Romans 7:1-6 he goes on to tell us that we have been delivered from under the law— especially in verses four and six. So, it is possible that some might say, "Paul, you are making the law synonymous with sin." So, Paul asks the question in Romans 7:7, "Is the law sin? Are sin and law synonymous?" He answers, "Certainly not!" On the contrary, says Paul, "I would not have known sin except through the law. For I would not have known covetousness unless the law had said, You shall not covet."

From this statement we see clearly that Paul is referring primarily to the moral law—what we call the Ten Commandments. Paul is saying here that sin and law are not synonymous. True, they are related in the sense that the law defines what sin is. But it is sin that is bad, it is sin that kills. The law simply gives sin the authority, because under the law we have to obey it in order to live (1 Corinthians 15:56).

Sin in the Heart

Notice the commandment Paul chooses from out of the 10 from which he could have chosen. "You shall not covet" deals not with an act but with a cherished desire. The Jews mistakenly defined sin as an act. In the Sermon on the Mount, Jesus in Matthew 5:22 and 28 corrects this mistake. The Pharisee stands up and says, "I have not murdered anybody." Jesus responds by saying, in effect, "If you hate somebody without a cause, even though you have not killed him, you have already in the eyes of God's law murdered him."

Temptation becomes sin when the mind says, "Yes." In human relationships, sin is sin only after an act is committed. For example, if a person sees a beautiful Porsche car and says to himself, "I wish I had that car," no policeman will accuse him of stealing. But he is breaking the law of God; he is coveting something that does not belong to him.

The Jews believed that sinning always involved overt acts, but Jesus corrects them and says, "If you hate somebody without a cause, you have already murdered that person in the heart."

When we realize that even cherished desires are sin, we begin to recognize how sinful sin is and how impossible it is for a person to save himself.

In Matthew 5:28 Jesus turns to the problem of adultery—another prevalent sin of our day. The Pharisee could stand up and say, "I have not committed adultery," but Jesus says, in effect, "If you look at a woman to lust, even though you have never committed the act of adultery, in God's eyes you have already done it."

James 1:14 and 15 tells us that temptation is a desire that is placed in our minds through the flesh. When the mind consents to that temptation, it becomes sin. Then comes the act and then comes death.

Paul is saying that mankind's problem when living under the law is that the law reveals that they are sinners. This is brought out in Romans 7:8, "But sin, taking opportunity by the commandment, produced in me all manner of evil desire. For apart from the law sin was dead."

In other words, if there was no law, sin would be non-existent. For example, if there were no speed limits posted on our roads, we would be breaking no law if we traveled 100 mph. But because there is a law, the moment we exceed the posted speed limit, we break the law. Paul is saying that sin is living in opposition to the demands of the law.

But he goes beyond that. He says, "But sin taking opportunity by the commandment produced in me all manner of evil desires." Paul is saying that sinful human nature is so desperately and utterly corrupt that when the law comes to us saying, "Do not do this," we deliberately desire to do it because of our rebellious nature. The law is not to blame for this—the law only reveals how sinful we are at our very core.

In Romans 7:9 Paul continues: "I was alive once without the law, but when the commandment came, sin revived and I died." Paul is not saying here that there was a time when he did not know the law. Paul was reared as a Pharisee, and a Pharisee grew up knowing the law from the very beginning of his conscious life.

When their children were only two years old, Pharisee parents would smear honey on the scroll of the law and make the child lick the honey so they would realize that the law was sweet as honey. By the age of 12, a Pharisee's child could recite the first five books of the Old Testament (Torah) from memory. Paul is not saying that there was a time when he (Paul) did not know the law. What he is saying is that he did not know the true purpose and function of the law.

As a Pharisee, Paul grew up believing that man is saved by keeping the law—a Jewish concept not taught in Scripture. In Philippians 3:4-6 Paul says that, regarding the righteousness of the law, he was blameless. Paul is telling us that before his conversion he lived as a strict, orthodox Jew, keeping all rules and regulations of his religion. He thought this would qualify him for heaven. He thought he was actually keeping the law. But, as Jesus reminded the Jews, what Paul was really keeping were the traditions of men (Matthew 15:1-3).

Perfect Motives

One day the Lord opened Paul's eyes to a sense of what the law demands, and Paul discovered that the law does not only demand perfect actions but perfect desires and motives. When he realized this, he knew he was a sinner, condemned to death under the law. In Romans 7:9 he says: "I was alive once without the law (*that is, as a Pharisee, keeping the rules of his religion*) but when the commandment came (*when I discovered the true meaning of the law*), sin revived (*I discovered I was a sinner and not a righteous man*) and I died." In other words, the commandments which he once believed could bring life actually brought death.

But was it the law's fault? No.

Romans 7:10 and 11 says: "And the commandment which was to bring life, I found to bring death. For sin, taking occasion by the commandment, deceived me and by it killed me."

We find an interesting statement in 1 Corinthians 15:56 that explains our predicament as sinful human beings under the law. "The sting of death is sin, and the strength of sin is the law."

That which kills us is sin. Sin is the cause of our death, but sin gets its authority to kill us through the law. If we are living under the law, every time we fall—every time we miss the mark, which is the definition of sin—the law condemns and curses us. Paul brings this out in Galatians 3:10: "Cursed is everyone who does not obey the law (*to do it at every point and all the time, continuously*)."

Paul discovered that the law does not save anyone. It simply gives sin the authority to bring death upon us. Romans 6:23 says "The wages of sin is death."

We read in Romans 7:12 and 13: "Therefore the law is holy and the commandment holy and just and good." Our problem with the law is not the law. The law is holy, just, and good. The problem is with our sinful nature, which does not change one iota after conversion.

True, the law cannot sympathize with our weakness or produce righteousness. The law can only command obedience and execute us when we fall. The law cannot even die for us. This is why we need a Savior to liberate us from under law and place us under grace. Under grace we live under the authority of Jesus Christ. In Hebrews 4:15 we are told that

Christ can sympathize with our weakness. Hebrews 2:18 tells us that Christ can help us and strengthen us.

In Romans 8:1 we will discover that Christ does not condemn the sinner—the believer under grace. In Romans 4:5 Paul tells us that God justifies the ungodly who believe. This the law cannot do—which is why we need to be delivered from under the law. This is not because the law is not good, but because the law and sinful human beings are incompatible.

Romans 7:13 says, "Has then what is good become death to me?" The answer is "Certainly not! (*God forbid! It is unthinkable!*)" Paul continues, "But sin, that it might appear sin, was producing death in me through what is good, so that sin through the commandment might become exceedingly sinful."

Sin kills, and without the knowledge of the law, we would not realize what sin does to us. In Jeremiah 17:9 the prophet makes it very clear that the heart is desperately wicked and deceitful above all things. The heart deceives its very owner, telling us that we can save ourselves by our own good works. The law says, "Impossible!" Paul tells us in Galatians 3:22-25 that the law is our tutor, our escort to lead us to Christ, that we might be justified by faith.

Having discovered that a holy law and sinful men are incompatible, let us begin to summarize by asking ourselves the question, "What was God's purpose in giving human beings the law?"

Purpose of the Law

When God declared the Ten Commandments and wrote them on tables of stone with His own finger and gave them to the Israelites during the Exodus, He knew that the Israelites could not keep them—that they were incapable of keeping His law. Then why did He give them at all?

The answer lies in the fact that what God knew, the Israelites did not know. When they heard the law being recited to them by Moses, they responded, "All that you say, God, we will do." In other words they said, "Don't worry, God. We will keep the law. You give it to us, we will do it." Yet within a few days, they were worshipping a golden calf.

We see, then, that the heart is deceitful above all things and desperately wicked. The law simply convinces us that we are sinful. Romans 7:7 says, "The law defines sin." Romans 3:20 says, "The law gives us the knowledge that we are sinners."

But there is a second purpose for the law. It shows us not only that we are sinners, but that we are exceedingly sinful. We read this in Romans

7:8. Sinful men are not only incapable of keeping the law but by nature rebel against the law. When the law says, "Do not do a certain thing," we deliberately do it. This is how exceedingly sinful we are.

This is society's problem. Though we make laws, the citizens deliberately break those laws simply because the laws exist.

While I was working as president of a mission college in Africa, our board authorized the purchase of a new tractor. The tractor was delivered and a rule made that no one was to sit on its fenders. If anyone did, he or she was to be fined about one dollar (then a lot of money in Africa).

A few days later, a student was found sitting on one of the tractor's fenders and was brought before me. I asked him why he had broken the rule. He replied: "I did it because you made a rule that we cannot do it. You challenged me and I defied you."

So I wrote out a slip of paper and told him to go to the business office, where he would be charged about one dollar.

The poor student fell on his knees and began pleading that he was very poor and could not afford such a fine. I replied that he should have thought about that problem before sitting on the fender.

But the student continued pleading, asking if there was any mercy. "Yes," I replied. "There is mercy, but mercy comes only through justice."

With that, I put my hand into my own pocket, took out some money, gave it to the student, and told him to go to the business office and pay the fine so he could go free. The student and I became good friends and today he is a pastor.

In the same way, Jesus paid the price for our sins and set us free from the condemnation of the law. Galatians 3:13 says that Jesus liberated us from the curse of the law, having been made a curse for us. While salvation is free and costs us nothing, we must never forget that it cost Jesus the cross to say, "You are forgiven."

The law does not forgive. It is God who forgives, for He has paid the price. He paid the penalty for our sins when He laid upon His Son, Jesus Christ, the iniquity of us all—when He did not spare His own Son but delivered Him up for us all (Romans 8:32).

Summary

So, what have we learned? First, that the law defines what sin is; second, that the law shows us our exceeding, utter sinfulness; and three, that in light of the two previous facts, mankind cannot save itself.

By the works of the law shall no flesh be justified. But there is hope. When Jesus redeems us, He not only redeems us from the curse of the law, He also liberates us from the jurisdiction of the law. Why? Because, when we accept Him and He places us under grace, no change takes place to our sinful nature. Our nature is potentially as 100 percent sinful as it was before our conversion—and will remain so until our dying day. It is only at the Second Coming of Christ, when this corruption shall put on incorruption, that we will be entirely delivered from our sinful nature.

So, even though we may not commit acts of sin, we are still sinners by nature, and if we were still under the law, the law would condemn us every minute of our lives. That is why Satan can accuse us day and night (Revelation 12:10). But in Jesus Christ we have been set free.

Remember Romans 6:14, 15. A Christian is no longer under law but under grace. But Paul is very careful that we not turn this good news into license to sin. Romans 6:15 says, "Shall we sin because we are not under law but under grace?" The answer is "Certainly not!" How can we who have said good-bye to sin through Jesus Christ and have come under grace condone sin? Grace does not give us the license to condone sin. Yes, we will struggle. We will be falling and, thank God, the law cannot condemn us. But we must never use this wonderful truth to excuse or condone sin. We must always remember that sin cost Jesus the cross. Sin was very expensive for God. This is why we must endeavor to walk continually in the Spirit (Galatians 5:16).

In the truest sense of the word, therefore, there is no such thing as cheap grace. An understanding of this wonderful truth sets Christians free from anxiety, free from guilt, free from the curse of the law, free from distress, and free to serve Jesus Christ.

Chapter 18

Wretched Man that I Am

Romans 7:14-25

We now come to the last section of Romans 7. Our two previous chapters covered verses 1-13, and now we will deal with a difficult, controversial passage in verses 14-25.

Like Romans 5:12-21, this passage has caused much discussion in the history of the Christian church. The great question is raised: "Is Paul referring to the struggle of Romans 7:15-25 as his own experience (*for the personal pronoun 'I' appears 25 times in this passage*)?" Is he discussing or explaining his struggle before his conversion, or is he presenting this passage in the light of his post-conversion experience?

This question has divided Christian scholars from the beginning of the Christian church. Origen, John Wesley, Weiss, Moffatt, C. H. Dodd— these great scholars of the Christian church all teach that this is Paul's pre-converted experience.

On the other hand, Augustine, Luther, Calvin, Anders Nygren, and John Stott insist that this is Paul's post-conversion experience. The question is not which side is right, but what Paul really is telling his readers.

Before, After—or Both?

To understand this passage, we must consider its context. Romans 7 is dealing with deliverance from the jurisdiction of the law. In verses 1-6 Paul tells the believers that when they are in Christ, through faith and baptism, they are delivered from under the law, because the law has dominion over a person only as long as he or she is living.

But the moment the believer accepts Christ and is buried with Him and rises to newness of life, he or she is no longer under law but under grace.

The apostle Paul then tells us that the reason we sinful human beings need to be delivered from the law is not only because the law condemns us, but because the holy law of God and sinful human beings are incompatible (Romans 7:7-13).

It is impossible for human beings in their sinful nature to keep the holy law. Paul covers this in Romans 8:7. He tells us that the carnal mind—the mind controlled by sinful nature—is not only at enmity with God, but is not subject to the law of God and never can be.

Since sinful natures do not change after conversion, the flesh remains a great enemy. The only change that takes place in believers, after conversion, is in their thinking. The word repentance means a change of mind. But human nature does not change one iota to its dying day or until Christ comes. Until then, the flesh will remain the greatest enemy in the Christian walk.

To understand what Paul is saying in this passage, we must put away our preconceived ideas and study it in its context. Having shown us the exceeding sinfulness of mankind through the law, Paul makes this concluding statement in Romans 7:14: "For we know that the law is spiritual." Paul has already mentioned in verse 12 that the law is holy, good, and just—and therefore spiritual. It is in harmony with the nature of God because God is a Spirit. Paul continues: "But I am carnal, sold under sin."

In dealing with the universal sin problem, Paul concludes in Romans 3:9 that both Jews and Gentiles are under sin. In Romans 5:19, then, he tells us that the reason we are under sin is that when Adam fell, all were made sinners. Paul is now saying that while the law is spiritual, this is not true of the Christian's nature. He has proven from every conceivable point that the believers remain carnal, sold as slaves under sin. They have no freedom to do righteousness apart from grace. They may choose and want to do what is good, but it is impossible from the true, godly point of view, because of their sinful nature.

Who Is "I?"

Now we look at the word "I" in this passage and at what Paul means when he says, "I am carnal. I am sold under sin." He is not referring to himself only. The personal pronoun "I" here is really a generic term. It refers to anybody. But Paul does have a specific people in mind when he uses the word "I" here. In Romans 7:1 Paul makes a statement in parentheses: "*(For I speak to those who know the law).*" Clearly he has the Jews in mind. The Jewish Christian believers of Paul's day insist that the law is still binding on the believer, as a requirement for salvation. This is the big issue in Acts 15:10, at the conclusion of the first Jerusalem Council. The disciples—especially Peter—say: "Why are you placing a burden on the Gentiles, a burden that neither we nor our fathers could carry?"

Sinful man and the holy law are incompatible because mankind, through Adam's fall, has been sold into the slavery of sin. A slave needs a deliverer. A slave cannot liberate himself.

Paul here proves a point especially useful for the Jewish Christians—the same one he proves in Galatians and leads him to ask in Galatians 4:21: "Tell me, you who desire to be under the law (*who want to contribute toward your salvation through the law*), do you not hear the law?"

Paul is showing that to live under law, or even to live partially under the law, is impossible, for the law is spiritual and mankind is carnal, sold under sin. Human nature does not change through conversion—only the believers' minds do. Through transformation of their minds they become God-centered as Christians, but their nature is still a tool of the devil.

In Romans 7:15 Paul simply proves this point. The word "I," used 25 times in this passage, does not refer to Paul specifically but to any human being who is trying to contribute to his or her salvation by living under the law. Here is the struggle of every believer who is trying to please God in his or her own strength.

"For what I am doing, I do not understand. For what I will to do, that I do not practice; but what I hate, that I do. If then, I do what I will not to do, I agree with the law that it is good" Romans 7:15,16. A Christian wants to do good and live a righteous life—a life in harmony with the law of God. Notice, however, that there is no mention of the Holy Spirit here.

Can Believers Live Holy Lives?

We ask the question, then, "Can Christian believers, who are born of the Holy Spirit, live holy, righteous lives?" Yes! Paul shows us in Romans 8:4 that through the Holy Spirit the righteous requirements of the law can be fulfilled in those who do not walk after the flesh, but after the Spirit.

But here he is dealing with those who want to remain under the law. Remember: Those who live under the law have to obey the law in their own strength. It is only under grace that the Holy Spirit gives power to live holy lives. Under law, no such assistance comes. Paul is saying in Romans 7:15 and 16, "I want to do what is right. I want to live a righteous life, but to put it into practice is impossible."

Paul says in Romans 7:17, "It is no longer I who do it, but sin that dwells in me." Here Paul deals with a problem facing all Christians, for sin is not only an act. Sin is also a force dwelling in mankind's very nature.

Paul here presents a third aspect of sin. Sin is the transgression of the law. As such, it is an act. True, sin also involves motives. But here Paul talks of sin dwelling in him. In verses 22 and 23 Paul points out that sin is also a force—a principle, a law just like the law of gravity—that dwells in our members, in our nature, in our humanity.

In Romans 7:18 Paul says: "For I know that in me that is, in my flesh (*in my human nature*) nothing good dwells (*because what dwells in our nature is sin*). For to will is present with me (*with his mind he can choose to do the right thing*), but how to perform what is good I do not find." We have a nature that will not comply with our converted wills.

In Romans 7:19 he continues: "For the good that I will to do, I do not do; but the evil I will not to do, that I practice. Now if I do what I will not to do, it is no longer I who do it, but sin that dwells in me." Twice in verses 17 and 20 Paul tells us that the culprit is sin dwelling in us—in every human being, even in the converted Christian.

Delighting in the Law

In Romans 7:21-23 Paul explains the heart of the problem. In verse 21 we read: "I find then a law (*a principle*), that evil is present with me, the one who wills to do good (*In other words, 'I find a conflict in my Christian experience. I in my converted mind want and choose to do good, but I find a principle in my nature that is evil, contradicting my good will'*)."

Then in verse 22 we continue: "For I delight in the law of God." Notice that Paul is not against the law. The desire of every converted Christian is to delight in the law of God, because the law, or principle, of sin in his or her members is a contradiction of God. The law is a revelation of the character of God. God is love and, as Jesus says in Matthew 22:36-40, love is the fulfillment of the law ("*I want to love God and my fellowmen, but my nature contradicts that law*" Romans 8:7).

In Romans 7:22 we read, "For I delight in the law of God according to the inward man. But I see another law in my members, warring against the law of my mind...." Here Paul is discussing a believer's experience. What he is making abundantly clear is that the law of God and sinful man are incompatible. Clearly the passage refers primarily to the experience of a believer. We know this because Paul moves from the past tense to the present continuous tense in verses 14-25.

If the "I" is referring to Paul, and if this is Paul's experience before his conversion, then it contradicts Philippians 3:4, 5. In Philippians he mentions no struggle as a Pharisee—only that he was blameless (verse 6).

No unbeliever delights in the law of God. Yes, the Pharisee's kept the law of God in their own thinking, but they did not delight in it. To them it was a necessary requirement. It was "do this" and "don't do that." This is Phariseeism. But the person in Romans 7 delights in the law of God. This must be a converted person; therefore it is clear that Paul has the Christian in mind.

The issue Paul is discussing can actually apply to both believer and unbeliever, since the nature of the believer and the nature of the unbeliever are identical. Sin dwells in both. The difference is that the believer delights in the law of God. He wants to do what is good. He delights in doing righteousness, but how to perform this desire—or delight—poses a quandary. This is because, while in his inward being (in his converted mind) he delights in the law of God, in verse 23 he says, "But I see another law in my members (*in my nature*) warring against the law of my mind and bringing me into captivity to the law of sin which is in my members."

Here Paul is describing the fundamental struggle of every genuine, born again, converted Christian. Before conversion, they see sin as only having to do with behavior or acts. But after conversion the believer discovers that sin is also a principle—a law and a constant force—in his or her nature.

The Christian U-turn

Paul tells us in Ephesians 2:3 that in the unconverted person the mind and the flesh are in harmony. They both belong to the realm of sin. They both agree with sinful desires. The unconverted mind and the unconverted nature are basically in harmony.

A Christian's mind, however, has made a turnaround—this is the meaning of repentance. The Greek word means a change of mind, a U-turn. Before conversion, the person hated God and was running away from God. He or she loved sin, but when conversion came (when he or she accepted Jesus Christ as Savior), there is a turnaround. Now they hate sin and love righteousness. They are not running away from God but daily communicate with Him. He is no longer a judge out to punish but their Friend—their Savior. The war they now face is a war within.

Paul calls the sin dwelling in them the "law of sin." We read in verse 23, "But I see another law in my members, warring against the law of my mind, and bringing me into captivity to the law of sin which is in my members." Not only is sin a force dwelling within, but it is a law. It is a constant, unending force. But willpower is not a law. Will is a force but not a law. It is not constant. Willpower can be strong at times and weak at other times. The will can change. The Christian can move in one direction by will one day but do the very opposite another day. Those with very strong wills can defy the law of sin, but they can never conquer it through willpower.

To illustrate this, hold a Bible with an outstretched arm. The law of gravity pulls the Bible down, but the Bible does not fall to the floor because it is being held up by muscle power. But muscle power is not a law. It is strong at times and weak at other times. Soon the arm will begin to feel weak, and the longer we hold the Bible, the weaker the arm will become. In the end, the law of gravity will pull the Bible down.

While it is true, good, and essential that Christians have the mind of Christ that delights in the law of God and wants to do good, it is impossible for the human mind to conquer the law of sin. When the believers discover this, they cry out as Paul says, in Romans 7: 24 : "O, wretched man that I am, who will deliver me from this body of death?" The body has been infiltrated with the law of sin. Every part of human nature is controlled by the law of sin, because of Adam's fall. This law of sin takes the mind into captivity and makes Christians do what they do not want to do. They then cry out as Paul says, "O, wretched man that I am, who will deliver me from this body of death?"

But Paul has a good answer to this question in verse 25: "I thank God through Jesus Christ our Lord!" Jesus has a solution to the law of sin.

True Wretchedness

To find that solution, let us first look at the word "wretched," found in verse 24. It appears only twice in all of the New Testament in the original Greek. Paul here applies it to anyone who recognizes that he or she has a sinful nature, incompatible with the law of God. This leads the Christian to cry out to God.

The second time the word appears, we find "wretched" used in Revelation 3. God is evaluating the seven churches of seven dispensations, through history from the beginning to the end of time. Christ is speaking to the church of Laodicea, the last generation of Christians before His Second Coming. Jesus, who calls Himself the True Witness, addresses this last church in Revelation 3:17: "Because you say, 'I am rich, have been wealthy, and have need of nothing'—and do not know that you are wretched…." This is a subconscious sin—a hidden sin that needs to be exposed. This is why verse 18 says, "Buy from Me…eyesalve that you may see." What needs to be seen? Their wretchedness! For Jesus says in Revelation 3:17, "You do not know (*or realize*) that you are wretched, miserable, poor, blind, and naked."

Incapable of God's Will

The deep need of every Christian living today is to realize that in and of themselves they are incapable of doing God's will. We know this from Paul's statement in Romans 7:25: "So then, with the mind I myself serve the law of God, but with the flesh the law of sin."

A Christian can serve the law of God with his mind and will, though his flesh is controlled by the law of sin. So when it comes to performance, all he does is sin.

Here we find a very important truth: "I myself" is not a strong enough translation of the original Greek in verse 25. Paul uses two Greek words here. One word ("ego") can be translated into English by the two words, "I myself." But Paul uses another Greek word ("autos") that means "left on my own, independent of God, grace, and the Holy Spirit." A converted Christian can only serve God with his converted mind, with his will. But when it comes to performance, all he is serving is the law of sin.

But there is hope for the Christian. This hope is declared in Romans 8, which we will cover in our next chapter.

As we conclude our study of Romans 7, we recognize that God's law and sinful human nature are incompatible, even after conversion. Only by grace can a Christian live a holy life. The believers are now free of their inability to live holy lives, by the power of the indwelling Holy Spirit. It is by grace they are saved, and only by grace can they live holy lives.

Chapter 19

Delivered from Sin's Bondage

Romans 8:1-4

In Romans 3:9-20 Paul explains our universal sin problem and makes it clear that both Jews and Gentiles are under sin. By this he means that mankind has a nature incapable of saving itself, sold as a slave to sin. Paul concludes in this passage that all human beings—the whole world— stands guilty, accountable to God under the law. This is the human predicament.

In Romans 6:14, we discover the good news to the believer who has accepted the gift of God—Jesus Christ and salvation through Him. The believer is no longer under the law but under grace.

In Romans 7, then, Paul explains how and why mankind has to be delivered from under the law. Those who by faith accept Jesus Christ and obey the gospel have a turn-around experience in their minds, though no change takes place in their human nature. It is just as sinful as it was before conversion.

This brings a predicament in the Christian life. A Christian who is justified by faith experiences a change of mind. He wants to do God's will. He delights in doing good. He wants to keep the law of God. But he still has a sinful nature, dominated by the law of sin (Romans 7:14-25), making it impossible for him, in and of himself, to do the will of God. We may delight in the law of God. We may choose and promise to do what is right and good, but how to perform that which is good, "we find not," Paul says. The Christian who has been justified by faith is crying (Romans 7:24), "O wretched man that I am! Who will deliver me from this body of death?"

Two Different Questions

Notice that Paul is not asking, "Who will save me? Who will justify me?" His is the cry of the believer who already has peace with God through justification by faith but has no internal peace because of his failure to live the Christian life. The Christian cries out for deliverance from the body of death—the body dominated by sin.

Paul's answer is found in Romans 7:25, "I thank God—through Jesus Christ our Lord!" We have a wonderful Savior! Not only did Jesus save us from the guilt and punishment of sin in His holy history, but the good news of the gospel is that Jesus can also save us from the power and slavery of sin. The gospel is not only the good news of justification, it is the good news of sanctification.

Paul tells Christians in 1 Corinthians 1:30 that in Christ they have justification, sanctification, and redemption. The salvation God obtained for the human race in the holy history of the Lord, Jesus Christ, is full and complete.

A New Problem

When new believers first come to Christ, their major concern is, "How can we be saved? How can we get to heaven? How can we escape the wages of sin, which is eternal death?"

Having discovered the good news of salvation by faith in Jesus Christ and peace with God, however, believers find a new problem. While they thank God for His forgiveness, they want more—they want to live holy, godly lives. They want to live lives pleasing to Jesus Christ. Jesus Himself says to His disciples in John 14:15, "If you love Me, keep My commandments." No longer do they see the law as a means of salvation but as a standard of Christian living, for the law is a revelation of God. God is love, and the New Testament is clear that love is the fulfillment of the law (see Galatians 5:14). Paul tells us in Romans 13:8-10 that when believers are controlled by the love of God and love their neighbors as themselves, they are fulfilling the law in spirit—as God wants them to.

But all new Christians discover that they are incapable, in and of themselves, of living holy lives. They do not want to live in a vicious circle of sinning and forgiveness, over and over again. Wonderful as forgiveness is, they want victory. But they find that no matter how much they resolve and promise to do good, they fail.

What they have discovered is the second problem of sin—that it is not only an act but a force, a power that dwells within sinful nature. This makes holy living, in and of itself, impossible. Paul expresses this in Romans 7:13-24. Here he is not dealing with sins as acts, but sin (singular) as a principle—a force controlling our human nature.

Paul's Biblical Solution

We find Paul's solution to this problem in Romans 8:1-4. Paul has told us in Romans 7:25 that there is a solution for sin as a force, a principle, and a law: "I thank God—through Jesus Christ."

In Romans 8:1-4, Paul explains how Jesus has set His followers free, not only from the condemnation and guilt of sin (Romans 3:21 and onward) but from the power and slavery of sin. His followers may indeed live holy and godly lives.

Sinful acts can be forgiven. But we need more—deliverance—from the slavery of sin. Paul shows us in Romans 8:1-4 how God saves believers from the slavery of sin. Because it is a difficult passage, we will study it thoroughly.

Paul writes: "There is therefore now no condemnation to those who are in Christ Jesus, who do not walk according to the flesh, but according to the Spirit. For the law of the Spirit of life in Christ Jesus has made me free from the law of sin and death. For what the law could not do in that it was weak through the flesh, God did by sending His own Son in the likeness of sinful flesh on account of sin; He condemned sin in the flesh that the righteous requirement of the law might be fulfilled in us who do not walk according to the flesh but according to the Spirit." Full of significance, this passage deserves step-by-step study.

Paul first says in Romans 8:1, "There is therefore now no condemnation to those who are in Christ Jesus." The believers' sins—acts of sin—do not make them sinners. Their acts of sin are simply proof of their sinful nature. Paul makes it clear in Romans 5:19 that because of Adam's one sin all are made sinners.

More than Willpower

Now, if believers build up their willpower and manage to live a sinless life for, say, two hours—even though they do not commit a sin in those two hours—they still stand condemned. For the law does not only condemn mankind for acts of sin, it condemns them for their sinful natures. Victory over sinful acts, therefore, is not enough to give the believers peace with God.

When the believers discover that sin is not only an act but a force—a power and a law that dwells in them—they begin to question if they really have been justified. The first good news Paul shares with them in Romans 8 is that they not only have peace with God and forgiveness of their sins, but they have no condemnation, despite having sinful natures.

In Romans 8:1 Paul tells the believers that in spite of their sinful nature (which is causing a great hindrance and opposition in their Christian living), there is no condemnation to those who are in Christ. Though they are struggling with the flesh (which is anti-Spirit, anti-God, and anti-law), there is no condemnation. Even though believers experience failures and may not yet have learned what it is to walk fully in the Spirit, there is hope.

The second part of Romans 8:1 poses a problem, in that the words are not found in all translations of the Bible. The second part of verse 1 reads: "Who do not walk according to the flesh, but according to the Spirit." In more modern translations such as the New American Standard Bible, the Revised Standard Version, the Good News Bible, and the New International Version, however, this last part is not found. Translators have omitted it because, though it is found in the manuscript used for translating the King James Version (KJV), it is missing in older manuscripts discovered after the publication of the KJV. This leads most scholars to believe that this last part of Romans 8:1 is a scribal addition.

The last part of verse 1 in the KJV indeed distorts Paul's theology of righteousness by faith. It makes sanctification the means of justification—the reverse of what Paul teaches. Therefore it should be omitted and the verse should read simply, "There is now therefore no condemnation to those who are in Christ Jesus."

Paul then tells us in Romans 8:2 why the law does not condemn the believer: "For the law of the Spirit of life in Christ Jesus has made me free from the law of sin and death." Notice the verb Paul uses. He is not discussing the subjective (sanctification) experience as Christians; he is dealing with an objective truth which took place in Christ some 2,000 years ago. It was then—at the cross—that the human race was set free from the law of sin and death in Jesus Christ, through the law of the Spirit.

Breaking the Law of Sin

When Christ came to save the world, He came not only to save mankind from its sins—which condemn us—but to liberate us from the principle—or law—of sin and death in our members. He accomplished this through the law of the Spirit.

Two laws—or principles—met in the humanity of Christ. These were the law of sin (which He assumed because He became one of us) and the law of the Spirit, which was His because He was born of the Spirit and was divine.

In Jesus Christ two constant, unending forces met. The first was the law of sin, which was ours and which He assumed, and which pulled Him down, trying to make Him act contrary to the will of God. This is why on more than one occasion He said, "I have come, not to do My will, but the will of My Father who sent Me" (John 5:30). The fact that He could talk of His will—in contradistinction to God's will—simply means He, as a human being, identified with our situation so that He might save us, not only from our sins but from our sin problem—the law of sin.

On the other hand, Jesus Christ from His very conception was born of the Holy Spirit. This is not true of us at our birth into this world. Jesus had in Himself the law of the Spirit. We discover that in the holy history of Christ, the law of the Spirit condemned and conquered the law of sin. Jesus demonstrated that the law of the Spirit is stronger than the law of sin. When the two meet, the law of the Spirit wins every time.

In Matthew 4:1-10 we discover a description of the threefold temptation Jesus faced in the wilderness. After defeating Satan, Jesus returned to Galilee, according to Luke, in the power of the Spirit (Luke 4:14).

The holy life of Jesus Christ did not come by human strength or by His own personal, divine power—the independent use of which He had laid down. Every victory Jesus obtained came by the power of the Holy Spirit, who conquered the law of sin. But Jesus did more than this, for the law of sin not only must be conquered, it must be condemned. Otherwise, we would still stand condemned.

When in Romans 8:3 Paul refers to the law ("*for what the law could not do*") he means the moral law of God. In Romans 7:1-6 we find that the law can neither sympathize with the sinner nor help weak, sinful human beings produce righteousness.

This is what Paul is saying in Romans 8:3: "What the law could not do, in that it was weak through the flesh." The law is incapable of producing righteousness in sinful flesh.

Likeness of Sinful Flesh

But what the law could not do God accomplished by "sending His own Son in the likeness of sinful flesh." We need to understand what Paul means by the word "likeness." Paul does not simply say, "God sent His Son in sinful flesh." If God had sent His Son in sinful flesh and not in the "likeness" of sinful flesh, Jesus Himself would have been a sinner in need of a Savior. Theologians today in many commentaries agree that the word "likeness" used here by Paul refers to the fact that, while His humanity was identical to our sinful human nature and that He assumed our sinful flesh just as we have it with the law of sin in it, He did not "have" a sinful nature. He assumed it, but He was still God (see, for example, C.E.B. Cranfield, *The International Critical Commentary on Romans 8:3*, 1982 edition).

In other words, God joined our sinful human nature to His sinless, divine nature. While He was God—sinless in and of Himself—He assumed our sinful nature. This did not make Him a sinner. He assumed something that was not His in order to save us from it.

Through the first five centuries, the majority of church fathers have agreed that Jesus could not save us from the law of sin without assuming that which needed redeeming. In other words, Christ could not save us from the law of sin or "the old man of sin"—He could not conquer, save, and deliver us from its condemnation without assuming it.

In his book *The Humanity of Christ*, p. 62, p. 63, Harry Johnson comments: "Jesus assumed 'fallen human nature', but He never added to this nature His will, and there was no break in fellowship between Himself and His Father. On the Cross, there took place the decisive battle between Jesus and the powers of evil, not simply powers that were external, but also the power of the 'fallen nature' that He had inherited. Here on the Cross there was the purging of human nature."

In the *Word Biblical Commentary*, 38a: 420-440, James Dunn writes: "Hence the importance of being able to affirm Christ's complete oneness with humankind's sinful flesh. For Paul the breaking of that power was achieved by Christ's death as a sacrifice whereby God condemned that sinful flesh. In the two phrases "for sin" and "condemned" lies the key to Paul's soteriology.... The logic of Paul's thought here is that sinful flesh could not be healed or redeemed, only destroyed.... God did not redeem flesh by an act of incarnation; he destroyed flesh by an act of condemnation."

What Romans 8:3 is saying is that what the law of God could not do in our sinful flesh God did in the flesh of Christ, which was like ours. In His flesh Christ condemned sin in the flesh. Paul is not talking here about sinful acts. The word "sin" in Romans 8:3 is in the singular. Sin in the flesh is synonymous with the sin mentioned in Romans 7:23, 20, and 17—which is "sin dwelling in me" or "the law of sin in my members." All these are synonymous with sin in the flesh.

The context tells us clearly that in Jesus Christ not only were the believers' sins condemned and they, themselves, set free from its condemnation, but that the law of sin in our members was both defeated and condemned. Because it was condemned on the cross, there is no condemnation for the believer, though they still possess the law of sin in their members.

But the believer receives more than deliverance from the condemnation of the law of sin. In Romans 8:4 Paul tells us that because of this dual salvation from sin(s) (both as acts and sin as a force), the believer not only has peace with God (in terms of his or her standing before Him), but that the righteous requirements of the law (which the believer was incapable of doing before conversion) now can be fulfilled.

Romans 8:4 tells us: "...that the righteous requirement of the law might be fulfilled in us who do not walk according to the flesh but according to the Spirit." This is not a requirement to go to heaven. The believers are saved by the doing and dying of Christ, that the power of the gospel might be manifested in them.

For the righteous requirement of the law to be fulfilled in them, however, the believer must do what Christ did in His earthly life—he or she must walk in the Spirit and not in the flesh (Romans 8:4).

The gospel is a wonderful truth. Not only are believers liberated from the condemnation of their many sinful acts through the death of Christ, they are liberated from the power of sin and its condemnation and slavery. This was accomplished on the cross and in the life of Christ. There is indeed hope for believers to live holy, godly lives—not as a requirement to go to heaven, but as a witness and demonstration of the power of the gospel in their lives (Titus 3:8).

We have a wonderful Savior. But for this experience to be ours, we must learn to walk according to the Spirit. The word "walk" in our text is in the present continuous tense. Paul will describe this in our next chapter, in Romans 8:5 and onward.

Chapter 20

Life in the Spirit

Romans 8:5-14

In our last chapter we covered Romans 8:1-4 and made an important discovery—one every born-again Christian should experience. We found that Jesus Christ on the cross not only saved mankind from the sins that condemn them. He also redeemed the believers from the law of sin and death that infiltrates every part of our beings and makes holy and righteous living, by our own efforts, impossible.

The greatest discovery any human being can make is that Jesus died for his or her sins. It is this knowledge that brings peace and hope to the sinful human race. But the greatest lesson for the believers—the born-again Christians who have already discovered justification by faith and are basking under the umbrella of grace and have peace with God—is that Christ has also liberated and redeemed them from the power and slavery to sin.

We discovered in our last study that Jesus also liberated the believer from the law of sin and death, which is in their members. Because of this, there is no condemnation for those who are in Christ. This is true, in spite of their still-sinful nature. Because Jesus liberated them and condemned sin in the flesh, the righteous requirements of the law can be fulfilled in them, not as a *requirement* for salvation but as the *evidence* of salvation.

Flesh and Spirit

Paul uses two words in Romans 8:4 worth reviewing: "flesh" and "Spirit." The word "flesh" appears many times in previous chapters, but here Paul introduces us to the work of the Holy Spirit. Here, the word "Spirit" refers, not to the human spirit, but to the Holy Spirit given to every born-again Christian—the Holy Spirit who indwells every believer.

The word "flesh" refers to that which Adam passed on to his descendents. This is our sinful nature, dominated by the law of sin and death. The "Spirit" is the third Person of the Godhead, the first phase of the gift of the eternal life that we have in Jesus Christ.

Romans 7 also makes another point worth reviewing. Paul made a distinction, especially in verse 25, between "flesh" and "mind." The "flesh" is the sinful nature inherited from Adam. The "mind" has been weakened by Adam's fall, but it is the human faculty that retains the capacity to choose. A Christian is one who, by his will or mind, has chosen to follow Jesus Christ. In the believer, therefore, the mind is pro-God, in harmony with God, delights in the law of God, and serves the law of God. But the "flesh" has not changed and remains unchangeable. Jesus said to Nicodemus in John 3:6: "That which is born of the flesh will always remain flesh." The problem for believers is that these two—the mind and the flesh—are at enmity. The mind cannot control, defeat, or conquer the flesh (Romans 7:15-24).

Every Christian must understand the issues of sanctification. The first battle in every Christian is between the flesh and the Spirit. In Galatians 5:17 Paul says: "The flesh and the Spirit are contrary to each other." They will never come together in harmony—they will never be at peace.

We also discover that the battleground between the flesh and the Spirit is the mind. The flesh, which wants to sin, cannot sin without the consent of the mind. The Spirit, likewise, cannot fulfill the righteousness of the law without the consent of the mind. The human mind is the battleground of the Christian life. Paul tells us that, apart from the Holy Spirit, the mind may choose to do what is right but cannot perform it. The flesh is much stronger than the mind. If a Christian has strong willpower, the mind may be able to defy the flesh for a season, but it can never conquer it. The flesh ultimately brings the mind into captivity and makes the person do what it—the flesh—wants to do (Romans 7:23).

Power in the Spirit

In our last study we also learned that the Holy Spirit—the law of the Spirit in Christ Jesus—conquered and condemned the law of sin. It is because of this act of Christ that the Christian is able to live a holy, righteous life—as he walks in the Spirit.

In John 15:5, Jesus says, "I am the vine, you are the branches; for without me you can do nothing." Jesus' advises in John 15:4: "Abide in Me, and I in you. As the branch cannot bear fruit of itself, unless it abides in the vine, neither can you, unless you abide in Me. I am the vine, you are the branches. He who abides in Me, and I in him, bears much fruit."

Believers cannot save themselves, but they can bear much fruit through their connection with Jesus. Without Him they can do nothing. Paul tells them that as they walk in the Spirit, the righteous requirement of the law will be fulfilled in them (Romans 8:4).

"How does one walk in the Spirit?" they ask. "What does it mean to walk in the Spirit?" Remember, the battleground of the flesh and the Spirit is the mind. With this background, we are ready to study Romans 8:5-14, where Paul describes the life in the Spirit.

Life in the Spirit

Romans 8:5 says: "For those who live according to the flesh set their minds on the things of the flesh, but those who live according to the Spirit, the things of the Spirit." Unlike the unbeliever who has only one nature—the flesh—the believer has become partaker of the divine nature through the new-birth experience. A born-again Christian still has sinful flesh but now also has the Spirit. Both of these natures want to control the mind. If the Christian's mind dwells on the things of the flesh, the flesh will control the mind. This defines the experience of the carnal Christian.

In 1 Corinthians 3:1-3 Paul divides believers—born-again Christians—into two groups, carnal and spiritual. He calls carnal Christians babes in Christ. They are born again and the Holy Spirit dwells in them (1 Corinthians 3:16). But it is possible for a born-again Christian to walk in the flesh. When a Christian does this, he is not bearing fruit for God nor witnessing the good news of salvation in his life. He is simply witnessing to what he is by nature—a sinful person.

Paul tells us in 1 Corinthians 3:3 that the Corinthians who were still carnal were living no differently than the unconverted. There was jealousy, fighting, enmity, and all kinds of problems in the Corinthian church, because they were not walking in the Spirit.

Saltless Christians

Unless Christians today learn to walk in the Spirit, they too will be unable to convince the world that the gospel is the power of God unto salvation from sin. Friedrich Nietzsche, a great pagan philosopher and son of a Lutheran pastor, once said to some Christians, "If you expect me to believe in your Redeemer, you will have to look a lot more redeemed."

The great liberator of India, Mahatma Gandhi, while in South Africa fighting the Apartheid system, said to the Dutch Reformed Church leaders: "When you Christians live the life of your Master, all India will bow down to Christianity."

The Middle East was swept by Islam in the seventh and eighth centuries for the same reasons Eastern European countries were swept by Marxism in the late 19th and the early 20th centuries—because the Christian church lost its saltiness. When the church loses its saltiness, Jesus says, it becomes worthless. It is useless to God and man and is fit only to be trodden underfoot (Matthew 5:13).

Christianity has been trodden underfoot in many parts of the world by pagan religions and humanistic ideas because Christians have failed to demonstrate to the world the power of the gospel.

The world is not concerned whether or not Christians are justified. What the world wants to see is the claims of the gospel demonstrated in the lives of Christians. The world wants to see the power of the gospel. In 1 Corinthians 4:20 Paul tells us that the kingdom of God is not in words but in power. For that power to be manifested, Christians have to walk in the Spirit. This means that their minds must be preoccupied with spiritual things.

Christians must ask themselves if their minds are dwelling on material things and fleshly concerns or on the things of God. Paul advises Christians in Philippians 4:8 to think on things that are honest, true, pure, and of good report. In Romans 12:2 Paul counsels them to put aside their worldly thoughts and renew their minds every day, offering their bodies as living sacrifices to the cause of God and the gospel.

Paul says in Romans 8:6 that if believers' minds are controlled by the flesh, they will eventually leave Christ and die spiritually. This is because the flesh—the sinful nature—still belongs to the realm of Satan. We are told in 1 Corinthians 15:50 that the sinful flesh—this corruption—cannot inherit incorruption. There must be a transformation—a change. This corruption must put on incorruption. This mortal must put on immortality. This takes place at the Second Coming of Christ, but until then, as Christians walk in the Spirit, they can have victory. The carnal mind—the mind controlled by the sinful nature—is at enmity with God. "It is not subject to the law of God, nor indeed can be" Romans 8:7. The next verse says that those who are in the flesh and allow the flesh to control them cannot please God.

We now read Romans 8:9 : "But you (*believers*) are not in the flesh but in the Spirit." In other words, "You have accepted the life of Christ (*the Spirit*) in exchange for the flesh." Paul continues, "if indeed the Spirit of God dwells in you."

The New Birth

The second half of verse 9 is saying, "Now, if anyone does not have the Spirit of Christ, he is not His." There are some Christians—mainly liberal ones—who think they can go to heaven without being born again. If a Christian is not born again, however, Christ cannot dwell in him. He may be a member of a Christian denomination and attend church services every week, but this does not make him a Christian. Faith-obedience to the gospel results in a new-birth experience. Otherwise they are living a sham—hypocrites. Paul tells us in Romans 8:9 that if the Holy Spirit is not dwelling in those who profess faith in Him, they do not belong to Him.

Romans 8:10 adds: "And if Christ is in you…." To Paul, the Holy Spirit dwelling within and Christ dwelling within are synonymous. The Holy Spirit is the Representative of Jesus Christ. If Christ is within, the body is dead, for the sinful nature was crucified with Christ when He condemned sin in the flesh (Romans 8:3).

If Christ is within, it is because the gospel has been obeyed. Baptism into Christ has occurred—into His death. We are told in Romans 6:10 that as Jesus died to sin, His followers likewise (verse 11) must consider themselves dead to sin in Christ. Jesus not only took humanity's sins upon Himself, He took humanity upon Himself. In the incarnation, the human race in its fallen condition was joined to the Lord, Jesus Christ. They became one; a holy God and sinful men were joined together. This is the mystery of godliness. Jesus linked Himself with a human race in need of redeeming. On the cross not only were their sins condemned, their sinful nature was likewise condemned. The law of sin and death was executed on the cross. The flesh (sinful nature) of those who belong to Christ, therefore, is dead—not literally, but by faith (Galatians 5:24). It died 2,000 years ago in Christ, the Source of salvation.

Killed by the Law

Paul very clearly describes the believers' position in Galatians 2: 19,20: "For I through the law died to the law (*The law killed me*)." Why does the law kill the believers? Because they stand condemned under the law. How and where does the law kill the believers? They have been crucified with Christ.

The death of Christ was a corporate death. It was not one man dying for all men. All mankind died in one man at the cross. This is why Jesus is called the second Adam. The word "Adam" means mankind—a collective significance. Paul has accepted this truth and can confess with all believers, "I have been crucified with Christ" (Galatians 2:20).

Paul continues: "But (*because of my faith obedience to the cross, to Jesus Christ and Him crucified*) it is no longer I who live but Christ lives in me (*through the Holy Spirit*); and the life which I now live in the flesh, I live by faith in the Son of God; who loved me and gave Himself for me."

As mentioned in earlier chapters, Christianity is not a transformation of the old life. It is an exchange of the old life for Christ's life. The believers surrender their lives to the cross of Christ. In exchange they accept the life of Christ—the life of the Spirit—so that they can not only go to heaven but may live lives of righteousness, in harmony with the holy law of God.

Now we return to Romans 8:11: "For if the spirit of him who raised Jesus from the dead dwells in you, He who raised Christ from the dead will also give life to your mortal bodies through his Spirit who dwells in you." What a tremendous statement! Here Paul is saying that Christ was raised from the dead by the power of the Spirit. "If the Spirit of Him (*God*) who raised Jesus from the dead dwell in you."

What has the resurrection to do with Christian living? Remember: the sting of death is sin and the wages of sin is death. The greatest power of sin, therefore, is death and the greatest manifestation of the power of sin is the grave. Do we know anyone, apart from Jesus Christ who has been able to conquer death?

Hitler tried to conquer Europe and nearly succeeded, but we thank God he failed. Rome conquered the world, as it was then known. It boasted military power over all the world, but Rome could not conquer sin. If we can conquer sin, we can conquer death. The fact that we cannot conquer death is proof that sin is greater than we are. But one Man did conquer sin—both sinful acts and sinful nature. He conquered it through His resurrection. Our sin could not keep Him in the grave. He assumed our flesh—the flesh that is dominated by the law of sin. This law of sin was executed and the body of Christ put in the grave. But the law of sin could not keep Christ in the grave, because He had conquered the law of sin. So the Holy Spirit raised Him up, as the greatest evidence of the power of the gospel.

Resurrected Proof

A few years ago in Ethiopia I was discussing the gospel with a Russian who was promoting Marxism. I asked the Russian if Marxism had conquered death. He replied, "Give us time. Science will one day find the solution to death."

"You can wait for that solution—which I believe science will never discover," I replied. "I already have the solution and do not need to wait as you do."

"What is your solution for death?" he asked.

"It is Jesus Christ," I replied. "He has conquered death. He has the keys to the grave. He can unlock the graves of every one who believes in Him." This is the wonderful news of the gospel.

In the context of Romans 8:11, Paul is saying that the resurrection of Christ is the greatest evidence that the Spirit of life in Christ Jesus is stronger than the law of sin and death. This Spirit in Christ, which gave Him victory over our flesh, is now in those who believe in Him. He who raised Christ from the dead will also give life to their mortal bodies.

We must remember that our bodies are still mortal—still flesh, still sinful. But through the Holy Spirit dwelling in the believer it is possible to live a spiritual life.

Paul now concludes in Romans 8:12-14: "Therefore brethren, we are debtors (*we have an obligation as Christians*) not to the flesh, (*because we have crucified the flesh in Christ, Galatians 5:24*) but to the Spirit." (*If we live according to the flesh, we will die because the flesh will take us to the grave*). "But if by the Spirit (*which is what we are debtors to*) you put to death the deeds of the body, you will live."

In other words, Christian living must bear fruit, for in the judgment each will be judged by their fruits. Though the fruits do not save anyone, they are the evidence of genuine justification by faith. In the judgment, Satan accuses humanity of its sins day and night (Revelation 12:10). Satan is technically correct, but Jesus vindicates His own by proving by their fruits that they have genuine justification by faith.

James 2:14-20 tells us that genuine justification by faith always produces fruits, for faith without works is dead. Works do not save, but present the evidence of salvation. These fruits come only by walking in the Spirit. Christians may not all produce the same fruits. Some may produce 30 fold, some 60 fold, some 100 fold, but all is evidence of justification by faith.

The more the Christian walks in the Spirit, the more he or she will reflect Jesus Christ. Paul concludes in Romans 8:14: "For as many as are led by the Spirit of God, these are the sons of God." In other words, the children of God behave like children of God.

Our desperate need today is for Christians who manifest the life of Christ. If they will walk in the Spirit and allow Him to set them free from the desires of the flesh, Christ will be manifest in them—Christ in them, the hope of glory (Colossians 1:27).

Chapter 21

The Blessed Hope

Romans 8:14-30

God intends the Christian life to be lived in the Spirit, as we discovered last chapter in Romans 8:5-18. Having saved and redeemed His followers from bondage, guilt, and punishment of sin, God does not leave them to live life on their own.

He sends the Holy Spirit to dwell in all who accept Jesus Christ as their Savior. The Holy Spirit makes real in their experience that which God has already obtained in the holy history of the Lord, Jesus Christ. He is the Communicator of the gospel. Having convicted the believer of the good news of salvation in Christ, the Holy Spirit now comes and dwells within.

Through the Spirit, the Christian gains a power—a strength—against sin's dominion. The unbeliever enjoys no such resource. Now, in Romans 8:14-30, Paul continues to proclaim the work of the Holy Spirit.

Adopted

In Romans 8:14 we read, "For all who are being led by the Spirit of God, these are the sons of God." A Christian is a person led by the Spirit of God. Through the gospel, Christ's followers are redeemed from the dominion of this world and are established in the kingdom of God. They are adopted as sons and daughters of God, through the Lord, Jesus Christ (1 John 3:1,2).

One evidence that they are God's children is the new birth experience. In Romans 8:15 we read, "For you did not receive the spirit of bondage again to fear, but you received the Spirit of adoption by whom we cry out, "Abba, Father."

Before conversion, theirs was a spirit of fear. Because they are sinful human beings, they had lived in slavery to the fear of death.

In Hebrews 2:14 and 15, we learn that Jesus partook of our humanity. He became flesh and blood through which He may deliver us from the fear of the bondage of death. But life without Christ is a life of fear and insecurity.

Those who receive Jesus Christ and experience the new birth, however, are no longer afraid of God. He is no longer a judge to them. He is a loving Father they can address as "Our Father." These words, in the original, mean "Dear Father."

Paul's explanation continues in Romans 8:16, The Holy Spirit Himself bears witness, Paul tells us, convincing Christians in their spirit that they are the children of God. What a privilege it is to be a Christian! Christians are no longer under sin or subject to Satan. They no longer belong to this world. They are citizens of heaven—children of God, their Father.

In Romans 8:16 we learn that the Holy Spirit gives assurance. Then in verse 17, we discover that those who are God's children become heirs of His kingdom—joint heirs with Christ, suffering with Him that they may also be glorified with Him. What a great privilege!

Remember that in Romans 5:12-21 we learned that the Christian receives far more from Christ than what he or she lost in Adam. In Adam—at his very best—humanity existed as third-class citizens of the universe. God came first, followed by the angels. Humanity was created a little lower than the angels (Psalm 8:5).

But Jesus raises up His followers and takes them to the very place where He is—at the right hand of God. The Christian becomes a joint heir with Christ. This may not be the experience yet, but one day Jesus will come and give His followers what He has already obtained for them in His holy history—the blessed hope.

Suffering—For Now

This blessed hope is future, and in the meantime His followers may have to suffer, just as Christ suffered in this world. He suffered socially, physically, and religiously. His own people rejected him. His ultimate suffering occurred on the cross, where He paid the ultimate price for their sins.

Christ's history was a corporate history, and by faith and baptism, His followers accept the history of Christ. His death becomes their death through baptism—as we saw in Romans 6. His suffering before His actual death and resurrection also becomes theirs. But His glorification—which took place at the end of His life—is also theirs. This is the blessed hope.

Paul continues in Romans 8:18: "For I consider that the sufferings of this present time are not worthy to be compared with the glory that is to be revealed to us."

This is the wonderful hope. Christians may indeed suffer in this world, for though they are citizens of heaven, they are still living in enemy territory. The world is still ruled by Satan and his angels, and this will bring certain suffering. But this suffering is as nothing compared to the wonderful experience of glorification when Christ comes. Though the suffering may seem terrible now, it is like a drop in the ocean compared to the glory and wonderful privileges in heaven, when Christ establishes His kingdom.

In 1 Corinthians 15:12 onward Paul tells Christians that if in this life only they have hope, they are of all people most miserable. The hope of the Christian is not in this world, not in this life—it is in the world to come, the life that God will fully establish at the Second Coming of Christ.

Christians eagerly await the day when they will experience the fullness of salvation as a tangible reality. Romans 8:20 says: "For the creation was subjected to futility, not of its own will but because of him who subjected it in hope that the creation itself also will be set free from its slavery to corruption into the freedom of the glory of the children of God."

Dominion Restored

When God created our first parents, Adam and Eve, He gave them dominion over all of creation (Genesis 1:26-28). David makes a wonderful statement in Psalm 8: "Oh Lord our God, how majestic is thy name." David explains the amazing things of God and how He has given us a wonderful privilege. In verse 3 onward he writes: "When I consider the heavens, the work of thy fingers, the moon and the stars which thou hast ordained, what is man that thou dost take thought of him and the son of man that thou dost care for him? Yet thou hast made him a little lower than the angels and dost crown him with glory and majesty."

God covered Adam and Eve with glory and majesty. He gave them dominion over all the beasts of the land and the birds of the air. David says in Psalm 8:6: "Thou hast made him to rule over the works of thy hands. Thou hast put all things under his feet, all sheep and oxen and also the beasts of the field, the birds of the heavens and the fish of the sea, whatever passes through the paths of the sea." Everything was placed under human dominion.

This text has a special meaning for me. While I was serving as a missionary to Uganda, a fellow missionary and I parked our car under a tree to have lunch. We looked up into the tree and saw two lions resting in the branches. The average lion in Africa weighs about 350 pounds and has such powerful front paws that it can break a man's neck with a single slap. Needless to say, the two of us remained in our vehicle as we watched the two lions and the lions watched us.

In most countries, lions like these are found only in cages, while people run free. In this instance, the opposite was true—we remained locked in my car while the lions were free.

After we finished our lunches, I turned the ignition key to continue our journey, but the car refused to start. I realized that the only way to start the car was to get out, lift the hood, and press a reset button. But one of the lions was now lying on a branch only a few feet above where I would need to stand to press the button.

Since lions can smell fear in human beings, to relax myself I began giving the lion a Bible study as I got out of the car and lifted the hood to press the button. I preached from Psalm 8 and told the lion, "You may be stronger than I am, more powerful. You may be the king of the beasts, but I want you to know, dear lion, that God has given man dominion over all the beasts of the field, and that includes you."

The lion looked at me as if to say, "What are you doing in my territory?" But the Lord kept the lion there in the tree, and when I pressed the button and started the car, the lion twitched his tail—a signal that he was about to pounce. But just in time I climbed back into the car and drove off.

All Creation Suffers

God did give mankind dominion over the earth, but we have failed to take care of the earth. When Adam sinned, not only did the curse of sin come upon mankind but on all creation. God said to Adam, "Cursed is the ground on which you stand. Thorns and thistles will come out of it."

Paul is referring to this in Romans 8. All creation is groaning, waiting for the redemption that will take place at the Second Coming of Christ.

Romans 8:22 says: "For we know that the whole creation groans and suffers the pains of childbirth together until now." When a woman prepares to deliver a child, she knows she will suffer pain. But she looks forward to being delivered of the baby she has been carrying for nine months. Paul says in verse 23 that not only is creation groaning for deliverance but so are Christians, as they eagerly await their physical redemption.

Patiently Waiting

Those who accept Christ have been redeemed. They stand justified before God and have peace with Him. They have become sons and daughters of God. They can call Him "Our Father." But they still have sinful bodies—bodies dominated by the law of sin and death. Christian life is a struggle between the Spirit and the flesh, for as Paul writes, the two are contrary to each other (Galatians 5:17).

Christians must wait patiently for the redemption of the body because, when Christ comes, this corruption will put on incorruption; this mortal will put on immortality. Then His followers will shout the shout of victory, "O sin, where is your sting. O death, where is your power?" (1 Corinthians 15:50, 51). Thank God through Jesus Christ for this victory!

Paul says in Romans 8:24. "For in hope we have been saved, but hope that is seen is not hope; for why does one also hope for what he sees?" Christians today are saved, but their salvation is a hope—it is not yet a fully tangible reality. They still possess sinful natures. They still live in enemy territory, but they have a hope, and that hope will be reality when Christ comes.

In Romans 8:25 Paul continues: "But if we hope for what we do not see, with perseverance, we wait eagerly for it." God wants us to wait patiently for the ultimate redemption that He has already obtained for us in Jesus Christ.

Holy Spirit Guidance

Meanwhile the Spirit is our constant guide, as Paul explains in Romans 8:26: "And in the same way the Spirit also helps our weaknesses. For we do not know how to pray as we should, but the Spirit Himself intercedes for us with groaning too deep for words."

Because mankind has a sinful nature, too often its prayers are egocentric. So God takes those prayers, polluted with self, and through the Holy Spirit intercedes for us. These prayers then go up to God as sweet-smelling incense. In the Old Testament, this process was portrayed in the Sanctuary service.

We continue reading Paul's words in Romans 8:27: "And he who searches the heart knows what the mind of the spirit is because he intercedes for the saints according to the will of God." Christians groan because they still have sinful natures. Their bodies are dominated by the law of sin and death. But their minds are converted, and the innermost desires of every true Christian are to live godly lives and glorify God.

Since the Holy Spirit can read the hearts of mankind, He knows what is inside us, and though we may be groaning because of our sinfulness and failures, He knows if our hearts are right with God. He brings this before God. What a wonderful blessing we have in the Savior, Jesus Christ! He has not left us alone. When He left this world, He said to the disciples, "I will send you another Comforter." The original Greek meaning for Comforter is "one who is by our side to comfort us, to help us, to guide us, to protect us, and to strengthen us in our battle with sin."

Working Together for Good

Christians have a wonderful Helper dwelling in them and able to give them all they need in the Christian walk. We read in Romans 8:28: "And we know that God causes all things to work together for good."

Paul is not saying that all things are good. He has already told us that Christians in this sinful world are suffering, but he is now saying that God is in complete control. He may allow us to suffer, but He will use all things for good. God's wants us to have the fullness of the power of the gospel, and He will turn everything—even bad experiences—to the good.

This is His purpose, for He is a God of love. He is sovereign, and He is able to do all things through Jesus Christ who intercedes for His followers.

Romans 8:29 says, "For whom He foreknew." God knows beforehand—this is the meaning of "foreknew." He knows in advance who will accept Jesus Christ as their Savior and who will reject Him. But God has not predetermined some to be saved and some to be lost. In fact, He has predestined all to be saved.

He has chosen all, in Christ. In John 3:16, we read that God so loved the world that He sent His only begotten Son. In 2 Corinthians 5:18 onward, we find that God does not count the sins of the world, because He laid them all on His Son, Jesus Christ, when He made Jesus sin for us.

Christ redeemed all mankind, but because God is love, He does not force anyone to accept that gift. We are created with free will. Paul says that those whom "God foreknew who would accept His Son and to them He has predestined to be conformed to the image of His Son that He might be the firstborn among many brethren." While God's desire is for all mankind to experience salvation, those who have accepted Christ as their personal Savior He has predestined to reflect the image of His Son.

Predestined for Sanctification

God has one goal for the human race and another goal for the believer. His desire for the human race is that none should perish—that all should accept His Son, Jesus Christ, and be saved (2 Peter 3:9).

But God has an additional goal for every Christian who has accepted Christ and has peace with God. That goal is to reproduce in them the character of His Son. As we have seen already, the Christian life does not consist of a mere transformation of the old life. Christianity is an exchange of the old life for a new one. We accept the life of Christ in exchange for the life that we were born with—a life of sin. We can say with Paul, "I am crucified with Christ, but I am still living. It is no longer I that lives; it is Christ who lives in me. And the life I now live, I live by faith in the Son of God that loved me and gave Himself for me" (Galatians 2:20).

Through the Spirit, God wants the believers to experience the character of His Son, Jesus Christ. The world desperately needs to see His Son in His followers. We read in Colossians 1:27, "Christ in you, the hope of glory." "For whom he foreknew, He also predestined to be conformed to the image of His Son, that He might be the firstborn among many brethren" Romans 8:29. The Holy Spirit pleads continually with every non-believer to accept Christ as their Savior. But God wants believers to walk in the Spirit so that He may produce through them the image of His Son.

Christ revealed God in the flesh. He is the firstborn (John 14:9). And now God, through the Spirit, wants to reveal Himself through the body of Christ—the church.

Paul concludes in Romans 8:30, "And whom He predestined He also called and whom He called, He also justified and whom He justified, these He also glorified."

These are the steps God takes with His followers. First He calls them to accept His Son. Then He justifies those whom He foreknew would accept His Son. He justifies—He declares them righteous. Ultimately He will glorify them. But until then He wants the image of His Son to be reproduced in them.

We live in a world where sin abounds, but Jesus tells us through Paul in Romans 5:20: "Where sin abounded, grace did much more abound." The gospel is applied, or received justification by faith, and its key text is found in the New Testament: "He that is justified by faith shall live" (see Galatians 3:11). This living begins the moment a person accepts Christ. From that moment the Holy Spirit comes and dwells in them.

Every believer wants to reflect the Son of God, Jesus Christ. Through the Holy Spirit this is possible. This is His function in the Christian walk. As Christians learn to walk in the Spirit, Christ is revealed in them, and the world no longer sees them, but Christ, in their behavior.

Chapter 22

God Is on Our Side

Romans 8:31-39

In Romans 3:21 Paul begins his presentation of the wonderful plan of salvation—the incredible good news of salvation in Jesus Christ. He shows from every conceivable angle that in Jesus Christ salvation is full and complete.

In Romans 8 He shows that this salvation is made real in the Christian's experience, through the Holy Spirit. Now in the closing verses of Romans 8, Paul brings this wonderful message of salvation to a conclusion. In Romans 9-11, then, he turns his attention to his own people—the Jews.

In Romans 8:30-39 Paul concludes his exposition of the gospel of the Lord, Jesus Christ. "What then shall we say to these things?" he asks.

In other words, what is the conclusion of the matter concerning the good news of salvation in Jesus Christ? "If God is for us, who can be against us?" The gospel has revealed a wonderful truth—that God is on our side.

God has told us through Paul in Romans 5:6-10 that while we were helpless, ungodly sinners and enemies of God, we were (past tense) reconciled to Him by the death of His Son. God has told us that in accepting this gospel we have become His sons and daughters and can now address Him as "Dear Father."

God With Us

If God is on the Christians' side, who can be against them? Paul does not mean that no one is against the Christian. There is opposition, even from within the church. Neighbors rise up against them, and they know for a fact that the devil opposes them. In Revelation 12:10 we read that the devil accuses the believers before God, day and night.

What Paul is saying is that if God is on the Christian's side, opposition is of no avail. How wonderful that the God of the Universe who sent Jesus Christ, defeated the devil, and redeemed us from his clutches is on our side!

In Romans 8:32 Paul provides ultimate proof: "He who did not spare His own Son, but delivered Him up for us all, how shall He not with Him also freely give us all things?"

To discover why God did not spare His own Son, we go to Gethsemane, where Jesus and His three closest disciples retreat just hours before He is arrested and crucified.

Jesus tells his disciples, "Wait here for Me and pray for Me" (Matthew 26:38, 39). Jesus then goes a little farther into the garden and falls to the ground, pleading with the Father in agony so intense that His sweat is mixed with blood. Jesus prays, "Father, if it is possible, please remove this cup. (*It is unbearable. My humanity cannot endure what is ahead of Me*)." Then the Father, who loves His Son and refers to Him as "My beloved Son in whom I am well pleased," says, "No." He does not spare His own Son the agony of the cross, because He has delivered His Son up for us all. If God had spared His own Son, we would be without hope.

Jesus in return says, "Father, not My will but Thine be done." The Son surrenders to the Father's will. He is obedient even unto death (Philippians 2:8). All this is done for us. God delivers His Son up for us all.

Always on Our Side

Since God delivered up His Son for us while we were still His enemies, how will He not also with Christ freely give us all things? (Romans 5:10). Christians who doubt their salvation need to read this text. Once salvation has been accepted, Christians must never doubt that God is on their side. They should never doubt His willingness and ability to save them.

Paul continues in Romans 8:33, "Who shall bring a charge against God's elect?" Some accuse the believers falsely—as the devil does. But God will never accuse them—the One who counts. For He justifies them and declares them righteous in Christ. He does not condemn those He justifies. God is true, honest, righteous, and just. Whom He justifies He never accuses.

Paul asks in Romans 8:34: "Who is he who condemns?" Certainly some may condemn the believer. The devil condemns the Christian. The Christian's conscience may condemn him. But Jesus Christ never condemns the believer, for He paid the price on the cross—the infinite price to remove the condemnation that rests on humanity. After paying such a price, how could He condemn the believers? Jesus Christ died to set humanity free from condemnation. Romans 8:1 says, "There is therefore now no condemnation to those who are in Christ Jesus."

No Separation

There is, however, yet another reason to rejoice. Paul says in Romans 8:34, "who also makes intercession for us." Not only did Jesus redeem the believers from condemnation, but He defends their justification against the accusation of Satan. He intercedes for His people against Satan's accusations, and one day He will say to Satan, "Get thee hence. I rebuke you. Is not this a brand plucked out of the fire?" (Zechariah 3:1-4).

Then we turn to one of the most wonderful passages in all of Scripture, one it would be well for us to memorize—Romans 8:35-39: "Who shall separate us from the love of God (*or the love of Christ*)?" The question is not, "Who will separate us from our love to God or Christ?" but "Who will separate us from God's, or Christ's, love for us?"

Continuing the passage, Paul asks, "Shall tribulation, or distress, or persecution, or famine, or nakedness, or peril or sword?" Paul lists these tragic experiences, for when a person accepts Jesus and all is going well, there is harmony between faith and feelings. But when the Christian comes under fire, facing tribulation or distress, something happens inside us. Our faith and our feelings part company.

Faith and Feelings

While serving in Uganda in the 1970s, my family was deported by Idi Amin and spent five years under a Marxist regime in Ethiopia. While waiting for our exit visas we were under duress, and my faith and feelings went their separate ways because I had agreed to write a book against Marxism. I developed a negative spirit and felt forsaken.

But my faith said, "Jesus says He will never forsake me." My faith said, "Jesus says He loves me with an everlasting love." I had to wrestle with the question, "Who is right, my faith in the Word of God or my feelings that come from inside me?" Romans 8:35-39 helped me tremendously.

Remember, the question in Romans 8:35 is, "Who shall separate us from the love of Christ?"

Paul says in verse 36 that because we are living in enemy territory—because citizens of heaven still live in a world dominated by Satan, the enemy of God—the believers are counted as sheep sent to the slaughter. But Paul adds in verse 37 that in all these things we overwhelmingly conquer through Him who loves us. The anchor of faith and assurance is the love of God. This love led God to send His Son to save humanity.

In Ephesians 3 Paul prays a very interesting prayer. He is writing from a Roman prison—a dungeon which consists of a hole in the ground with a small window at the top to give light and air. Many of his flock are becoming discouraged and saying, "If God is not able to protect this great apostle Paul, what hope is there for us as lay people?"

Paul has heard about this and, though he is suffering greatly in that Roman prison, he has no concern for himself, for the truth has set him free. What does concern him is his flock. Paul is not just a theologian. He is a pastor—a shepherd of the flock. In Ephesians 3:13 he says, "Therefore I ask you (*his dear flock*) not to lose heart at my tribulations on your behalf for they are your glory" (NASB). In other words, "Do not give up hope just because I am in prison for preaching the gospel. But because you are distressed (*because your faith is dwindling and you are losing your confidence in God*), I am praying for you."

Paul's prayer is recorded in Ephesians 3:14: "For this reason, I bow my knees before the Father, from whom every family in heaven and on earth derives its name, that He would grant you (*believers who are distressed and discouraged*) according to the riches of His glory, to be strengthened with power through his Spirit in the inner man (*converted mind*); so that Christ may dwell in your hearts through faith; and that you, being rooted and grounded in love, may be able to comprehend with all the saints what is the breadth and length and height and depth, and to know the love of Christ which surpasses knowledge, that you may be filled up to all the fullness of God." What a powerful passage!

Inner Strength

Paul is praying that the believers may be strengthened inwardly, through the Holy Spirit and be rooted and grounded in the love of God, that Christ may dwell in their hearts by faith. The statement in verse 17 "that Christ may dwell in your hearts through faith," bothered me for a while, for Paul is not writing to the unbelievers. He is writing to believers who have already accepted Christ, experienced the new birth, and have Christ dwelling in their hearts. Is Paul implying that they are unconverted when he prays "that Christ may dwell in your hearts"?

The key to understanding this statement is the word translated "dwell." In the Greek language used by Paul, two different words can mean "dwell." One means to lodge, or dwell temporarily. If we stop overnight at a motel, we "dwell" in the motel—a temporary dwelling.

The other Greek word means to "dwell permanently." Paul uses this word, praying that Christ will find a permanent dwelling in the lives of the Ephesians.

Christ, by the Holy Spirit, dwells in every born-again Christian. But is Christ's dwelling in us permanent? For that to happen, we must be rooted and grounded in the *agape* love of God. This is the love that passes understanding.

The question asked in Romans 8:35, "Who shall separate us from the love of Christ?" is answered in verse 37, "In all these things (*persecution, distress, famine*), we are more than conquerors through him who loved us." This is the anchor of the soul.

Unconditional Love

Unlike human love, which is reciprocal, conditional, changeable and self-centered, God's love is unconditional, everlasting, and self-emptying. This is why New Testament writers use a unique word when describing the love of God. This word is the noun *agape* (pronounced ah-GAH-pay). We covered this in Romans 5, but it bears repeating that there is no English word equivalent to the Greek word *agape*. The English word "love" does little justice to God's love. In English we use the same word "love" to apply to both God's and mankind's. Yet the two are so different. God loves us unconditionally and everlastingly. He said to the Jews in Jeremiah 31:3, "I have loved you with an everlasting love."

Paul tells us in 1 Corinthians 13:8, "Love never fails." John tells us in John 13:1, "Having loved his own, He loved them to the end."

God loves us unconditionally and everlastingly. His love for us never changes. This is the grounds for our salvation in Jesus Christ. God so loved the world unconditionally that He sent His only begotten Son, not to condemn but to save the world (John 3:17). Once the believers have accepted Him, they need to be rooted and grounded in this love so that when the storm, persecution, distress, famine, or the sword come, they are able to stand. They can be more than conquerors because they know that God's love will never leave them.

Romans 8:38 and 39 assures us: "For I am convinced that neither death, nor life, nor angels, nor principalities, nor things present, nor things to come (*terrorism?*), nor powers, nor height, nor depth, nor any other created thing, shall be able to separate us from the love of God, which is in Christ Jesus, our Lord." Memorize this passage! A Christian's hope transcends every experience he will ever pass through life.

One day I visited a woman who was so sick she could no longer recognize her husband. For six months he'd lovingly fed, clothed, and cared for her in every way. Without the hope that Christ had given him, he did not know how he could have handled the tragedy.

No tragedy, distress, tribulation, persecution, loss of a job, hunger, destitution, peril, or sword—nothing whatsoever—can remove the Christian from the sphere of God's unconditional love.

The Christian can say, "I am convinced beyond every shadow of doubt that nothing in my experience—death or life, angels or the powers of the evil one, present experience or the things that bring fear or despair and insecurity—will ever separate me from the love of God" (See Romans 8:38, 39).

The evidence that God will never forsake us is found in Christ Jesus, the Lord. Jesus was obedient unto death because He loves humanity unconditionally. God spared not His Son—despite terrible agony on the cross—because He loves us. Ours is a God of love. When John says in 1 John 4:8: "God is love," John does not mean that one of the attributes of God is love. He means God is Love—Himself. No matter what we go through—and God may allow us to go through many trials and difficulties—He will work all of this together for good (Romans 8:14-29).

Resting in God

But now, in the closing verses of Romans 8, Paul says that the ultimate aim of the gospel is to produce a people who are fully resting in the love of God, who has redeemed them in the holy history of Christ.

Christians represent a God who loves them unconditionally—whose love will never change, and loves them more than He loves Himself. This is what Jesus Christ revealed on the cross. Three times, using human agents, the devil tempted Jesus to come down from the cross and save Himself. Jesus knew He could do this. Pitting His divine power against the will of God, He could come down from the cross and confound His tormentors. But He submitted to death because He loved us more than He loved Himself.

This is what God reveals on the cross. Let us be rooted and grounded in this love, that we may know this truth that sets us free.

CHAPTER 23

The Jewish Tragedy

Romans 9:1-33

While Paul makes it clear in his epistle that he is set aside by God as the apostle to the Gentiles (Ephesians 3:8), he still has a great burden for his own fellowmen, the Jews.

Having explained the essentials of the gospel clearly in Romans 3:21 to the end of Romans 8, he directs himself to his own people in Romans 9-11. The central issue in these three chapters is whether God has failed to keep his promise to Abraham, Isaac, and Jacob (Romans 9:6).

God has promised that through these three fathers of Israel all of their descendants will be saved in the kingdom of God.

In Matthew 23:38 Jesus says to the Jewish nation, "I leave your house desolate." This seems to contradict the promise of God to Abraham, Isaac, and Jacob. But in Romans 9-11 Paul proves that God does indeed keep His promise and presents his conclusion in Romans 11:26.

What is Israel?

Before he can do this, however, he has to answer two main questions: "What constitutes Israel?" and, "Where did the Jews fail and why did God reject them?"

Paul also shows that righteousness by faith is the only way humankind—Jew or Gentile—can be saved. Having laid this foundation, we prepare to study Romans 9, where Paul very clearly explains God's meaning of the word "Israel." But first we need to review Romans 2:28 and 29 to lay the foundation.

In Romans 2 Paul defines the real Jew as God sees him: "For he is not a Jew who is one outwardly, nor is that circumcision which is outward in the flesh, but he is a Jew who is one inwardly, and circumcision is that of the heart, in the Spirit, and not in the letter; whose praise is not from men but from God."

From these two verses it becomes clear that God defines the words "Jew" and "Israel" differently than do the Jews themselves.

Paul's Burden

In Romans 9:1-5 Paul expresses deep concern for his nation—his own people who had been especially blessed by God. The Jews considered Paul a traitor. They hated him. In Acts 21:28-30, we read that Paul is arrested by his fellow men and accused of three things by his own people: Of being against his own people; of desecrating God's temple in Jerusalem; and of undermining the law.

But despite this hatred, Romans 9:1 and onward tells us of the great love Paul felt toward his own people: "I tell the truth in Christ, I am not lying, my conscience also bearing me witness in the Holy Spirit, that I have great sorrow and continual grief in my heart. For I could wish that I myself were accursed from Christ for my brethren, my kinsmen according to the flesh, who are Israelites, to whom pertain the adoption, the glory, the covenants, the giving of the law, the service of God and the promises; of whom are the fathers and from whom, according to the flesh, Christ came, who is over all, the eternally blessed God. Amen." Paul clearly wants the Jews to understand that he has a great burden for them.

This statement is amazing in its selflessness, especially verse 3: "For I could wish that I myself were accursed from Christ for my brethren, my kinsmen according to the flesh."

Paul is saying that his love for his fellow men, despite their hate, is greater than his own concern and love for himself. This is a man who is reflecting the self-emptying, unconditional *agape* love of God. He says in so many words: "This is the truth; my conscience is bearing witness before God Himself, before the Holy Spirit, that I am willing to be lost if this will save my fellow Jews."

Blood Not Enough

Having expressed his deep concern for his fellow Jews, in Romans 9:6 he begins to explore the first major problem with Israel: "But it is not that the word of God has taken no effect. For they are not all Israel who are of Israel." (The first "Israel" in this verse refers to the nation of Israel; the second "Israel" refers to Jacob, whose name was changed to "Israel" Genesis 32:22-27).

In Romans 9:6-8 Paul's makes the point that possessing the blood of Abraham, Isaac, and Jacob fails to qualify a person as an Israelite in God's eyes, for not all descendants of these three ancestors are Israelites, even in the physical sense.

He continues in Romans 9:7: "Nor are they all children because they are the seed of Abraham; but, 'In Isaac your seed shall be called.' "Those who are the children of flesh, (*the natural descendants of Abraham*), these are not the children of God; but the children of the promise are counted as the seed." These verses are crucial in defining Israel on God's terms.

God gave Israel three fathers—Abraham, Isaac, and Jacob. Throughout the Bible these three names occur again and again, as a unifying thread woven through and through. The Sadducees once asked Jesus what would happen in heaven if a wife had been widowed seven times on earth by seven different husbands—with whom will she be married in heaven? Part of Jesus' response in Matthew 22:32 was, "God is not the God of the dead, but of the living. He is the God of Abraham, Isaac and Jacob." In other words, these three men represent the living.

"Why did God give Israel three fathers?" we ask. We must answer this question if we are to understand Paul's meaning of "Israel." As we study carefully what God says about them, we find that Abraham stands for faith. He is the father of all who believe. In Romans 4:11 we read: "And he (*Abraham*) received the sign of circumcision, a seal of the righteousness of the faith which he had while still uncircumcised, that he might be the father of all those who believe, though they are uncircumcised (*or Gentiles*)." (See also Galatians 3:6-9).

The natural descendants of Abraham do not necessarily constitute Israel. Ishmael can claim Abraham as his father, but he does not belong to Israel. Esau can claim both Abraham and Isaac as his father, yet Esau does not belong to Israel.

To understand what Paul is saying, we must read Romans 4:18, where Abraham's faith is described: "Who (*that is, Abraham*), contrary to hope (*because his wife had passed the age of childbearing*), in hope believed, so that he became the father of many nations, according to what was spoken, 'So shall your descendants be.'"

Galatians 4:23-28 tells us that Abraham had two sons, one through the flesh and one through the promise. The promised son is the one who represents the Christians, the true people of Israel.

Abraham the Faithful

Abraham represents faith. If we have the faith Abraham demonstrated, we become the children of Abraham. This is very clear in Galatians 3:27-29: "For as many of you as were baptized into Christ have put on Christ. There is neither Jew nor Greek (*Gentile*), there is neither slave nor free, there is neither male nor female, for you are all one in Christ Jesus. And if you are Christ's then you are Abraham's seed, and heirs according to the promise."

Abraham stands for faith. The word "father" here does not mean natural father, but prototype or example. So Abraham is the father—the prototype or example—of all those who believe.

Isaac Born from Above

Now what is so special about Isaac? In the Old Testament we discover nothing significant about Isaac's spiritual life. But there is something special about his birth. He was born from above. God came to Abraham when he was 75 years old and promised him a son. Abraham believed God. Yet eight years passed and no son arrived, and Abraham's faith began to fade.

Then God comes to Abraham again, in Genesis 15, and asks him why he doubts His promise. Abraham responds, in effect, "God, You promised me a son eight years ago. Human beings take nine months. How long does it take You to give me a son? Am I to consider the son of my slave Eliezer the promised son?"

God replies, "No, the son I have promised is the one that will come out of your loins." Then God shows Abraham the stars and asks, "Abraham, how many stars can you count?"

"Impossible to count!" Abraham replies.

"This is how many children you will have," God promises. "An uncountable number like the sands of the sea."

Genesis 15:6 says, "And Abraham believed in the Lord, and He accounted it to him for righteousness," a verse Paul often quotes.

Two years later, Sarah says in effect to Abraham, "God promised you a son through your loins, but I do not believe He can produce a son through me. Why don't you help God by going to Hagar, my slave woman? Use her as a surrogate mother, produce a son, and help God keep His promise." Abraham agrees to the idea and he and Hagar produce a son, Ishmael.

But Ishmael is not accepted by God as the promised son. God waits approximately 14 years, until it becomes impossible—medically, scientifically, and humanly—for Sarah to have a child. She has now passed the age of childbearing. Abraham and Sarah have exhausted all possible human resources to produce a son, and now God gives them the promised heir, Isaac. Abraham is 100 years old and Sarah about 10 years younger.

Why does God wait 25 years to fulfill His promise to Abraham? Why does He wait until it is humanly impossible for Sarah to have a child through Abraham? Because Isaac represents those who are born from above. Jesus basically tells Nicodemus in John 3:6, "That which is born of the flesh is flesh, but, Nicodemus, if you want to be a child of God and go to heaven, it is not enough to have the blood of Abraham, Isaac, and Jacob in your veins; you need to be born from above. You need to be the spiritual son of Isaac."

After proving that we are saved only through the New Covenant (represented by Isaac), Paul says in Galatians 4:28, "Now we, brethren (*believers who have accepted Christ and experienced the new birth*), as Isaac was, are children of the promise." While Abraham represents faith, Isaac represents the new birth.

Jacob who Persevered

Now then, what does Jacob represent? The name Jacob can mean schemer or supplanter. Jacob is promised the birthright which normally, in the Jewish custom, goes to the firstborn. But Jacob has the misfortune of not being the firstborn. His twin brother Esau is. As Esau is being born, Jacob holds onto Esau's heel, as if to say, "Come back, Esau, I am supposed to be the firstborn."

All through his life, Jacob tries to obtain the promised birthright through scheming and deception. When Esau returns from hunting, empty handed and hungry, Jacob tries to trade the birthright for a bowl of lentil stew.

Later he tries to secure the birthright by deceiving Isaac, who is by then very old and blind. Jacob and his mother kill a lamb and cook Isaac a meal, then put the skin of the lamb on his hands to impersonate Esau, who is very hairy, and asks for Isaac's special blessing.

The history of Jacob's life is that he tries to fulfill God's promise in his own strength—a struggle all Christians face. After accepting Christ as their righteousness and experiencing the new birth, Christians often earnestly try to fulfill God's will in their own natural strength. In that sense, all new Christians are like Jacob.

But Jacob's schemes cause endless problems, and he is forced to flee from his brother into exile. After many years, however, he returns to his homeland, still fearing that Esau may not have forgiven him for all his schemes—especially for robbing him of his birthright. So he sends gifts to Esau and moves his family ahead of him. He then goes out alone by a river, confesses his sins, and lies down to sleep.

While he is sleeping a hand touches him, and his first thought is that Esau, his brother, is taking his revenge. A wrestling match begins and continues all night long—a terribly exhausting experience. As dawn breaks, the one with whom Jacob has been wrestling manages to dislocate Jacob's hip and he realizes that this is no ordinary man, but the angel of the Lord. In terrible pain, Jacob holds onto the angel and says, "I will not let you go until you bless me."

The angel asks, "What is your name?"

"Jacob (*which means schemer or supplanter*)," comes the reply.

The angel then blesses him, saying in Genesis 32:22-28, "No longer will you be called Jacob. I shall give you a new name. Your name shall be Israel (*which means 'one who has persevered with God'*)."

It is not enough to believe in Jesus Christ or to be a born-again Christian. Jesus Himself makes it clear in Matthew 10:22, as does Paul in Hebrews 10:38 and 39, that faith must endure to the end. It must persevere. Revelation 14:12 reads: "Here is the patience of the saints." Here are they that endure unto the end.

Faith, Birth, and Perseverance

To be a true Israelite, one must have the faith of Abraham. The believer must also be born from above, as Isaac was. And one's faith, like Jacob's, must endure unto the end. Paul teaches in Romans 9 that only those who have these characteristics will sit down in God's kingdom with Abraham, Isaac, and Jacob.

In Romans 9:10 Paul tells us: "And not only this, but when Rebecca also had conceived by one man, even by our father Isaac (*for the children not yet being born, nor having done any good or evil, that the purpose of God according to election might stand, not of works but of Him who calls*)." Salvation is a gift of God. It does not come through our efforts, our earnings, or our flesh. It comes as we respond in faith when He calls (Mark 16:15, 16).

"Flesh" refers to anything that is true of our natural state—our birth, lineage, or performance when we depend on it fully or in part for our salvation. If we depend on our flesh we fall from grace (Galatians 5:4).

In verses 14 and onward Paul reveals that God is sovereign and that His salvation and mercy are based on His sovereignty and not human right. Romans 9:14-29 makes this plain. The potter has a right to take the clay and make a vessel to be used by kings or for menial use; the clay has no say in this. God, in His sovereignty, has chosen to save us out of His mercy and love. Mankind's part is to believe, to accept, to experience the new birth, and to persevere to the end. Salvation is by faith alone, from beginning to end (Romans 1:17).

Two Big Problems

The Jews' first problem was their failure to accept righteousness by faith. God promised salvation to Abraham, Isaac, and Jacob through righteousness by faith in Jesus Christ. Jesus says in John 8:56: "Your father Abraham rejoiced to see My day, and he saw it and was glad."

The Jews' second problem was their failure to understand God's way of saving sinful man. They refused to accept that it is not those who are the literal descendants of Abraham, Isaac, and Jacob who become heirs to the promise, but those who have the faith of Abraham, who experience the new birth like Isaac, and whose faith endures unto the end like Jacob's. This is true Israel.

God did not fail to keep His promise to Israel when He, through Jesus Christ, says to them in Matthew 23:38 "I leave your house desolate." This is because the promise was fulfilled in Jesus Christ and in God's sight Israel does not mean those who have the blood of Abraham, Isaac, and Jacob. Israel consists of those who have the qualities of these three men—the faith of Abraham, the new birth experience of Isaac, and the perseverance of Jacob. All believing Jews and all believing Gentiles together make up all Israel. God is keeping His promise. All Israel will be saved.

God Keeps His Promise

But God has a concern for His people. Paul's cry to the Jews is, "God did keep His promise. The promise was Jesus Christ. He is the promised seed (Galatians 3:16). The Messiah did come. Please do not turn your backs on Him." There is still hope for the Jews, as Paul explains in Romans 11.

But as we move forward to Romans 10, we see the Jews' fundamental problem. Why did God say through Jesus Christ, "I leave your house desolate?" Did God fail to keep His promise, or did the Jews reject the promise?

May we as Gentile Christians witness to our Jewish friends that Jesus Christ is still their Messiah and that, if they believe in Him as Abraham did, there is hope. Jesus says, "Abraham saw My day and rejoiced" (John 8:56).

CHAPTER 24

Who Constitutes True Israel?

Romans 10:1-21

In Romans 9 we discover that in God's eyes the true Israelite—the Jew—is by no means always a descendent of Abraham, Isaac, and Jacob. The true Jew is one who has Abraham's faith, Isaac's new-birth experience from above, and Jacob's perseverance to the end. These three qualities define true Israel.

Now, to introduce chapter 10 we turn to the final verses of Romans 9, where Paul reveals the core problem faced by the Jews of Christ's day. We read in Romans 9:30-33, "What shall we say then? That Gentiles, who did not pursue righteousness, have attained to righteousness, even the righteousness of faith; but Israel, pursuing the law of righteousness, has not attained to the law of righteousness. Why? Because they did not seek it by faith, but as it were, by the works of the law. For they stumbled at that stumbling stone. As it is written: Behold, I lay in Zion a stumbling stone and rock of offense, And whoever believes on Him will not be put to shame."

The Jews mistakenly believed that if one was descended from Abraham, Isaac, and Jacob, they were God's children. True, God did give the literal Jews a special privilege. Paul tells us in Romans 3 that unto them were given the oracles of God. Unto them God gave the promise, and God kept His promise.

Then why say to the Jewish nation, "I leave your house desolate" (Matthew 23:38)? In Romans 10 Paul shows why God has rejected the Jewish nation while leaving open wide the door of salvation for all individual Jews.

God did indeed keep His promise, Paul tells us. The Jews were rejected as a nation because they rejected God's promise, Jesus Christ.

That They May Be Saved

Paul begins Romans 10 in much the same way as he began Romans 9, though he approaches things in a slightly different way. He says in Romans 10:1: "Brethren, my heart's desire and prayer to God for literal Israel is that they may be saved."

Paul has the heart of a true Christian and genuine pastor. The Jews bitterly hate Paul and see him as a traitor. Yet Paul's heart's desire is for Israel's salvation. In Romans 9:3 he says, in effect, "I am willing to be cursed—lost forever—if this would mean the salvation of my countrymen."

Now, in Romans 10:1 he says that his heart's desire is that Israel might be saved. In verse 2 he explains, "For I bear them witness that they have a zeal for God, but not according to knowledge. For they being ignorant of God's righteousness, and seeking to establish their own righteousness, have not submitted to the righteousness of God."

This is the core problem with the Jews of Christ's day. Yes, they have zeal for God. They spend hours praying. They fast more than the Old Testament laws require. Yet they fail because they are ignorant of God's righteousness, man's only means of salvation. The Jews try to produce their own righteousness, which God rejects. This is also a major problem with many Gentiles.

Paul then makes another key statement, in verse 4: "Christ is the end of the law for righteousness to every one who believes." Paul is not saying that Christ did away with the law when He saved mankind through grace. Christ makes this clear in the Sermon on the Mount in Matthew 5, especially in verse 17 and onward: "I did not come to destroy the law but to fulfill."

The End of the Law

What does Paul mean, then, with the phrase, "the end of the law"? The Greek word for "end" can mean either "fulfillment" or "termination." Both can apply to verse 4. Paul could be saying that at the cross Christ brought legalism—that is, the law as a means of salvation—to an end.

Since human beings are legalists by nature, when Christ died on the cross He discredited—brought to an end—any attempt by man to save himself by his own good works. Paul clearly states in Romans 3: 28, "Therefore we conclude that a man is justified by faith apart from the deeds of the law," and in Romans 3:20, "Therefore, by the deeds of the law no flesh will be justified in His sight...."

The second meaning—"fulfillment"—is that in Christ's perfect life and sacrificial death, which meet the law's positive demands and justice, Jesus satisfies the law on behalf of sinful man. We can interpret Romans 10:4 to mean that Christ has fulfilled that which the law of God requires of us. Christ is the fulfillment of the law for righteousness to every one who believes. The moment we believe in Jesus Christ, God looks at us, not as failures and sinners, but as if we are His Son. Remember God's words about Jesus at His baptism, "This is My beloved Son in whom I am well pleased" (Matthew 3:17). This applies to all who are in Him!

Jesus satisfies all the positive demands of the law as well as its justice. The moment we believe, the righteousness of Christ fully satisfies the law and becomes ours. In this sense Christ is the fulfillment—the end—of the law for righteousness to everyone who believes.

Since Paul is discussing the Jewish nation, he also means that on the cross Jesus brought legalism to an end. He declares that the only way the Jew will be saved is by faith in Jesus. In verse 5 Paul adds, "For Moses writes about the righteousness which is of the law. The man who does those things shall live by them."

There are great differences between salvation by law and salvation by grace. If we come to the law and say, "I believe in all your commandments," the law cannot justify us. The law justifies only those who obey it perfectly and continually—something none of us have done.

In Galatians 3:10 Paul tells us, "Cursed is the person who is living under the law," for the law requires this person to keep it continually and perfectly. According to the law mankind is saved by performance. But in salvation by grace the believers are saved on the basis of God's promise fulfilled in Jesus Christ. The works of Christ justify under grace. The human part, from beginning to end, is faith. Paul presents this in Romans 10:6.

Faith Vs. Works

The righteousness of faith says: "Do not say in your heart, Who will ascend into heaven?" Paganism in Paul's day—and even today— teaches that mankind saves itself by appeasing an angry God and reaching heaven's gates through good works (the spiritual meaning of Babylon).

But the righteousness which is by faith does not try to reach up to God nor descend to the depths of the grave to find salvation. Christ defeated death (verse 7) and ascended to heaven (verse 8): "But what does it say? The word is near you, even in your mouth and in your heart (*that is, the word of faith which we preach*): that if you confess with your mouth the Lord Jesus and believe in your heart that God has raised Him from the dead, you will be saved."

"Dear Jewish people," Paul is saying. "There is only one way to truly be a child of God and honestly belong to God's Israel. It can only happen by faith in Jesus Christ."

Paul then says in verse 10: "With the heart one believes to righteousness and with the mouth, confession is made to salvation."

A true Christian is one who rejoices in heart and word in Jesus Christ and has no confidence in the flesh (Philippians 3:3). This is Paul's goal for his fellow Jews. Paul says in verses 11-13, "For the Scripture says, Whoever believes on Him will not be put to shame. For there is no distinction between Jew and Greek (*Gentile*), for the same Lord over all is rich to all who call upon Him. For whoever calls upon the name of the Lord shall be saved."

There is only one way to reach heaven. The Jews' history is recorded for our benefit and theirs, that we may all turn for salvation to Jesus Christ as Messiah (1 Corinthians 10:11).

Proclaiming Salvation

"Whoever calls upon the name of the Lord shall be saved," Paul says in verse 13. Then he introduces the steps of faith by asking a series of questions, beginning with verse 14: "How then shall they call on Him in whom they have not believed?"

In other words, how can the Jews confess Jesus Christ if they do not believe He is their Messiah and Savior?

Then again, "And how shall they believe in Him of whom they have not heard?" We cannot believe in Jesus as our Savior if we have not heard about Him. That much is obvious. "And how shall they hear without a preacher?" Paul continues.

Preaching is central to God's plan of salvation. Before He left this earth after His resurrection, Jesus commissioned His disciples to "Go into all the world and preach the gospel to every creature. He who believes and is baptized will be saved, but he who does not believe (*who deliberately turns his back to this gift of God*), will be condemned" Mark 16:15-16. This commission remains for Christians today, living in the 21st century.

But in Romans 10:15 Paul carries us several steps beyond preaching, asking, "And how shall they preach unless they are sent?" God sends His followers for all time to proclaim the gospel to every creature, including their Jewish brothers and sisters. Paul then reflects, "How beautiful are the feet of those who preach the gospel of peace."

The gospel is good news of peace. At Jesus' birth the angels proclaimed to the shepherds of Bethlehem, "I bring you glad tidings of great joy, of peace, that are for all men" (Luke 2:10).

In verse 16 Paul at last expresses the problem that caused Jesus to say to the Jews, "I leave your house desolate" (Matthew 23:38). "But they all had not obeyed the gospel," Paul says. This is the problem. God has not failed to keep His promise to Abraham, Isaac, and Jacob that through one of their descendants the seed (Messiah) would come.

The Promise Came

Paul says clearly in Galatians 3:16 that the word "seed" is in the singular and refers to Christ. Through a single descendant of these three patriarchs God has blessed all nations of the world. True, the Messiah was to be a descendant of Abraham, Isaac, and Jacob. But salvation is not based on being a blood relative of these men, for Abraham, Isaac, and Jacob are prototypes of every true believer.

In the end, however, the Jews as a nation did not obey the gospel. To prove his point, Paul quotes the prophet Isaiah in Romans 10:16, "Lord, who has believed our report?" He then concludes in Romans 10:17: "So then faith comes by (*from*) hearing, and hearing by the word of God (*preaching*)."

In other words, the steps of salvation are, first, to hear the gospel; second, to believe the gospel; and third, to obey the gospel and pass from death to life, from condemnation to justification.

The Jews chose to reject this progression. They heard the gospel. But they refused to believe and obey the gospel of the Lord, Jesus Christ. They fulfilled Isaiah's prediction, "Who shall believe our report?"

"But I say, Have they not heard?" Paul asks in Romans 10:18. Has the Jewish nation of his day not heard the gospel? Is this the problem? No, Paul says, "Their sound has gone out to all the earth, And their words to the ends of the world." Here, "the ends of the world" refer to the world known as the Roman Empire—primarily the Middle East.

We read on in verses 19 and 20, "Did Israel not know? First Moses says, I will provoke you to jealousy by those who are not a nation. I will anger you by a foolish nation (*the Greek says, 'a nation that does not understand'*). But Isaiah is very bold and says: I was found by those who did not seek Me: I was made manifest to those who did not ask for Me."

Gentiles Welcomed

"Those" refers to the Gentiles. The Gentiles accepted righteousness by faith, while the Jews as a nation held onto their righteousness by works of the law. We see this clearly in Romans 9:30-33.

Paul then concludes Romans 10 with these words: "But to Israel he says: All day long I have stretched out My hands to a disobedient and a contrary people (*an obstinate people*)."

Paul has already reassured the Jews that Jesus died for them and has redeemed them. God has kept His promise to Abraham, Isaac, and Jacob. The seed did come, and that seed is Jesus Christ. Jesus came to save all men—Jews and Gentiles alike. God so loved the world (human race) that He gave His only begotten Son that whoever believes, whether Jew or Gentile, shall not perish but have everlasting life. Yes, God first made the promise to the Jewish nation, and He has kept that promise. If any Jew is lost, it is not because God has failed to keep His promise. Death comes only through deliberate, persistent and ultimate rejection of the fulfilled promise in Jesus Christ.

We are dealing here with a serious situation. God never fails to keep His promises. But while God did keep His promise and reconciled the whole world unto Himself through the death of His Son (Romans 5:10; 2 Corinthians 5:19), God created humankind with free will. He does not force salvation on anyone. This is why God wants positive responses, irrespective of race. The only way God can save mankind is by faith alone in Jesus Christ. God is the God of Jews and Gentiles. There is no difference, for all have sinned and come short of the glory of God (Romans 3:23). In and of ourselves we are all in the same condition, 100 percent sinners with only one hope—faith in the grace of the Lord, Jesus Christ.

Hope for All

Unless we accept God's Son as our only hope of salvation, we will be ashamed in the judgment. Our own righteousness, wonderful as it may be in our eyes, cannot qualify us for heaven. The law of God demands not only perfect performance but perfect motives and perfect natures (see Matthew 7:21-23).

We were all born with sinful natures and stand condemned, for sin cannot enter the kingdom of God. Paul says in 1 Corinthians 15:50 onward, "This flesh and blood cannot inherit heaven because corruption cannot inherit incorruption."

But if we believe Jesus is the Messiah and that God did keep His promise, we will accept Jesus Christ as our Savior. The Jews do not need to become Gentiles to be saved, but all must accept Jesus Christ as their Savior.

I was returning home on foot one evening from a meeting in England. As I walk down the street, a woman calls to me from a second-story window: "Excuse me, sir, would you please come and do me a favor."

I stop and reply, "What would you like me to do?"

She says, "Would you please come and turn on my lights?"

The window is high and I can see only her head from the neck up, and I imagine she must be disabled and in need of help.

"Yes," I say. "I will be glad to turn on your light." I climb the steps and go to the door with the number she has given. I knock and am surprised when the woman opens the door herself.

This puzzles me: Surely, if she can open the door, she can turn on the light.

The woman sees the strange look on my face and says, "I know this is a strange request, but I am an Orthodox Jew and it is a sin for us to turn any light on once the sun sets on Friday and the Sabbath begins." (Turning the light on was to her "kindling a fire," spoken of in Exodus 35:2-3).

She has no idea, of course, that I am a Sabbath keeper on my way home from Friday-evening vespers. So I ask her: "Doesn't that law also say that the stranger within your gates should not work?"

Shocked that I, a Gentile, know the fourth commandment, in her embarrassment she says, "Yes, this is true, but you are a Gentile." In other words, "There is no hope for you."

So I say, "Sister, do you have a Bible?" She says yes, she has a copy of the Old Testament. I ask her to turn to 1 Samuel 16:7, where God tells Samuel, "Do not look at his appearance (*referring to Saul*) or at the height of his stature, because I have refused him. For the Lord does not see as man sees, for man looks at the outward appearance (*or outward performance*), but the Lord looks at the heart."

"What has this to do with my request?" she asks.

I reply, "Everything. But let me first turn your light on." I go to the wall and flip on the switch, then turn to the woman and say, "Your problem is this. While it was I who turned on your light, I was not doing my will but yours. As far as God is concerned, you turned the light on yourself. You only used me as a tool. You have broken the Sabbath and lost salvation."

"You are making this all very difficult for me," she says.

"No sister—not hard, impossible!" I reply. "I learned this from a Jew whose eyes were opened by God. His name is Paul and he says, 'By the works of the law shall no flesh be justified.' Sister, your only hope is to accept Jesus Christ as your Messiah."

This is my prayer for every Jew reading this book. Let us know this truth that sets us all free.

Chapter 25

God Keeps His Promises

Romans 11:1-36

Paul begins Romans 9 by expressing deep concern for his own people, the Jews. God has not failed to keep His promise to Israel, but Paul says the Jews have failed to realize that God's promise is to the spiritual descendants of Abraham, Isaac, and Jacob.

The believer must have Abraham's faith, Isaac's new birth experience from above, and Jacob's perseverance. These are the attributes of God's chosen people as portrayed in Romans 9.

In Romans 10 Paul explains that if the Jews are lost, it is entirely their own fault, for God's promised salvation came in Jesus Christ. Only when the Jews deliberately, persistently, and ultimately rejected Jesus Christ as the Messiah did they commit the sin of unbelief. The Jews clearly must accept the blame, Paul says in Romans 10, for they heard the gospel, were convicted of the gospel, but did not obey the gospel.

Rejection Not Absolute

Now we turn to Romans 11, where Paul concludes his discussion of the Jews. He points out two important facts: First, that Israel's rejection is not total. When Jesus says in Matthew 23:38: "Your house is left desolate," He does not mean that it will be impossible for any Jews to be saved. What He is saying is that no longer will the Jewish nation represent Him to the world. He has taken the torch from their hands and is giving it to the largely Gentile Christian church.

Second, Paul points out in Romans 11 that God's rejection of Israel is not absolute. There will come a time when in a remarkable way He will make the gospel available to the Jewish nation.

In Paul's day, many Jews accepted Christ, as many Jews are doing in our day. In Romans 11 Paul shares his own experience. Paul (formerly Saul) had persecuted the early Christian church. But God met Paul on the road to Damascus, where Paul accepted Jesus as the Messiah.

He tells us in Romans 11:1, "I say then, has God cast away His people?" In other words, "Is there no hope for the Jewish people?" "Certainly not!

(*God forbid!*)," he replies. Is Paul not an Israelite of the seed of Abraham, of the tribe of Benjamin? There is still hope for the Jew who says, "I am now convinced that Jesus is the Messiah and I accept Him as my Savior."

In Romans 11:2 Paul says, "God has not cast away His people whom He foreknew." What does the word "foreknew" mean? In Greek it consists of two words joined together—"before" and "to know." Paul is saying that God did not cast away those whom He knew beforehand would accept His Son, Jesus Christ, as their Savior. We must not confuse the word "foreknowledge" with "fore-ordain." God has fore-ordained all men to be saved, but He also "foreknows" which of the Jews will accept Jesus as their Messiah. But that does not stop Him from pleading with all mankind to accept His Son (2 Peter 3:9).

Still Pleading

Paul continues in Romans 11:2: "Or do you not know what the Scripture says of Elijah, how he pleads with God against Israel." In 1 Kings 19:10 and 14 Elijah says, in effect, "They (*the Jews*) have killed your prophets; they have torn down your altars and I am the only one who is faithful to you and they are seeking my life."

God effectively replies to Elijah, "You do not realize that I have reserved for myself not two, or three, or a handful, but 7,000 men (*heads of families*) who have not bowed to Baal."

As human beings we judge outwardly, but God knows the heart and He knew in Elijah's day that 7,000 families had not turned their backs on Him.

In Romans 11:5 Paul says that a remnant remains, according to the election of grace. Not all Jews have rejected the Messiah. Paul says there are faithful ones who have not turned their backs on the truth.

The word "remnant" means those who remain faithful through times of persecution and general apostasy. In this passage Paul is saying that even though the Jewish nation had turned its back on the true God and Jesus Christ, the Messiah, many had not turned their backs on God's gift. These are called the "election of grace." The word "election" means chosen ones. God did indeed choose all men to be saved—the New Testament is very clear on this. Many universal texts clearly teach that God loved the world, that He saved the world, and that He reconciled all men unto Himself.

Romans 5:18, for example, clearly says, "By one man's obedience, justification unto life came to all men." What does Paul mean, then, by the word "election?" God elected all men to be saved, but He created us with free will. He lets us choose to accept or reject His election. When we accept the gift of God (Jesus Christ), we elect to be saved according to the election of grace.

In Romans 11:6-8 we find this to be entirely biblical: "And if by grace, then it is no longer of works; otherwise grace is no longer grace. But if it is of works, it is no longer grace; otherwise work is no longer work." Paul is saying that God's promise to Israel was not salvation by keeping the law. It was not salvation by works of the law or good works. It was salvation by grace—salvation by the doing and dying of the Lord, Jesus Christ. Jews who accepted Jesus as the Messiah are called the election of grace, for they have elected God's method of saving mankind, in contradiction to men's method of saving himself through his good works and keeping the law.

Paul is not discussing the fruits of salvation which result in many good works. When he talks of works in Romans 11, he is not referring to the fruits of salvation. He makes it clear in Romans 12 and onward that genuine justification by faith—salvation by grace—produces a people zealous to do good works. But here he uses the word "works" to refer to works as a means of salvation. Our works contribute not one iota to our salvation. Entirely free to sinners, it is made effective by faith alone.

Now we read Romans 11:7: "What then, Israel has not obtained what it seeks, but the elect have obtained it." Somehow the Jews had become sidetracked from what God promises them in the Old Testament. God promises them a Messiah, one who would live a perfect life and meet the wages of sin for them. God gave the law, not as a means of salvation or of solving the sin problem, but to show them that they were sinners in need of grace. The Jews unfortunately perverted that which was to lead them to the Savior and used it as a substitute method of salvation (read Hebrews 4:2).

God's Sovereignty

Paul continues in Romans 11:8 (KJV): "Just as it is written: 'God has given them a spirit of stupor.'" This statement and several like it in the Bible cause difficulty for many. "God has given them a spirit of slumber." Such statements, found especially in the Old Testament, give the impression that God is responsible for the Jews sidetracking the gospel.

In Exodus 9:12 we read that God hardens Pharaoh's heart. Isaiah 45:7 says, "I (*referring to God*) created evil." Readers in the Western Hemisphere read these texts and say, "See, God is to blame. He is the one who hardened Pharaoh's heart. He is the one who created evil. He is the one who caused the Jews' stupor."

But we must understand these statements in the context of the Old Testament concept of the sovereignty of God. Because God is sovereign, nothing happens without His permission. Because He has allowed Satan to tempt Adam and Eve and bring sin into the world—because He has allowed the Holocaust, for example, and many other things—He assumes the blame until the judgment day. Then He will show the Universe and the world that the real culprit is Satan and that He allowed Satan the freedom to cause havoc on this earth. He allowed Satan to do terrible things so that man would realize how terrible a thing sin is.

When God told Adam and Eve that sin was evil, to them it was only a theory. Only later did they begin to fully realize how terrible sin is. Someday everyone will confess that God is right. But until then He assumes the blame. God did not harden Pharaoh's heart; He simply allowed Pharaoh to harden his own heart. But God accepts the blame for it. God did not create evil, but He allowed evil to develop and grow in this world. For this He assumes the blame until the judgment day. When that day comes, all will confess to God, "Just and true are thy ways" (Revelation 15:3).

Nor did God cause the Jews to misunderstand the Old Testament and sidetrack them from His great promise to Abraham—of salvation by faith alone in the righteousness of the Messiah. This is clearly brought out in the Epistle to the Hebrews.

Many terrible things happen in this world that God does not stop. He allows them for a purpose and assumes the blame, because He is sovereign. On judgment day, however, everyone will confess that God is just. The Bible says that then Satan himself will admit God is right. Until then, by faith we must believe that God is a God of love—that He wants none to perish.

Called to be Special

Now Paul continues, quoting David's words that the Jews face the same difficulties everyone faces. God did indeed call them to be a special people, but He did not exempt them from the devil's fiery darts when they deliberately, persistently rejected God and the Messiah, Jesus Christ. Only then does Jesus say of them in Matthew 23:38, "I leave your house desolate."

Now we read Romans 11:11: "I say then, have they stumbled that they should fall? Certainly not! But through their fall, to provoke them to jealousy, salvation has come to the Gentiles."

Paul is an exceptional theologian. He sees God from every angle. When the Jews reject the gospel, God sends it forth to the rest of the world, creating in at least some Jews a sense of jealousy at the Gentiles' newfound peace, hope, and salvation. This leads them to turn to Jesus.

The Olive Tree

But this is not the ultimate end of the Jews. Paul presents an interesting illustration in Romans 11:15-24, using the olive tree as a metaphor for spiritual Israel. The tree's roots and sap represent Christ, Paul says. As the tree depends on the roots for life, so the life of the church is Christ, the Source of our hope, peace, righteousness, and right to eternal life. Christ represents the roots and the sap which keep the tree alive.

The olive tree has natural branches, which represent the Jews, because salvation first came through them. Jesus Himself was a Jew. But because the Jews rejected Christ, Jesus takes the branches, which represent the unfaithful Jews, and breaks them off. Then He grafts in wild olive branches—the Gentiles—who become partakers of the life which is Jesus Christ.

In Romans 11:18 Paul says to the Gentiles: "Do not boast against the branches." In other words, "Do not brag because the natural branches have been broken off. You were not grafted because you are better than the Jews. You were grafted because you accepted the gift of God by faith, the righteousness of Christ which is by faith alone. If you begin to brag, then you will face the same problems as the unfaithful Jews."

If God can break away the natural branches, it is no problem for Him to break off the wild branches. There is no room for boasting in the gospel. There is room for everyone to be saved, Jews and Gentiles, but once we accept the gospel we are all on the same level. We are 100 percent sinners, saved by grace.

Unbelief is a deliberate rejection of the gospel. It is the only sin God cannot forgive, since Christ did not die for the sin of unbelief—the sin against grace (Hebrews 10:26-29). The sin that deprived the Jewish nation of salvation was not the breaking of the law but the rejection of Jesus Christ, the unpardonable sin.

Now the Gentiles are grafted into the tree. The Jews are broken off because of unbelief and the Gentiles are grafted in through their belief. Paul warns the Gentiles to remember what happened to the Jews who, through unbelief, were unfaithful to the promise.

Paul makes a stirring statement in Philippians 3:3: "We Christians are the truly circumcised who worship God in the Spirit, and have no confidence in the flesh because we rejoice in Jesus Christ and Him alone."

Romans 11:21 tells us that if God did not spare the natural branches, He can do the same with the Gentiles, and verse 23 adds, "And they also, if they do not continue in unbelief."

If the Jews, today, would turn back to God and say they were sorry and had made a mistake, admitting that they had crucified the Messiah and that Jesus is Savior of the world, God would gladly graft them back. If He can graft wild olive branches into a good olive tree, He can surely graft natural branches back onto the olive tree.

None Should Perish

As Gentile Christians, let us share this wonderful message of salvation with our Jewish brothers. God wants none to perish—either Jew or Gentile. He has obtained salvation, full and complete, for all human beings. Many Jews and Gentiles will reject this message. What a tragedy, for God is love and does not coerce. He will give them what they have chosen—death.

Paul concludes in Romans 11:24, "For if you were cut out of the olive tree which is wild by nature and were grafted contrary to nature, into a good olive tree, how much more will these who are the natural branches (*the Jews*) be grafted into their own olive tree?" Then Paul makes this powerful statement in verse 25: "For I do not desire, brethren, that you should be ignorant of this mystery (*this secret that was kept hidden*), lest you should be wise (*or proud*) in your own opinion, that hardening in part has happened to Israel (*the literal Jews*) until the fullness of the Gentiles has come in."

Paul is telling us here that God gave the Jews 1,500 years to proclaim and accept the gospel. Then He fulfilled His promise and the Messiah came. When they rejected Him, God gave the gospel to the Gentile Christian church. Both Jews and Gentiles were given the hope of salvation through Jesus Christ.

Not all Jews rejected the Messiah and not all Gentiles will accept Him as their Savior. But in Romans 11:25 Paul says that God will give the Gentile world the full opportunity, as He gave the Jews. All believing Jews and all believing Gentiles—together—form Israel. God will keep the promise He made that all of Abraham's children will be saved.

By "all of Abraham's children" God did not mean only the physical descendants of Abraham, Isaac, and Jacob, but their spiritual descendants.

Jews and Gentiles who believe—together—constitute Israel. This Israel will be saved; God will keep His promise. This is God's goal for all of us.

Paul has clearly proven in Romans that Jews and Gentiles alike are sinners. None are righteous, none does good, and none deserves salvation. We all belong in the same category. In Romans 3:23 Paul says there is no difference between Jews and Gentiles; all have sinned and come short of the glory of God.

In Romans 3:9 we read that all Jews and all Gentiles are under sin. But in Romans 11:32 Paul tells us that God saves out of mercy. Jew and Gentile alike are saved by grace alone, through faith alone, because of Christ alone.

Paul ends this wonderful chapter with verses 33-36: "Oh, the depth of the riches both of the wisdom and knowledge of God! How unsearchable are His judgments and His ways past finding out! For who has known the mind of the Lord? Or who has become His counselor? Or who has first given to Him and it shall be repaid to Him? For of Him and through Him and to Him are all things. To Him be glory forever. Amen."

Our only choice—our only hope—is Jesus Christ and salvation through Him. It makes no difference whether we are Jew or Gentile. Every person who goes to heaven is a 100 percent sinner, saved by grace. Only those who believe the gospel will experience, subjectively, the salvation God has obtained for all men.

Chapter 26

Living the Christian Life

Romans 12:1-8

With this study of Romans 12, we delve into the final section of this epistle. In Romans 12 through 16 Paul turns his attention to Christian ethics. How should a person who stands justified by faith in Jesus live in this world while waiting for Jesus to come?

The gospel is more than a theory—it brings change in the believer's life. This becomes absolutely clear as we study Romans 12-16. Paul tells us that those who experience the wonder of justification by faith will undergo complete transformations of life. Their lifestyle and attitudes will change.

A Glance Backward

But first, what is Paul is telling us so far in Romans? After introducing himself and his great theme (Romans 1:15-17), Paul presents in detail the universal sin problem (Romans 1:18-3:20). He concludes this passage by painting a dark, dismal, hopeless picture of mankind. He says in Romans 3:12, "There is none righteous, not even one. There is none that doeth good." Both Jews and Gentiles are under sin.

But in Romans 3:21 he introduces the incredibly good news of salvation—the gospel. He defines the gospel as the righteousness of God— planned by God, initiated by God, obtained by God, fulfilled by God, and made available to us by God—in Jesus Christ.

Paul explains the gospel from Romans 3:21 to the end of Romans 8, presenting it from every conceivable angle. Then he spends three chapters (Romans 9-11) dealing with his deep concern for his fellow Jews who have unfortunately turned away from God's gift, Jesus Christ. Hope remains for the Jews, Paul says, and he hopes to bring them back to Christ.

Paul then focuses on Christians—both Jewish and Gentile believers— and tells them how they should live as they allow the gospel to affect their daily lives. In this study we consider Romans 12:1-8.

A Call for Sanctification

Paul begins in Romans 12:1: "I beseech you therefore, brethren...." In other words, "I appeal to you; I exhort you, dear brethren." The word "brethren" means fellow believers, Jews and Gentiles.

Paul appeals to them "by the mercies of God that you present your bodies a living sacrifice, wholly acceptable to God which is your reasonable service and do not be conformed to this world but be transformed by the renewing of your mind that you may prove what is that good and acceptable and perfect will of God" (Romans 12:1, 2).

Paul is telling us in a nutshell what it means to be a Christian in terms of lifestyle. First he says believers should present their bodies as living sacrifices. The word "present" is in the past tense. Paul calls on the believers to be decisive and once and for all present their bodies as living sacrifices—not as sacrifices to death but as living sacrifices.

To understand what Paul is saying, we need to review what takes place when a person accepts Christ. First comes a change of mind, which the Bible calls repentance (the word "repentance" is translated from two Greek words that mean "a change of mind"). A Christian's mind is now turned toward God, and he says, "Thank-you for Your gift, Jesus Christ."

No change, however, has yet taken place in the repentant Christian's nature. Though the believer's mind is now in harmony with God, his nature remains in harmony with sin. Paul brings this out in Romans 7:25: "So then with my mind I serve the law of God but with my flesh (*sinful nature*) I serve the law of sin." In other words, when Christians decide to live for Christ, those decisions run diametrically contrary to their sinful natures.

Left alone, new Christians fail miserably to live up to their decisions. Only by the power of the Holy Spirit dwelling in them can their sinful natures be deprived of the sin for which they crave.

Living Sacrifices

Christian living then becomes a living sacrifice—holy and acceptable living unto God, which is our reasonable service.

Other texts in the Bible help us understand how this can be. In Hebrews 2 the writer discusses the situation of our Lord, Jesus Christ, not as God but as a man who took our place.

In Hebrews 2:17 onward we discover some important facts: "Therefore, in all things He (*Christ*) had to be made like His brethren, that He might be a merciful and faithful High Priest in things pertaining to God to make propitiation for the sins of the people."

To qualify as our Savior, Christ united Himself with the human race He came to redeem. This took place at the incarnation.

Hebrews 2:18 then expands on this relationship: "For in that He Himself has suffered, being tempted, He is able to aid those who are tempted." When we face temptation and struggle with our sinful, addicted natures, we do well to remember that we have a Savior who can understand our struggle and sympathize with our problems. In Hebrews 4:15, in fact, we are told that He too was tempted in all points as we are, yet without sin. Jesus never consented to sin. He conquered temptation, yet He can sympathize with our struggles, for He suffered. Every time He gained the victory over temptation through the power of the indwelling Holy Spirit, He suffered.

Suffering Under Temptation

We ask where did He suffer? In Hebrews 2:18 the writer is not referring to His suffering on the cross, but of Christ's suffering from being tempted. Jesus was tempted all His life, just as we are. The answer to where He suffered is found in 1 Peter 4:1: "Therefore, since Christ suffered for us in the flesh (*sinful nature*), arm yourselves also with the same mind, for he who has suffered in the flesh has ceased from sin."

Christ assumed the same humanity we possess—a humanity infiltrated by the law of sin. Paul says in Romans 8:2 that the believers have been set free from the law of sin and death through the Spirit of life in Christ Jesus. This law of sin constantly tried to force Jesus to go against the will of His Father. In Gethsemane, three times with the sweat of blood He pleaded with the Father, "If possible, remove this cup. Nevertheless, not My will but Thine be done." When He surrendered His will to the will of His Father, His humanity—His flesh—suffered.

In the same way, when God gives us victory over sin, our sinful natures will suffer, for we will be depriving them of their natural desires. A Christian is a converted person. He stands justified before God, but his nature is still sinful. His nature still belongs to the devil and the realm of sin.

Paul is saying that when Christians make definite decisions to present their bodies to Christ in terms of their reasonable Christian service, they present them as living sacrifices. They deny their bodies what they crave, and this brings suffering. This is why Paul uses the term "a living sacrifice."

Nonconformity to the World

We now return to Romans 12:2 to discover how Christians can present their bodies as living sacrifices and the important decisions they must make.

"And do not be conformed to this world," Paul says. (*In other words, "Do not fit yourselves into the mold of this world."*) "But be ye transformed by the renewing of your mind that you may prove what is the good and acceptable and perfect will of God."

Justification by faith says, "Not I, but Christ." But Christian living must also use the same formula.

Paul tells us in Galatians 2:20 (KJV): "I am crucified with Christ; nevertheless I live; yet not I, but Christ who liveth in me. And the life which I now live in the flesh I live by the faith of the Son of God, who loved me, and gave Himself for me."

The Lusts of Life

What does Paul mean by "the world" in this passage? Two New Testament passages help us define it: James 4:1-6 says, "Where do wars and fights come from among you? Do they not come from your desires for pleasure that war in your members? You lust and do not have. You murder and covet and cannot obtain. You fight and war. Yet you do not have because you do not ask...."

In other words, the problems we face in this world—the terrible atrocities that take place—happen because man allows himself to be controlled by his sinful nature.

But the very next verse, James 4:7, offers a remedy: "Therefore submit to God. Resist the devil and he will flee from you." A Christian must not allow the flesh to control him. In James 1:27 we find more guidance: "Pure and undefiled religion before God and the Father is this, to visit orphans and widows in their trouble, and to keep oneself unspotted from the world." James does not mean here that we hide ourselves away from the world, having no contact with people.

In 1 John 2:15, 16 we find more help in defining the Bible meaning of the word "world": "Do not love the world or the things in the world. If anyone loves the world, the love of the Father is not in him. For all that is in the world, the lust of the flesh, (*the sinful desires of our human sinful nature*) the lust of the eyes (*we want what we see, the sin of covetousness*) and the pride of life (*the goal of life is self-first*) is not of the Father but is of the world."

John tells us in this verse that three basic drives control the unconverted man. When we accept Christ, surrendering our humanity to the cross of Christ, our attitude toward these three basic drives completely changes.

In Galatians 5:24 Paul addresses those Christians who walk in the Spirit: "And those who are Christ's (*believers*) have crucified the flesh with its passions and desires." In Romans 13:14, Paul tells us to put on the Lord, Jesus Christ, and make no provision for the flesh. We cannot conquer the flesh, though our minds may be converted and we have chosen to do good and live righteous lives. We cannot conquer the flesh and its ways without the power of the Holy Spirit. It is through the Spirit that we overcome the lust of the flesh, the lust of the eyes and the pride of life.

Paul then continues: "Do not be conformed to the world." In other words, do not allow these three drives to control you, but be transformed by the renewing of your minds. Notice that the renewing takes place in the mind. Although the flesh can be overcome, God will not give us the victory if our minds have not been surrendered to the truth as it is in Christ. We must renew our minds daily, saying, "Not I, but Christ." Then the Spirit will take over and fulfill the good and acceptable and perfect will of God.

Paul in Philippians 2:12 says, "Work out your salvation with fear and trembling for it is God who wills and performs in you."

Romans 12:3 and 4 adds, "I say through the grace given to me to everyone who is among you not to think of himself more highly than he ought to think but to think soberly as God has dealt to each one a measure of faith." The gospel completely changes our attitude toward ourselves. Philippians 3:3 says that a Christian is one who rejoices in Jesus Christ and has no confidence in the flesh—one who recognizes that all are 100 percent sinners, saved by grace. Therefore we do not boast about what we are or what we do, like the Pharisees in Christ's day. Our glorying is in the Lord and what He has done.

Members of One Body

Moving forward, Paul says in Romans 12:4 and 5: "For as we have many members in one body, but all the members do not have the same function, so we, being many, are one body in Christ, and individually members of one another."

Paul here touches on the vital issue of "one body in Christ." Like a human body with its many parts, members of the body of Christ have many functions. But the church is one body and God's greatest desire is that it should remain united. Many theologians try to promote unity in the church through dialogue. But only the gospel can produce that unity.

Only Jesus Christ and Him crucified and His followers' surrender in faith and obedience to that gospel can produce a united Christian body. Though there are many members, there is but one body. Each member has a different function, but each serves the whole body (1 Corinthians 12:4-7).

Paul continues in Romans 12:6 and 7: "Having the gifts differing according to the grace that is given to us, let us use them: if prophecy, let us prophesy (*proclaim the Word of God*) in proportion to our faith; or ministry, let us use it in our ministering...." If God has given us the gift of helping others then let that be our gift. If God has given us the gift of teaching then let us use that gift. If we have been given the gift of counseling, let us use it to glorify God.

"He who gives with liberality, he who leads with diligence, he who shows mercy with cheerfulness...." As the human body has different functions—the feet to move us about, the hands to do things, the eyes to see, and the ears to hear—so every member in the church is given one or more gifts, so that the whole body—the church—may grow to maturity and unity (Ephesians 4:7-13).

In stadium sports, a handful of overworked contestants toil while thousands sit around and watch. Not so in the Christian life. As members of the body of Christ, every member has a position to play.

In the human body, if the right arm becomes paralyzed, the whole body no longer functions at 100 percent. In the same way, the Christian church today is paralyzed because many Christians are not using their gifts. They are just pew warmers.

Paul says that converted Christians must first present their bodies as living sacrifices to live for Christ; then they must put their gifts to use, whatever those gifts may be.

In 1 Corinthians 12:7 onward, Paul tells us that the gifts God gives to the Christian believer are for the benefit of the whole body. Christians cannot live for themselves. They live for Christ and for each other, for they are one body.

In 1 Corinthians 12:26 and 27 Paul says that when one member suffers, all members suffer. When one member rejoices, the others—far from being jealous—rejoice with that one member, for in the body of Christ, what happens to one happens to all.

If a time comes when all Christians unite under one faith, one baptism, and one truth, it will not be through dialogue or promotional programs but by virtue of the gospel of Jesus Christ and Him crucified.

When all Christians surrender to the cross and say, like Paul, "I am crucified with Christ; it is no longer I but Christ lives in me through the Holy Spirit, the Spirit of Christ will bring unity. He cannot do this if we do not present our bodies as living sacrifices. He cannot do this if we do not renew our minds daily and determine not to be conformed to this world. As we are transformed into the image of Jesus Christ, the lust of the flesh, the lust of the eyes, and the pride of life will be replaced by the words, "Not my will, but Thine be done."

The Christian church has failed miserably to reveal the power of the gospel, leading many to reject it. As Christians present their bodies as living sacrifices, the character of Christ will be seen in each one. Then the world will recognize that the gospel is the power of God unto salvation.

Chapter 27

Into His Likeness

Romans 12:9-21

In this study we turn again to the final section in Paul's epistle—Romans 12-16. Here the great apostle explains how the fruits of the gospel come through practical application of the wonderful doctrine of righteousness by faith.

In our last study we laid the foundation for our study of the Christian life by looking at Romans 12:1-8. This study covers verses 9-21. But before we begin, let us remind ourselves that the chapters ahead deal with Christian ethics. Chapters 12-16 must be studied in the context of Romans' theme: "The just shall live by faith" or "Righteousness By Faith."

This theme is based on Habakkuk 2:4, a text Paul loves to quote in his writings. But Judaism had misinterpreted this text to mean "He who is just by his *(that is, man's)* faithfulness shall live." This, of course, led Judaism into legalism.

In Romans Paul explains the correct meaning of the text. He says that man is totally bankrupt when it comes to trying to produce righteousness and salvation (Romans 1:18—Romans 3:20).

In Romans 3:21 to the end of Romans 8, Paul then goes on to make it clear that man's only hope is the righteousness of Christ—a righteousness that becomes his (is made effective) by faith alone. When we put together the righteousness of Christ and the human response (faith), we come up with the doctrine of righteousness (or justification) by faith. The Jews had missed this wonderful truth, and Paul deals with this situation in Romans 9-11.

Now in this final section, Romans 12-16, Paul writes to believing men and woman who have experienced the peace that comes through justification by faith. They have enjoyed the new-birth experience that results from righteousness by faith. Genuine righteousness or justification by faith is transforming their attitude and characters. Paul here addresses born-again Christians—justified people who have experienced the power of the gospel and have the Holy Spirit dwelling in them. Paul tells them that those who are justified by faith will live in a way that glorifies God and reflects his Son, Jesus Christ.

True Love

With this foundation, we are ready to read Romans 12:9-15 onward: "Let love be without hypocrisy. Abhor what is evil. Cling to what is good. Be kindly affectionate to one another with brotherly love, in honor giving preference to one another; not lagging in diligence, fervent in spirit, serving the Lord; rejoicing in hope, patient in tribulation, continuing steadfastly in prayer; distributing to the needs of the saints, given to hospitality. Bless those who persecute you; bless and do not curse. Rejoice with those who rejoice, and weep with those who weep."

To understand this we must remember that Romans 12 is really a continuation of Romans 8. Romans 9-11 is an interjection. Because of Paul's great burden for the salvation of his own Jewish people, He writes at some length about their condition. But now we return to what, in effect, is a continuation of Romans 8:29, which reads: "For whom he foreknew, he also predestined to be conformed to the image of his Son that he (*Christ*) might be the firstborn among many brethren."

We know that the word "foreknew" simply means that God identifies beforehand those who will accept the gift of salvation obtained for all men in Jesus Christ. While the gospel is incredible good news for all mankind, not all will go to heaven, for God created human beings with free choice. They can accept or reject His gift.

In Romans 8:29 Paul is saying that God knows beforehand who will accept. To those who will accept the gift of salvation in Jesus Christ, He not only offers good news (*the gospel, offered to all mankind*), but He tells them, in effect: "I have a plan. My purpose is to transform you so that you conform to the image of My Son, Jesus Christ—the firstborn among many brethren."

Christ is not only the world's Savior, He is also the Christian's example—the prototype of the believer. To the world Christ is a Savior; to the believer Christ is also an example—someone to imitate. Since human beings cannot do this by themselves, to those who have accepted Christ by faith, God sends the Holy Spirit. One function of the Holy Spirit is to reproduce in the believer the character of our Lord, Jesus Christ (2 Corinthians 3:17,18).

The church is the body of Christ. He is the head; believers are the body. It is God's purpose that the body reflect the head. Christ is the Firstborn; Christians are the harvest of the Firstborn.

Hypocritical Love

As we study Romans 12:9 and onward in detail, we find that Paul says, in effect: "Behave as Christians. Let your love be without hypocrisy." The Pharisees' love was hypocritical. The word "hypocrisy" comes from the Greek word used to describe actors in a theater. In Paul's day, actors did not present themselves as they do today. They wore masks that portrayed various emotions, including sadness, laughter, and anger. The word "hypocrisy" was applied to this masked playacting. Characters might pretend to love others on stage, when in real life no such love existed.

So it is in life today. Outwardly we may show love to someone, but inwardly we may hate them. Hypocritical love saturates our society, but Paul says true Christianity loves sincerely. Christianity is not built on playacting; Christian living does not pretend to be something it is not. Christian living simply reflects what we are in Jesus Christ. We are righteous in Him and in Him we have perfect love. Jesus loved us unconditionally, unselfishly, with changeless, everlasting, love.

Paul says in so many words, "Now Christians, let that love—that righteousness that you have accepted in Jesus Christ—be revealed in your life through the work of the Holy Spirit in you. Let that unconditional love be manifested in you so that the love that the world sees in you is genuine."

Not I, But Christ

We find in John 13:34 that before Jesus ascends to heaven, He tells His disciples that he wants them to love each other just as he has loved them. John then adds in verse 35, "By this (*unconditional agape love that you manifest toward each other*) all men shall know that you are My disciples." The formula for Christian living is "Not I, but Christ." The Holy Spirit in the Christian reproduces the character of Jesus Christ. He is the communicator of Christ's righteousness.

What, then, does the character of Jesus Christ do? First, it loves without hypocrisy; and second, it abhors evil. Paul says, "Abhor that which is evil, cling to that which is good."

All that is good, righteous, and genuine lovely comes from God and is to be reproduced in the believer. The result, as we read in Romans 12:9 and 10, is that Christians will follow the counsel, "Be kindly affectionate to one another with brotherly love." The church, we have learned, is one body; therefore members are all interconnected through Jesus.

Christian Kindness

When I was a high school student in Kenya, our favorite sport was soccer. We could not afford football or soccer boots, so we played barefoot. Once when I was running across the field with the ball, my toe struck a stone. My toenail literally ripped apart, and suddenly my hands flew to my feet to try to ease the terrible pain. My hands did not say to my feet: "You are dirty. You have been running without shoes. We will not dirty ourselves." Instead my hands showed instinctive concern for the toe, for the injury to my toe brought suffering to my whole body.

In much the same way, Paul says we must love each other as members of one body. We must be diligent in our Christian living. We must abound in love, in sharing, and in helping each other. We must remain fervent in spirit. Paul says in Romans 12:11 that we are to be found "serving the Lord, rejoicing in hope, patient (*enduring*) in tribulation, continuing steadfast in prayer, distributing to the needs of the saints, given to hospitality." Christians should be the kindest, most loving people in the world.

Where Christians Fail

The government in some countries has taken over care of the homeless and unemployed. In these areas, the Christian church has failed to accomplish what it should be doing. Christianity should be foremost in showing what it means to help the homeless and manifest the unconditional love of God to society. This is what Paul is saying in Romans 12.

In Romans 12:14 Paul continues giving counsel to born-again Christians: "Bless those who persecute you; bless and do not curse them."

Let us pause and go to the Sermon on the Mount where Jesus is teaching much the same thing to His disciples. In Matthew 5:43 Jesus says, "You have been taught (*this is what Judaism taught you*), love your neighbor and hate your enemy." Jesus says, "No, this is not Christianity."

In the very next verse, Jesus offers a powerful alternative: "Love your enemies. Pray for those who despitefully use you (*do not hate them*). Do good to those that hate you that you may be the children of your Father who is in Heaven." Jesus then goes on to explain the love of the Father—the unconditional love of God.

He says in Matthew 5:45 that "God brings the rain on the good and the evil. He brings sunshine on the righteous and the unrighteous." God's love knows no discrimination. God blesses us in unique ways, and we must not think that God blesses us only because we are good or special. Everyone is special in God's eyes and He blesses good and bad alike.

In Exodus, God's people are rebellious—yet God feeds them miraculously. He keeps them warm in the cold desert night by being a pillar of fire for them. He keeps them cool in the hot desert sun by being a cloud canopy over them. Yet the book of Hebrews and other New Testament passages make it very clear that He was displeased with them for 40 years. He blessed them because His love is unconditional.

Christ tells His disciples from Matthew 5:44 to the end of the chapter that they must love as He does. Of what good is God's love if we love only our friends? He asks. Even the worst sinners love their friends! The love Christians must display will be unique—a kind of love selfish human beings cannot generate on their own. But when the Holy Spirit takes control of Christians' lives, He manifests in them the love revealed in Jesus Christ. Then the Christian will be able to truly bless those who curse and persecute him.

In Romans 12:15 Paul says: "Rejoice with those who rejoice, and weep with those who weep." Here Paul explains how we should relate with other Christians within the church. In 1 Corinthians 12:6, 7, Paul tells Corinthian Christians that the church is the body of Christ. When one person is in pain, the whole body suffers. When one person rejoices, the whole group of Christians rejoice. There should be no schism in the body. This is Paul's point in Romans 12:15. Let the world see the unity and love in the body of Christ. This is the most powerful witness of the power of the gospel to the world.

The Golden Rule

In Romans 12:16 Paul continues: "Be of the same mind toward one another." In other words, treat others as you would treat yourselves. "Do not set your mind on high things, but associate with the humble. Do not be wise in your own opinion." In true Christianity all glory— all boasting—is in Christ.

Paul continues in verse 17: "Repay no one evil for evil. Have regard for good things in the sight of all men. If it is possible as much as it depends on you, live peaceably with all men." Christians do not start quarrels with neighbors, Paul is saying. The world wants and needs to see the love of God among Christians. The famous philosopher Friedrich Nietzsche says, "If you expect me to believe in your Redeemer, you will have to look a lot more redeemed." When the world sees jealousy and fighting in the church, how can they believe that the gospel is the power of God to redeem man from the condemnation of the law—let alone the power and slavery of sin? Such behavior is no different than the world's (1 Corinthians 3:3).

Isaiah 53:6 says: "All we like sheep have gone astray; We have turned, every one, to his own way." Human beings are egocentric by nature and performance. Only the presence of the gospel in their lives can set them free.

Paul continues in Romans 12:19 and 20: "Beloved, do not avenge yourselves, but rather give place to wrath; for it is written, 'Vengeance is Mine, I will repay,' says the Lord. Therefore if your enemy hungers, feed him; If he thirsts, give him a drink; For in so doing you will heap coals of fire on his head." Paul quotes these words about kindness to enemies directly from Proverbs 25:21 and 22.

He concludes the chapter with this concise admonition, "Do not be overcome by evil, but overcome evil with good." Such counsel directly contradicts human impulse and behavior. When we look at world conditions today, we see in the former Yugoslavia, for example, the deadly results of ethnic and religious grudges. The tensions were held in check by communism for many years. But with the coming of freedom, long-repressed hate and animosity boiled over. The same can be said of Rwanda and many other countries. Truly the only solution to our human problem is the gospel of Jesus Christ.

True *agape* love cannot be promoted with signs that read "Make Love, Not War." The moral influence theory offers a solution in one sense, for the love of God must indeed constrain us. But the moral influence theory unfortunately denies need for a legal atonement—as we've previously studied. What we need to realize is that no human effort to bring world peace will work. Moral rearmament and communism tried to bring peace, but both failed miserably. The only solution is the gospel.

The Book of Acts tells us that the early Christian church is made up of men and women who are of one mind. There is no fighting among them. Those who possess lands and money give to the church and distribution is made according to need. This is the biblical solution (Acts 4:32-25).

Summary of Christian Ethics

In concluding this study, let us sum up how Christian living works through the power of the gospel.

1. God takes the first step. He takes the initiative. He comes with the good news of salvation. He tells us that while we were sinners, enemies, and ungodly, He reconciled us to Himself by the death of His Son. He gives us a new history—a new status—in which we stand righteous, fully qualified to live in heaven forever.

2. Because mankind was created with free will, there must be a human response to God's initiative. We can either say "Yes" or "No." The Bible definition of "Yes" is faith. Faith is a human being's response to God's love and His gift. "God so loved the world that He gave His only begotten Son." God did the loving; God did the giving; human beings do the believing. The moment they believe, they pass from condemnation and death to justification and life, as Jesus makes clear in John 5:24.

3. Jesus then sends the Holy Spirit to dwell in his followers. They become born-again Christians, and the Holy Spirit works to reproduce in them the life of Jesus Christ, the Son of God. The Holy Spirit brings with Him that wonderful ingredient Christians can never generate on their own—God's unconditional *agape* love.

Paul tells us in 1 Corinthians 13 that this love of God is the supreme gift of the Holy Spirit and comes, not that it may go back to God vertically, but that it may go horizontally to others, that all may see God manifested in the body of Christ.

When men and women see this love of God revealed in Christians' relationships with each other in the church and with the world, they begin to realize that the gospel is not just a theory but is the power of God to redeem man, not only from the condemnation of sin, but from its power and slavery.

This is the gospel Paul is talking about in Romans 12. Christians are called to act in the power of the Holy Spirit as justified, righteous, and holy people. Through God's blessing they can truly reflect Jesus Christ.

Chapter 28

Loyal Citizens
Romans 13:1-7

Paul lays the foundation of Christian ethics in the first half of Romans 12 and tells the Roman believers how they should relate to one another. In the chapter's second half he turns to the Christian's relationship to civil authority and continues the theme in Romans 13:1-7.

A Christian's Obligation

A Christian has an obligation to civil authority, says Paul. While Christians may indeed be citizens of heaven, they still live in this world and have civil obligations. "Let every soul be subject to the governing authorities (*the Greek means civil authority*)," Paul says in Romans 13:1.

He begins Romans 13 this way to counteract any misunderstanding of Romans 12:2, where he tells believers not to be conformed to this world or its mould. Paul knows that Christians could take this statement and refuse to pay their taxes or obey civil authorities. Paul wants no misunderstanding: What he means in Romans 12:2 is that Christians should not allow the lust of the flesh, the lust of the eyes, and the pride of life to control them.

Now in Romans 13:1 he says Christians are to be subject to civil authorities: "For there is no authority except from God and the authorities that exist are appointed by God."

Christians have struggled with this statement, especially those living in communistic countries or where government itself persecutes Christians. Does God put these governments in authority?

To better understand what Paul is saying, we must remember that God is sovereign. Nothing happens without His permission. When a communist government takes over a country, though that may not be God's will, He permits it for a reason. In this sense, no authority exists today except as God permits it.

But Paul is not commenting on systems of government but on how to deal with authorities common to every governmental system—capitalist, democratic, communist, or socialist.

Whatever the system, a government has God-appointed responsibilities to keep law and order. This is Paul's message in Romans 13. God uses civil authorities everywhere to curb lawlessness. Romans 13:3 says: "For rulers are not a terror to good works, but to evil. Do you want to be unafraid of the authority? Do what is good and you will have praise from the same."

We lighten the load of our policemen if we live good, righteous, upright lives. Christians should never become nuisances to higher authorities.

How does this fit into Paul's concept of the gospel? He explains that when sin entered this world with Adam's and Eve's rebellion, not only did they come under condemnation, their very natures became sinful. We, their descendants, are born slaves to sin, as Paul clearly shows in Romans 7:14: "The law is spiritual but I am carnal, sold (*as a slave*) under sin."

In Romans 3:9 Paul says that both Jews and Gentiles are under sin. The word "under" means to be ruled by or to be dominated by. We are dominated by sin, and if God did not restrict sin through civil authorities, men would kill each other and the human race could become extinct.

Where law and order fail, men simply wipe one another out. Civil authority curbs lawlessness. Therefore, Christians should not resist civil authority. Romans 13:2 says clearly, "Therefore, whoever resists the authority, resists the ordinance of God, and those who resist will bring judgment on themselves." God has ordained the civil authority. We may not agree with some of its laws or its behavior, but Christians should be law-abiding citizens. God forbids Christians to set themselves against the laws of their country, though the men enforcing those laws may be corrupt. Misuse of authority is part of the sin problem, but Paul is not addressing that question in this passage. Paul is simply saying "Do not disobey your civil authorities."

No Religious Authority

While God has appointed civil authorities to keep law and order, He has given them no right to interfere with the people's religious convictions. Their work is limited to keeping law and order—curbing evil and protecting society from corruption. But God never gives civil authorities license to interfere with individual religious convictions. Separation of religion and government is mandated in some countries, including the United States of America, whose founders wrote this separation into the Constitution.

The biblical principle is clearly presented in Acts 5:28, 29, where the authorities demand that the apostles put aside their religious convictions. The Book of Acts gives a historical account of the early Christian church, and here the chief priest of the ruling Jewish council, the Sanhedrin, demands of the apostles, "Did we not strictly command you not to teach in this name?" The apostles had been given fair warning; they had been commanded not to preach in the name of Jesus Christ. "And look, you have filled Jerusalem with your doctrine," he accuses them. They have disobeyed the will of the high command, filling all Jerusalem with a knowledge of Jesus Christ. Now the people are turning against their Jewish leaders, accusing them of wrongly crucifying Christ.

Peter's response as spokesman of the apostles comes in verse 29: "Then Peter and the other apostles answered and said: "We ought to obey God rather than men." In other words, "Your command not to preach in the name of Jesus goes beyond your authority. God did not give you that authority. You have no right to restrict us in preaching Jesus Christ."

Paul indeed is saying in Romans 13, "Yes, Christians, obey your civil authorities as long as they do not interfere with your religious convictions."

But this can create problems, for religious convictions vary and who decides what is religious and what is not? Christians need to understand clearly, from the Word of God, what is religious and what is civil. For example, the Jews in Christ's day charged a temple tax, and some Pharisees accused Jesus of not paying that tax.

Jesus does not argue with these men. He tells Peter in Matthew 17:27, "Go fishing and you will find a coin in the belly of the fish. Give it to the temple as payment of the tax."

Caesar's and God's

Later, the Pharisees try to trap Jesus by bringing him a Roman coin with Caesar's inscription on it and asking a difficult question, "Who should we listen to; Rome, which is ruling Israel, or God, who is our Lord?" Jesus wisely answers that we have an obligation to government as well as God. We should not confuse the two. We should "render unto Caesar" that which belongs to Caesar and to God that which is God's.

There is a definite demarcation between state and religion. The Bible is clear—when it comes to obeying the rules of a country, such as civil and traffic laws, it is God's will that we as Christians obey the government.

Paul in Romans 13:5 says: "Therefore you must be subject, not only because of wrath, but also for conscience sake." The Christian's motivation for obeying the civil authority is not to avoid punishment, but because of their love for God. A Christian's obedience to civil authority must not be motivated by egocentric concerns, such as fear of punishment or desire for reward. Obedience must flow from love for God and mankind—love that does not harm others, does not steal, does not covet, and does nothing to cause suffering to others. True Christianity loves neighbors unconditionally in the same way Christians spontaneously and unconditionally love themselves.

Jesus makes this abundantly clear to a young lawyer who comes to Him in Matthew 19:19: He tells the young man, "Love your neighbor as you love yourself." Paul is saying the same thing in Romans 13:8. Christian behavior is motivated by a love relation with others.

Romans 13:6 contains an important reminder as we face the tax authorities: "For because of this, you also pay taxes, for they are God's ministers attending continually to this very thing."

These civil authorities are paid from tax money. True, sometimes tax money is misused, but the authorities must answer to God for this. In Romans 13:7 Paul says, "Render therefore to all their due: taxes to whom taxes are due, customs to whom customs, fear to whom fear, honor to whom honor."

Paul has already said in Romans 12:21: "Do not be overcome by evil but overcome evil by good." In verse 19 he says: "Beloved, do not avenge yourselves, but rather give place to wrath; for it is written, 'Vengeance is mine; I will repay,' says the Lord."

When civil authorities misuse tax money, God deals with that. The Christian's primary work is to reflect the character of their Lord, Jesus Christ. He was mistreated but He kept silent. He was falsely accused but He did not fight back. He did not take out revenge. He could have called thousands of angels to come and strike His enemies dead, but He did no such thing. Paul says in Romans 13:7 that Christians need to pay their taxes, not because the government requires it, but because Christians need to support the men and women who are carrying out God's appointed work of keeping law and order.

When I left Kenya in 1958, it was still a British colony. When I returned in 1965, it had become independent. One day my wife and I went to a market—an African market where men and women laid their goods on mats to sell what they could. Growing bored after awhile, I noticed some elderly men handcuffed and guarded by a policeman. I saw that the men looked discouraged, so leaving the shopping to my wife, I went over to speak with them.

"What crime have you committed that you are handcuffed like criminals? You look like good men," I began.

One of the older men replied, "When is this independence coming to an end?"

"What do you mean?" I asked. "You people fought for independence. Now you have it. Do you want it to end and have the British return?"

"Yes!" he said.

"Why?" I asked.

"The problem is that when we were fighting for independence, we had the idea that once we had it we would not have to pay tax," he replied. "We thought we were paying tax because the British were exploiting us. But now that we're an independent country, we discover that not only do we have to pay tax, but the tax has increased and the new civil authorities are stricter than the British. So we prefer British rule to our own government."

These dear old men had failed to realize what independence means. So I explained to them that as an independent country, Kenya no longer was depending on some other nation to take care of things. Kenya had become independent, which meant that the Kenyan people were now responsible for their own survival and upkeep. Their government had to take care of the roads and keep law and order, and it had to collect money to do these things. Taxes had gone up because the country was now independent and had no other source of income. This is part of the responsibility that comes with being independent.

The old men were not happy with my little speech, but I think they recognized that with independence comes responsibility.

Governments cannot function without money, so they charge taxes. In Romans 13:4 Paul is saying that Christians should be law-abiding citizens. They should be without reproach. Though a Christian does not belong to this world, he still lives in this world. He is a physical part of this world and has an obligation to his government and its civil authorities. Christians should be exemplary citizens in their relationship to civil authorities.

An Eye for an Eye

Paul is saying in summary that Christians should obey civil authorities because they are appointed to keep law and order and curb lawlessness. Believers should not resist these authorities, for they are ordained of God to bring judgment on those who disobey. God has given the civil authorities certain rights. In the Old Testament the Jews misinterpreted Leviticus 24:17-20 where God says, "an eye for an eye and a tooth for a tooth."

To whom does God give this law? To civil authorities. It is not given to individuals to put it into practice personally. The Jews unfortunately took this statement and applied it to their personal relations with their enemies and used it to take revenge on those who had mistreated them.

Jesus corrected this mistake and said in the Sermon on the Mount, "This should never be so."

What God is saying to civil authorities in Leviticus is that when a person commits a crime—robbery, assault, or murder—let that person be punished with a punishment equivalent to his crime. If a person takes someone's life, the civil authorities have a right to practice capital punishment. But the families of the victim of murder should not try to apply this law themselves. This law was given only to civil authorities.

Romans 13 tells us that God has given certain responsibilities to governments, one of which is to take vengeance on those who disobey the laws of the land. God gives them permission to do this. And He gives government the right to practice capital punishment, put people into prison, and penalize those who disobey civil laws. Paul is saying that we should pay our taxes and obey civil authorities, not for fear of punishment, but for conscience's sake.

"Please be law-abiding citizens," Paul exhorts the Roman Christians. Let the government find no fault in the Christian church in matters of civil law. Only when the civil authorities go against the will of God and try to make you do something contrary to your faith, then and only then we have a right to say, 'No. I have to obey God first and then the civil authorities.' But in everything else we must obey the civil governments so that our reputation may be one that is above reproach and governments can say that Christians are the most law-abiding citizens of the country. By doing this we will uplift the name of Christ. We will raise the name of Christianity as a religion that produces men and women who live good, noble, righteous, and honest lives."

Chapter 29

Fulfilling the Royal Law

Romans 13:8-14

Last study we focused on the first half of Romans 13, where Paul discusses the Christian's relationship to civil authorities—or government.

Now we study the second half of Romans 13, beginning with verse 8, where Paul discusses the love relationship Christians should have with their neighbors. A neighbor may live next door or be a one-time contact. Jesus is clear that anyone who needs help in our sphere of living becomes our neighbor.

Christian Neighborliness

How should Christians deal with their neighbors? We read in Romans 13:8-14: "Owe no one anything, except to love one another, for he who loves another has fulfilled the law. For the commandments, 'You shall not commit adultery,' 'You shall not murder,' 'You shall not steal,' 'You shall not bear false witness,' 'You shall not covet,' and if there is any other commandment are all summed up in this saying, namely, 'You shall love your neighbor as yourself.' Love does no harm to a neighbor, therefore love is the fulfillment of the law. And do this knowing the time that now it is high time to wake out of sleep; for now our salvation is nearer than when we first believed. The night is far spent, the day is at hand. Therefore let us cast off the works of darkness, and let us put on the armor of light. Let us walk properly, as in the day, not in revelry and drunkenness, not in licentiousness and lewdness, not in strife and envy. But put on the Lord, Jesus Christ, and make no provision for the flesh to fulfill its lust."

What a tremendous passage about Christian neighborliness! As we've already learned in this chapter, a Christian is not of this world but still lives in this world. Because the Bible teaches that we are not of this world, many Christians (especially in the past) chose to live in seclusion where they would have little or no contact with the world. This is not God's plan for the Christian. In Jesus' prayer to His Father in John 17:15, He clearly says, "I pray that You do not take them out of this world but that You keep them from the evil of this world."

One of the great purposes God has for every Christian is to reflect the love they have experienced through the gospel. In Romans 13:8 Paul clearly states that he who loves another has fulfilled the law.

Law—in Letter and Spirit

We can look at God's law in two ways—in its letter or in its spirit. We can see the law as a method of salvation or as a standard of Christian living. The Jews unfortunately chose to see the letter of the law as a method of salvation. To them the law was "do this" or "do not do that."

We find in Matthew 22:36 where some great scholar of Judaism approaches Jesus and asks Him a question: "What is the greatest commandment of the book of the law (*the Torah*)?"

Instead of giving rules, Jesus answers that the greatest commandment found in Scripture, in the book of the law, is loving God with all your heart, with all your soul, and with all your being. And the second is like the first, loving your neighbor as yourself. On these two laws rest all the law and the prophets (i.e., the whole Bible).

To God the law is not a set of rules. Man has turned it into a rulebook, but to God the law is a relationship of love toward Him and mankind. Later in this chapter we will study more deeply into the distinctions between the law as a method of salvation and the law as a standard of Christian living. Paul is saying here that the fulfillment of the law as God sees it means loving one's neighbor as one's self (Romans 13: 9, last part).

Love's U-turn

To understand this statement, we must first recognize that human love as we know it has taken a U-turn away from God's unconditional love. When God created Adam and Eve, the book of Genesis tells us they were created in His image. In 1 John 4:8 we read that God is love. Clearly, when God created mankind He created humankind with a nature in harmony with His nature and character—with unconditional, self-emptying, and changeless love.

When Eve sins and brings the forbidden fruit to Adam, he surely realizes that she is going to die. But he loves her even more than he loves himself, for in his nature this unconditional love makes him willing to die with her. This is how much Adam loves his wife before he sins. But the moment he eats the forbidden fruit, his nature makes a U-turn. The love that has gone out unconditionally to Eve and others now changes direction and focuses on his own interest.

That evening God comes to visit Adam and Eve after they have sinned, and Adam blames God for giving him a defective wife. Now where is Adam's selfless love for Eve? It has made a U-turn toward self.

Human love today has all the qualities of God's love—except its direction. Like Adam, we now love ourselves unconditionally, everlastingly, and more than we love anyone or anything else. This is our human predicament. Paul says here that genuine law-keeping is loving our neighbor in the same way that we naturally love ourselves, unconditionally and everlastingly.

A Human Impossibility

Man unfortunately cannot do this on his own. We find an example of this deficiency in Matthew 19:16: A young man asks, "What good thing must I do to have eternal life?"

This young man is a sinner, trying to do good to be saved. Jesus attempts to correct him by saying that there is nobody good except God. "But," He adds, "if you want to go to heaven by being good, keep the commandments."

"Which ones?" asks the young man. Jesus quotes him the commandments that Paul quotes in Romans 13:9—those that refer to relationships with neighbors. He completes them the same way Paul does: "Love your neighbors in the same way that you love yourself."

In other words, citizens of heaven are to love their neighbors spontaneously and unconditionally, just as they naturally love themselves.

Not realizing what Jesus is really saying, the young man answers, "All these things I have kept since I was a youth. What do I lack?"

Jesus is testing him to see if he really loves his neighbors as himself, and to prove that the man has no such love, Jesus says, "Take your wealth, which means so much to you, and give it to the poor, your neighbors, then follow Me and I will give you My wealth."

Jesus is offering a tremendous bargain, but the young man has not accepted Jesus as the Son of God, so he considers it a sacrifice—a sacrifice he is unwilling to make. So he leaves Jesus sorrowfully.

Jesus is showing his disciples that it is impossible for unconverted men and women to love their neighbors in the same way they love themselves. But Paul in Romans is advising Christians to do that very thing. The only way they can attain to this kind of love is by following his counsel in Romans 13:14: "Put on the Lord, Jesus Christ, and make no provision for the flesh, to fulfill its lusts."

Only through the indwelling Spirit of Christ can we love our neighbors the same way we spontaneously, unconditionally, and everlastingly love ourselves. In 1 Corinthians 13 Paul presents love—God's character—as the supreme gift of the Holy Spirit to every believer.

Standard or Method of Salvation?

What distinguishes the law as a method of salvation from the law as a standard of Christian living? Let me tell you a story.

I attended the 1980 National Council of Churches Conference in Nairobi, Kenya, held only for pastors. The featured speaker was the famous John Stott and there were about 1,500 attendees, from approximately 83 denominations.

Stott gave us a series of studies from the book of Thessalonians and in the third study said, "We evangelicals know how to preach the good news but we have failed to preach the good life. The reason for this is that we have done away with the law." Then he added, "The law was never done away with as a standard of Christian living."

The New Testament makes a distinction between the law as a method of salvation and the law as a standard of Christian living. In Romans 3:28 and Romans 9:30-32, Paul makes it clear that God never gave the law as a method of salvation—though the Jews mistakenly believe it can save them.

But now in Romans 13, Paul lifts up the law as a standard of Christian living while previously opposing it as a method of salvation. What are the differences? There are at least four.

The first distinction is that when Christians keep the law as a method of salvation, they follow the letter rather than the spirit of the law—they see only "do this" or "don't do that."

The Jews made the law of God into rules. In Matthew 23:23, for example, Jesus speaks about these rules—the 248 rules and 369 prohibitions the Jews had established under the law. Keeping these were considered essential to salvation.

On the other hand, when Christians keep the law as a standard, motivated by faith that works, love becomes the fulfillment of the law. The gospel creates in the Christian a deep gratitude for what God did for them in Jesus Christ. He redeemed them and reconciled them, so they now respond by a faith motivated by love. The Holy Spirit brings this important ingredient of God's *agape* love. This love of God constrains the Christian to reproduce in himself the character—the life—of Christ, which is in harmony with the law.

In Galatians 5:22 onward Paul talks about the fruits of the Spirit—love, joy, peace, long-suffering, and so on. He concludes by saying that against such there is no law. In other words, these fruits of the Spirit fulfill the law. The law does not condemn the fruits of the Spirit; they are in perfect harmony with its requirements. The law as a method of salvation keeps the letter of the law. The law in the spirit keeps the law from the heart, motivated by love.

The second distinction is that when the law is kept as a method of salvation, it produces only external righteousness. Jesus says in Matthew 15:8-9, quoting from the book of Isaiah: "These people draw near to Me with their mouth, and honor Me with their lips, but their heart is far from Me. And in vain they worship Me, teaching as doctrines the commandments of men."

The Jews took a law that was based on the love of God and turned it into rules, regulations, and prohibitions. In keeping these rules, they prided themselves on keeping the law. But their law-obedience—this keeping of the rules—was only external righteousness. Their hearts were far from God.

When Christians begin keeping the law as a standard, the law becomes a delight, an inward obedience. It never becomes a set of rules. A person who keeps the law as a standard, controlled by the Holy Spirit and motivated by love, keeps the law from the heart. This is what the New Covenant is all about (Hebrews 8:10).

I once presented week of prayer services at a Christian college that had very strict rules. I preached to the students for a whole week on the wonderful message of salvation by grace. Toward the end, one of the faculty members asked me, "How do we as an institution practice righteousness by faith?"

I answered, "First, you must make a distinction between the rules your college has set up and Christianity itself. Every college has rules— including government colleges. Let the students realize that these rules are rules of the college. Do not link them with Christianity, for if you do, the students will look upon these rules as Christianity itself, a requirement for salvation.

"Christianity is not a set of rules," I continued. "It is a relationship with God and our fellowmen. It is justification by faith. The fruit is holiness of living. Make sure the students know about Christ, so they become converted men and women. Give them Christ in such a way that the love of Christ constrains them, so that they can say with Paul, 'For me to live is Christ.'"

During that week of prayer, I ate my meals with the students and discovered two groups: About 90 percent had come to the college with its strict rules because they wanted to be there. The other 10 percent came there because they were sent by parents who wanted to reform them. Those who came of their own free will did not need the rules—they were already converted Christians. They were already living lives in harmony with the rules of the college, so they did not need the rules. But the 10 percent sent by their parents found the college—as one student put it—to be "hell." She told me, "Please do not tell my mother that this is a wonderful college."

"Why not?" I asked.

She answered, "I do not want three more years of hell." To her, being in this Christian college was like being in prison.

Righteousness by faith begins from the heart. God works from the inside, outward. Legalism—the law as a method—is only concerned with external performance.

The third distinction between law as a method and law as a standard is that external righteousness (which law-keepers produce when they keep the law as a method of salvation) may look good to men, but to God it is an abomination. In Isaiah 64:6 we are told that all our righteousness is, in God's eyes, filthy rags.

In Luke 16:15 Jesus concurs with Isaiah. We read, "And he said to them (*the Pharisees*), 'You are those who justify yourselves before men, but God knows your hearts. For what is highly esteemed among men is an abomination in the sight of God.'" God looks at our hearts; man looks at the external performance.

When a Christian, saved by grace, controlled by the Spirit, and motivated by love, obeys the law, it is not simply a set of rules for external righteousness. It is God—Christ—living in him by faith. In Hebrews 8:10-13 the writer tells us the meaning of the New Covenant. In legalism, the law is written on tables of stone; in the gospel, the law is written on the believers' hearts.

God promises to put the basic ingredient for law-keeping—His *agape* love—in our hearts, so that we may have a loving relationship with our neighbors as God has with us.

The fourth and final difference is that the righteousness of the law, when used as a method of salvation, glorifies man. Remember the Pharisee who prays in the temple, "God, I thank You I am not a sinner like this Publican at the back of the temple. I fast twice a week; I do this and I do that; I pay tithe."

The Publican at the back, hardly looking up at God, says, "God, forgive me, a sinner." Jesus says that it is the Publican who goes home justified (see Luke 18:11-12). Man is only concerned about himself and how good he looks to others, but a Christian who is keeping the law as a standard considers himself a sinner and does not look down on others, for he is living a life of love toward others. Like John Wesley, he says when he sees a sinner: "There go I but for the grace of God."

The Law as a Standard

Paul is saying in Romans 13:8 onward that a true Christian has already been justified in Christ and does not look at the law as a method of salvation. Instead he sees the law as a standard of Christian living and allows the Holy Spirit to produce the obedience that reflects the love of God and character of Jesus Christ.

In Romans 13:11 Paul says: "And do this, knowing the time, that now it is high time to awake out of sleep; for now our salvation is nearer than when we first believed."

Even though Christians are saved in Jesus, Paul is saying that the consummation—the reality—of salvation is future. It is important as we close the study of this passage that we realize this New Testament teaching about salvation. Many Christians claim to be saved—and stop there. Yet, salvation as a subjective experience in the New Testament is presented in all three tenses—past, present, and future. A person who has been justified by faith and has received the gospel by faith and Christ as His Messiah and Savior can confess, "I am saved." A Christian is already saved in terms of the guilt and punishment of sin. But a Christian must not stop there. He must go on and say, "I am being saved" in the continuous present tense. We are being saved daily from the power and slavery of sin. This is what God saves us from daily through the Holy Spirit, as we put on the Lord, Jesus Christ.

Finally, the Christian must also say, "I will be saved" from the nature and presence of sin. A Christian is saved because he is justified by faith. He is being saved because sanctification is a daily process that goes on throughout his lifespan. He can say, "I will be saved" in terms of glorification, for when Christ comes, this corruption will put on incorruption and this mortal will put on immortality. In Jesus Christ the Christian has salvation full and complete. But in experience it is not enough to say simply, "I am saved." The world needs to see that salvation in daily living produces true law-keeping that loves our neighbors in the same way that we love ourselves. When this happens the world will realize that the gospel is the power of God unto salvation.

May Christians today be His in both word and action, as they await the day Christ comes to take them home.

CHAPTER 30

Christian Relationships

Romans 14 1-23

As we begin our study of Romans 14, we discover that Paul continues to exhort the Christians at Rome—and through them Christians today—how they should live in this world.

Paul explains and applies in this chapter the great principle of love that dominates relationships among Christians.

The church consists of all types of believers. Some are mature and some are babies in Christ. How should these Christians with different levels of experience relate to each other? This is where Romans 14 begins.

Paul says in verse 1, "Receive one who is weak in the faith but not to disputes over doubtful things for one believes he may eat all things but he who is weak eats only vegetables. Let not him who eats, despise him who does not eat. And let him who does not eat, judge him who eats for God has received him."

Gray Areas Disputed

When a person accepts Christ and joins the church, he or she may not see eye to eye in every aspect of Christian living. Some things a Christian clearly does not do—he does not steal, he does not commit murder, he does not commit adultery, and so on. But there are gray areas. Many Christians in Paul's day, for example, feel that it is a sin to eat food that has been offered to idols.

Pagans are bringing meat and produce from their gardens and offering it as sacrifices to pagan gods. The priests of these gods are then selling this food in the market as a source of income. Because the priests do not pay anything for this food and because the food is normally of good quality, they sell it for a lower price. Christians of limited means can buy this good-quality food at a savings.

Some Christians, however, see this practice as sinful and raise the issue as a matter of dispute.

On a related issue, some Christians in Paul's day feel that they should deprive their bodies of the good things of this earth. These Christians are mainly of Greek origin. The Greeks believed that the soul and the body were two distinct, unrelated parts of man—that the soul was immortal and good and the body was evil, for it was made of matter. In the Greek view, the good and immortal soul was imprisoned in a sinful body. To liberate the soul, therefore, the body had to be deprived.

In this passage, Paul is not discussing the health laws God gave to the Jews in Leviticus. This is not an issue at all, and Christians should not take Romans 14:1 and 2 and apply it across the board to dietary questions being raised in some churches today.

What Paul is addressing is the issue of judging and looking down on fellow Christians. How should a mature Christian who is resting fully in Christ and has peace with God look upon a weak believer who is still struggling? No Christian has a right to condemn another Christian in terms of behavior. Why? The argument Paul gives at the end of Romans 14:3 is that if God has received a believer, who are we to condemn him? In Romans 14:4 Paul says, "Who are you to judge another's servant?"

When I was a missionary in Africa, some national pastors began complaining that their salaries were lower than foreign missionaries'.

Amid this controversy, an African pastor spoke up and made an excellent point: "If my neighbor sends his garden boy to cultivate my garden, paying him a salary more than I earn myself, I will not complain. He is doing me a favor, cultivating my garden. I am not paying him. My neighbor is paying him, and whatever my neighbor is paying him is none of my business. I simply tell my neighbor, 'Thank you for sending your garden boy to dig my garden.' Likewise, the foreign missionary is not paid by the local congregation."

In some denominations in the United States, congregations pay the salaries of missionaries they send to Africa. What the American church pays the missionary is none of the nationals' business, this African pastor was saying. African pastors should be grateful that the missionaries are coming to their country and serving at no cost to them.

Paul is saying much the same thing to the Romans. A Christian lives for Jesus Christ, his Savior and Master. Christians have no right to judge someone else's servant. In the second half of Romans 14:4 Paul says, "To his own master, he stands or falls. Indeed, he will be made to stand, for God is able to make him stand."

In other words God is responsible for each of His servants. Do not meddle with other Christians.

Observance of Days

In Romans 14:5, Paul says, "One Christian esteems one day above another. Another esteems every day alike. Let each be fully convinced in his own mind."

The Christian church in Rome consisted of both Jews and Gentiles, and even though the Jews had accepted Christ, many still kept the feast days of the Old Testament. The Gentiles saw no reason to keep these feast days. Paul is saying in so many words, "If you Jews want to keep the feast days, that is all right. But do not condemn the Gentiles for not keeping the feast days. And you Gentiles, do not look upon the Jews as legalists. They are not keeping the feast days in order to be saved. They have accepted Christ as their Savior. Therefore, let each person be convinced in his own mind how he should live unto God."

Verse 6 says, "He who observes the day observes it to the Lord; and he who does not observe the day, to the Lord he does not observe it. He who eats, eats to the Lord, for he gives God thanks; and he who does not eat, to the Lord he does not eat, and gives God thanks."

Verse 7 continues this line of thinking, "For none of us lives to himself, and no one dies to himself."

A Christian does not live an independent life. Christians are human beings who have dynamic relationships with their Savior. They serve a living God, One who was raised from the dead through the power of the Holy Spirit.

Romans 14:8 says, "For if we live, we live to the Lord; and if we die, we die to the Lord. Therefore, whether we live or die, we are the Lord's." Here Paul is saying that Christians are under the rulership of Jesus Christ. He is the head of the Church and it is to Him they have to answer, not to each other.

Two Fundamental Principles

Paul lays down two fundamental principles we must always keep in mind when it comes to Christian living: First, whatever Christians do, they must do in terms of their relationship to God. And second, because God's love controls them, they must do nothing that will cause their fellow believers to stumble.

Christians live unto God because He is their Lord and Master and has redeemed us. And they live in such a way that they do not become stumbling blocks to their neighbors. This is Christianity!

The love of God constrains (controls) them. It is the motivating factor in all their performance and relationships. Paul continues in Romans 14: 9: "For to this end, Christ died and rose and lives again that He might be the Lord of both the dead and the living."

Jesus is not only the Savior of the believing Christian, He is their Master and Lord. In many of his epistles, Paul refers to himself as the slave of Jesus Christ. Christians are not afraid to be slaves of Jesus Christ, because Jesus is a benevolent Master. He redeemed them at the cross. He paid the price for their sin. Since He bought them back from Satan by shedding His blood, Christians love to be the slaves of Jesus Christ. He is their Master.

Judgment for Believers

In Romans 14:10, Paul continues, "Why do you judge your brother? Or why do you show contempt for your brother? For we shall all stand before the judgment seat of Christ."

Some Christians today believe there is no such thing as a judgment for the believer, but Paul clearly states that we shall all stand before the judgment seat of Christ. He is specifically addressing believers who are justified by faith.

In Romans 14:11 he continues, quoting from Leviticus: "For it is written: 'As I live says the Lord, Every knee shall bow to Me and every tongue shall confess to God.' (*Therefore, we must live to God irrespective of what man says*)."

Paul is saying that every human being, believer or unbeliever, has to give an account to God. Of the unbeliever, God will ask only these questions, "What did you do with My Son whom I gave to you at infinite cost to Me, but to you as a free gift? What did you do with the salvation that My Son obtained for you in His doing and dying?"

And when the unbeliever admits that he has deliberately, persistently, and ultimately rejected this gift, God will say to him in the spirit of Matthew 25:41: "Go into everlasting fire which was prepared for the devil and his angels. Since you insisted on believing the devil's lie and rejecting the gospel of salvation, you have chosen to be exterminated with Satan and his angels."

The reason the Christian must stand before the judgment seat of God is not that God must decide if he or she is good enough to save. Salvation is by grace—grace that saves not only from guilt and punishment but from the power and slavery of sin. They stand before God to simply give an account. What did they do with the Holy Spirit dwelling in them?

What did they do with the power of the gospel that became theirs through faith?

Every one will stand before the judgment seat of God. Only God has a right to judge them. Christians are accountable to God alone—not to their fellowmen, not even to their fellow believers. So Paul tells Christians to stop judging each other (Romans 14:10). Each Christian will give an account to God. Let God be the judge, since only He can read hearts and render true judgment.

Paul says in Romans 2 that God's judgment will be true and righteous—Christians must wait for it, for it is an end-time event.

Paul adds in Romans 14:12, "So then each of us shall give account of himself to God. Therefore, let us not judge one another anymore, but rather resolve this, not to put a stumbling block or a cause to fall in our brother's way."

The Law of Love

Paul now once again explains the law of love, approaching it from a different angle than in Romans 13. In Romans 14:14 he says, "I know and am convinced by the Lord Jesus that there is nothing unclean of itself; But to him who considers anything to be unclean, to him it is unclean."

We should not equate this statement about uncleanliness with the health laws of Leviticus 11. Paul is not discussing the health issue. He is discussing food offered to idols. Is it right or is it wrong for a Christian to buy market food which was offered to idols?

He answers that the food offered to idols and sold in the market is not in and of itself clean or unclean. This is not the issue. Whether we see it as clean or unclean is a matter of attitude—of point of view. To some Christians who realize where the food comes from, it is unclean. Other Christians, who realize that the food itself is not unclean (even though it is sold by the priests who receive it from the pagan worshipper), eat it with a clear conscience.

One feels the food is unclean because it was offered to idols. The other group feels the food is clean because the food itself had not been contaminated by being offered to idols. Paul says to let each believer be persuaded in his own mind.

Clearly Paul is not discussing rules of healthful living given to Moses, which are still viable to Christians. When God gives health laws in Leviticus, He is not giving these rules as requirements for salvation. He is giving them for the good of His people.

God is not only our Savior, He is our Creator. As our Creator, He knows what is best for our health. He wants our bodies, our souls, and our spirits to be kept blameless (1 Corinthians 1:8) until the coming of the Lord. God gave health rules and many other rules. We take these rules and apply them ourselves, as Christians, not because we want to be saved but because we want to have bodies that are healthy so that God can use us more fully for His glory.

At this point it may be useful to share three basic rules for relationships among Christians: 1. In fundamentals there must be unity; 2. In non-fundamentals there must be charity; and 3. In nonessentials there must be liberty.

Paul in Romans 14 is discussing relationships when challenged by areas of dispute. To some Christians, eating food given as offerings to pagan priests is wrong; to others it is acceptable. Romans 14:15 says, "Yet if your brother is grieved because of your food, you are no longer walking in love. Do not destroy with your food the one for whom Christ died."

Suppose a Christian who finds it perfectly all right to buy and eat food offered to idols goes to market. There he meets a weak Christian and they fall into step together as they shop. For the strong believer to buy food offered to an idol in the presence of the new believer could be a stumbling block. In such circumstances, and for the sake of the new believer, Paul is saying to the stronger believer, do not buy that food.

As mentioned before, Christians do not live for themselves. They live for God and their fellowmen. Things that touch a brother's or sister's spiritual sensitivities—even though the matters are not moral issues—should be respected, out of concern for the weaker Christian. Romans 14:17 says, "For the kingdom of God is not food and drink, but righteousness and peace and joy in the Holy Spirit."

Christians must never take the guidelines God gives in the Old Testament regarding lifestyle, eating, or dressing, as requirements for salvation. Men and women are saved only one way—by grace. True justification by faith creates a relationship to God and fellowmen that differs radically from the pre-conversion way of life. Before conversion, human beings live as they please. They do as they please—it's no one else's business. But now they live for God, uplifting Him before all, doing nothing to cause either believer or unbeliever to reject Christ.

Genuine Christians live unto God and for the sake of others. These become controlling factors in whatever they do. Paul says in 1 Corinthians 10:31 that whatever Christians do, eat, or drink, let it be to the glory of God. God wants Christians to live for others.

In Romans 14:18-23 we read, "For he who serves Christ in these things is acceptable to God and approved by men." What a wonderful statement! Christians should live lives that please God and bring honor to the cause of God. Verse 19 says, "Let us pursue the things which make for peace and the things by which one may edify another."

Christianity Brings Peace

True Christianity brings peace between human beings—not only between man and God. Justification by faith gives peace with God but also produces a lifestyle conducive to peace between man and man.

Paul continues in verse 20: "Do not destroy the work of God for the sake of food. All things indeed are pure, but it is evil for the man who eats with offense." What excellent counsel!

Verse 21 continues, "It is good neither to eat meat nor drink wine nor do anything by which your brother stumbles or is offended or is made weak."

The gospel's fundamental principle is the golden rule. Christians should do nothing that will hurt someone else. We do to others what we would want others to do to us.

Romans 14:22 continues: "Do you have faith? Have it to yourselves before God. Happy is he who does not condemn himself in what he approves."

In this verse Paul is turning to the Christian's relationship to God. Whatever the Christian does must be done in a love relationship with God. Christians must do nothing that builds barriers between them and their holy God. They must do nothing to offend a fellow believer. These are two fundamental principles of Christian living.

Paul adds in verse 23: "But he who doubts is condemned if he eats, because he does not eat from faith; for whatever is not from faith is sin." This is a new definition of sin. Normally we look at sin as transgression of the law. But Paul here sees sin not as breaking some rule but as breaking a relationship—whether the relationship between the believer and God or between the believer and his fellowmen.

The three basic drives that control an unbeliever are the lust of the flesh, the lust of the eyes, and the pride of life. The unconverted man lives for himself and thinks for himself. But the believer has crucified the flesh with all its desires. Jesus says in Luke 9:23, "If any man follows Me, let him deny himself and take up the cross and follow Me."

Christian living involves a cross—self-denial (Luke 9:23). In exchange,

Christ lives within. The life Christ lived 2,000 years ago He can live in the Christian today, for He is the same yesterday, today, and forever.

The world needs to see, not how good Christians are, but how the goodness of God can be manifested in them.

In other words, Paul says, "You are God's children. Please behave as God's children. Let the world see. Let the Christian church be an example of the unity of the Trinity. Let us be of one heart—one mind—so that the world recognizes that the gospel is the power of God to redeem us from selfishness as well as condemnation."

When Christians know and practice this truth, the world will truly know they are disciples of Jesus Christ.

Chapter 31

Burden Bearing

Romans 15:1-33

As we turn to Romans 15, we are nearing the end of Paul's epistle. Here we find the final counsel Paul gives on Christian ethics to the believers in Rome—and through them to us.

The first seven verses of chapter 15 continue chapter 14's theme of relationships. In Romans 14:1-13 Paul admonishes believers to accept one another because Christ has received them. If Christ accepts them—sinners as they are—who are they to question their fellow believers whom Christ has received?

The second half of Romans 14 says that believers should edify one another. Now in Romans 15:1, Paul says, "We then who are strong ought to bear with the scruples of the weak, and not to please ourselves." We need to clarify here that Paul is not distinguishing between the weak in faith and the strong in faith. In Romans 14:1, Paul speaks of two groups of Christians— the weak in faith and the strong in faith. The weak in faith are those believers who are justified by faith but still have legalistic tendencies. On the other hand, the strong in faith clearly understand justification by faith and are living under the full blessings of grace.

Adult and Baby Christians

In Romans 15, however, Paul is not discussing the same two groups when he speaks about the weak and the strong. Paul instead is contrasting the mature Christian and the babe in Christ. The moment we receive Christ, we become spiritually newborn creatures—babes in Christ. We have received the Holy Spirit and experienced the new birth, but we now have to learn to walk in the Spirit, as any child born into this world has to learn to use his legs.

Paul tells us that we who are mature and have experienced the power of the gospel need to help those who are weak. We are not to criticize or condemn them but take them under our wings.

What do adults normally do when babies are first learning to walk? Do we scold them, rebuke them, or undermine them because they fall?

Of course not. We pick them up, comfort them if they are hurt, and help them as much as we can to learn to use their legs. Paul says the same applies in the spiritual realm. Christians need to help one another. The Christian church contains babes in Christ as well as mature Christians. Should the mature Christians say, "We do not know why they are taking so long with these problems. We succeeded without difficulty!"

No! The mature Christian understands that the reason he is not having the same problems as the babe in Christ is that by the grace of God he has learned to walk in the Spirit.

For this growth to take place in the baby Christian, the Bible says there must be love. Paul describes this love in 1 Corinthians 13 as the supreme gift of the Holy Spirit to the believer. First Corinthians 13:4 and 5 lists some qualities of this love. The mature Christian should follow this counsel in dealing with babes in Christ.

"Love suffers long and is kind," says Paul. "Love does not envy; love does not parade itself, is not puffed up; does not behave rudely, does not seek its own, is not provoked, thinks no evil." Then, in verse 6 Paul adds that it "Does not rejoice in iniquity, but rejoices in the truth."

In other words, a mature Christian is one who is controlled by *agape* love and has deep sympathy and concern for the babe in Christ.

In Romans 15:3 Paul explains why mature Christians should do these things: "For even Christ did not please Himself; but as it is written, The reproaches of those who reproached You, fell on Me. (Psalm 69:9)."
Christ was willing to bear the sins of the whole world, and in that spirit mature Christians must bear the infirmities, weaknesses, and struggles of those in need of assistance.

The Bible calls this corporate identity, based on the fact that the Christian church is one body. The various parts of the human body have empathy for one another (Romans 12:5). Likewise, believers should show concern for each other because they belong to one body. When all is said and done, we are members of one another.

God's Word the Standard

Paul continues in Romans 15:4: "Whatever things were written before were written for our learning, that we through the patience and comfort of the Scriptures might have hope."

The measuring stick of a Christian experience must be the Word of God. Let the Word of God guide, direct, rebuke, and control the Christian's life. The Bible should become the blueprint, not only of salvation, but of Christian ethics.

In 2 Timothy 3:16 Paul makes important statements about the ideal Christian relationship with the Word of God. We live today in an age of many Bible scholars—many of them liberal theologians who no longer accept the authority of Scripture. They have made reason and scientific method the measuring rod of truth. But Paul says: "All scripture is given by inspiration of God and is profitable for doctrine, for reproof, for correction, for instruction in righteousness, that the man of God may be complete, totally equipped for every good work." The Bible is full of divine guidance we should study at length.

We read in Romans 15:5-6 more counsel of relationships: "Now may the God of patience and comfort grant you to be like-minded toward one another, according to Christ Jesus, that you may with one mind and one mouth glorify the God and Father of our Lord, Jesus Christ." The greatest power of the gospel comes when Christians in unity love each other. Paul here is referring to the believers of Rome, both Jews and Gentiles. Normally Jews and Gentiles were antagonists, but Paul says the gospel must set them free of such feelings.

A pastor from Tanzania once visited me in Nairobi, Kenya, at a time when Tanzania was at war with Uganda. While we were talking in the living room, a knock came on my door. My wife opened the door and there stood a Ugandan pastor, dropping by for a visit.

As my wife welcomed him into our home, I wondered how the Ugandan pastor would relate to the pastor from Tanzania—since their two countries were at war. For a split second they stood staring at one another, then each ran toward the other and met in a hug of Christian love.

"Here is the power of the gospel in the lives of two men whose countries are at war," I thought. As far as they were concerned, they were one in Christ. This is exactly what Paul is saying to the Jewish and Gentile believers in Romans 5:6, "Glorify God by your love and concern for each other." What a witness this would have been to the power of the gospel in Rwanda during the genocide of 1994.

In Luke's historical record of the early Christian church, we read in Acts 4:32, "Now the multitude of those who believed (*this is the Christian church at its inception*) were of one heart and one soul." They were perfectly united. They may not have agreed on everything but, in spite of diversity in minor areas, they were united in Christ.

"Neither did anyone say that any of the things he possessed was his own, but they had all things in common." This is biblical, Christian oneness. Marxism legislates sharing and compels unity. But here the unity of the church is not something enforced by the apostles. It comes instead from an inward experience of the power of the gospel: "And with great power the apostles gave witness to the resurrection of the Lord Jesus. And great grace was upon them all."

Sharing Openly

Luke goes on to explain in verse 34 that those who possess lands and money are giving it to the church and distribution is made to each according to need. There is no compulsion, for in the very next chapter (Acts 5:4) we learn of Ananias and Sapphira, who lied to Peter. Peter rebukes them, saying, "When the land was yours, no one forced you to sell." In other words, "There is no compulsion in the Christian church. Why did you lie to the Holy Spirit?"

The fruits of the gospel are seen in the Christian church in terms of relationship. Christians come from different parts of the world and cultures. We may not think alike, but when we come into the church of Christ, our unity makes a tremendous impact on the world.

With this in mind, we read Romans 15:7 onward: "Therefore receive one another, just as Christ also received us, to the glory of God." God makes no distinction—nor does the gospel—between Jew and Gentile. Paul makes this clear in Romans 3:23. There is simply no difference. Both have sinned and come short of the glory of God. Both are saved by grace alone, through faith. God does not have one way of saving Jews and another for Gentiles. All mankind is saved by faith in the precious Savior, Jesus Christ.

Just as Christ removes all barriers to receive the Christian, so Christians should practice the power of the gospel in their lives.

A Promise for All

Romans 15:8 says: "Now I say that Jesus Christ has become a servant (*the actual Greek word means "deacon"*) through the circumcision for the truth of God, to confirm the promises made to the fathers."

God came to the fathers of Israel—Abraham, Isaac and Jacob—and promised them a coming Messiah. That Messiah would be their descendant and would be the Savior of the world. But in that promise God included the Gentiles, for verse 9 reads: "And that the Gentiles might glorify God for his mercy, as it is written, 'For this reason I will confess to You among the Gentiles, And sing to Your name.' And again he says, 'Rejoice O Gentiles with His people.' And again, 'Praise the Lord, all you Gentiles! Laud Him all you peoples!'"

Isaiah 11:10 clearly says: "Therefore there shall be a root of Jesse; And He who shall rise to reign over the Gentiles, In Him the Gentiles shall hope." Salvation is through the Jews, because Jesus Christ is a Jew. But His salvation embraces both Jews and Gentiles. Since God has accepted the Jews and Gentiles in Jesus Christ, we must together glorify God.

Note the progression in the promise made in verses 9-12. In verse 9 Paul says, "(*Jews*) glorify God among the (*Gentiles*)." Then in verse 10, he adds, "(*Gentiles*) rejoice with the (*Jews*) because together you have been saved in Jesus Christ."

Then in verse 11, Paul says, "(*Jews and Gentiles*) praise God together. No more division among you." Finally in verse 12, Paul says Christ will be their Lord. Christ is the Source of salvation for both Jews and Gentiles. Therefore there should be no distinction between them in the Christian church.

Paul concludes in verse 13: "Now may the God of hope fill you with all joy and peace in believing, that you may abound in hope by the power of the Holy Spirit." Paul's great desire is that Christians should rejoice together. All distinctions must go. In Galatians 3:27 and 28 Paul says that when believers are baptized into Christ, all worldly distinctions cease, for in the church there is no male or female, no Jew or Gentile, no rich or poor, no educated or uneducated—and may I add, no distinction between black and white. All are one in Christ, and when the world sees this it will be known that the gospel is the power of God unto salvation.

Unity Through the Spirit

This unity of the faith between brethren, however, cannot be produced by promotional programs or incentives. It comes from walking in the Spirit and allowing the Holy Spirit to bring joy, peace, unity, and hope among the believers.

In Romans 15:14 onward Paul reminds Gentile believers of the great commission God has given him. We will cover this step by step in verses 14-33, but first let us summarize. In verses 14-17 Paul says he was called by grace to be an apostle to the Gentiles, to minister the gospel to the Gentiles for God's glory: "Now I myself am confident concerning you, my brethren, that you also are full of goodness, filled with all knowledge, able also to admonish one another because of the grace given to me by God. That I might be a minister of Jesus Christ to the Gentiles, ministering the gospel of God, that the offering of the Gentiles might be acceptable, sanctified by the Holy Spirit. Therefore, I have reason to glory in Christ Jesus in the things which pertain to God."

The Jews in Paul's day believed that the salvation God promised through Abraham, Isaac, and Jacob was only for them. Here Paul is saying "No." The mystery that was hid in the past is now made perfectly clear—that the Gentiles are indeed included in Jesus' salvation, by the power of God (verses 18 and 19).

In Romans 15:20-24 Paul says that this is being accomplished according to God's plan: "And so I have made it my aim to preach the gospel, not where Christ was named lest I should build on another man's foundation (*Paul desired to go into unentered areas*), but, as it is written, To whom he has not announced, they shall see and those who have not heard shall understand (*referring to the Gentiles*), for this reason I also have been much hindered from coming to you."

In the opening verses of the Epistle to the Romans, Paul says that he was hindered from coming to them earlier because God had told him that he could go to Rome only after he had visited all unentered areas of Asia Minor. But now we read in Romans 15:23 that Paul is in a position of "….no longer having a place in those parts." He has carried the gospel to every sector of Asia Minor.

Now he says, "Having a great desire these many years to come to you, whenever I journey to Spain I shall come to you. For I hope to see you on my journey, and to be helped on my way there by you, if first I may enjoy your company for a while."

Paul is concerned about visiting Rome, for he has been uniquely chosen as an apostle to the Gentiles. His calling also came in a unique way, while he was doing evil, persecuting the Christian church. He was the most feared man among the believers, until on the road between Jerusalem and Damascus he met Jesus Christ.

Paul then made a complete turnaround and at God's bidding became a messenger for Jesus to the Gentile world. His fellow Jews are scandalized and see him not only as a traitor but as a preacher of a message woefully out of harmony with their interpretation of the Word of God.

Most Jews of Paul's day believe that man must make some contribution to his own salvation. Paul on the one hand is recognized by many believers as a great apostle of God. But by many others, especially Jewish believers, he is seen as a self-appointed apostle preaching heresy.

Setting the Record Straight

One reason Paul writes the Epistle to the Romans is to prepare them for his visit with a personalized message about what he is really preaching. In this epistle, Paul makes it clear that Christians are saved by grace alone, activated by faith in Christ alone. But this grace by no means allows the believer to live as he pleases. Grace does not give the believer license to sin!

In Romans 12 to 15 Paul is saying that true justification by faith transforms the way Christians live their lives. That transformation lovingly affects their relationships with God, their neighbors, civil authorities, and fellow believers. They become loving and submissive as they dedicate their lives to the well-being of others. No genuine believer who reads Romans can accuse Paul of preaching cheap grace.

But now Paul wants to prepare the believers' minds to accept him when he arrives. So in Romans 15:25-33, He asks the Gentiles to minister to the Jews in appreciation for the Jews' part in bringing the gospel to them. In turn he asks the Jews not to undermine the Gentiles, since all are one in Christ. When he arrives, he hopes to find love and unity, for he is coming not as a tourist, but so the blessing of the gospel may be witnessed in their lives.

"But I know that when I come to you, I shall come in the fullness of the blessing of the gospel of Christ," Paul writes in Romans 15:29. "Now I beg you brethren, through the Lord, Jesus Christ, and through the love of the Spirit, that you strive together with me in your prayers to God for me."

Paul is asking them not to become his enemy. He wants them to pray for him "that I may be delivered from those in Judea who do not believe; and that my service for Jerusalem may be acceptable to the saints."

Paul is concerned that the Jews—especially those of Jerusalem—may have rejected the gospel because they think Paul is a traitor. In verse 32 Paul continues: "That I may come to you with joy by the will of God, and may be refreshed together with you. Now the God of peace be with you all. Amen."

Paul had to stop in Jerusalem before coming to Rome, and he still fears that the Jews who rejected Christ may destroy him. He who had been a chief agent in the destruction of the Christian church has become its most fervent advocate. Paul is not afraid to die for Christ, but he fears that these Jews will prevent him from coming to Rome. His premonition is partially fulfilled: Though Paul eventually reaches Rome, he arrives as a prisoner and witnesses powerfully—though confined to house arrest.

Paul's theme is always the wonderful gospel of Jesus Christ—of justification by faith and its fruits of holy living. It is a gospel of salvation by faith alone, not faith plus works. But it is salvation by faith that works. Paul says that the salvation of Jesus Christ is revealed in lives lived through the power of the Holy Spirit. The Christian's great love for the Savior will lead to good works, not out of fear of the judgment, but out of fear of letting down their beloved Master.

Chapter 32

One in Christ

Romans 16-1-27

We now begin our final study in the Epistle of Paul to the Romans. Many tend to ignore Romans 16, for it consists mainly of greetings to people Paul knew but whose names are meaningless to us.

But Romans 16 has some important lessons and contains a section of important warning. And we should by no means ignore Paul's benediction.

First let us summarize chapter 16; then we can deal with a key phrase in this chapter, central to Paul's theology.

Greeting the Saints

In Romans 16:1-16, Paul greets 26 persons by name and two unmentioned saints. While it is true that Paul has not yet visited Rome, many Roman believers have been with or worked with Paul in Asia Minor. So Paul knows some of them personally and in these verses he greets them as friends.

"Thank God for loyal supporters," we can say, as we read this section. Every pastor—every worker for God—needs loyal supporters, for we live in a hostile world.

False Teachers

In Romans 16:17-20 Paul warns against false teachers—especially Judaizers who pervert the gospel. We find out more about this in the Epistle to the Galatians, Paul's strongest letter against the Judaizers. The Judaizers have convinced the Galatian believers to give up the doctrine of salvation by grace alone and add circumcision and law-keeping as requirements for salvation.

In Romans 16:21-24 Paul honors nine faithful co-laborers who have worked with him and are now in Rome. And finally, in verses 25-27 Paul writes a benediction in his own hand. Paul typically dictates his epistles, but when he comes to the end of an epistle, he takes the pen and writes the benediction himself. He does this for two reasons.

First, he wants to provide evidence that this is a genuine Pauline letter; and second, he wants to express his personal concern and benediction for those to whom he is writing.

"In Christ"

Now let us cover in more detail the first 16 verses of Romans 16. These verses are full of names, but one phrase runs through them all. No matter whom he addresses, Paul applies the phrase "in Christ" to them all.

This phrase runs through all of Paul's epistles. If we were to remove it, there would be very little left of Paul's exposition of the gospel.

Paul sometimes varies the phrase, writing "in Christ Jesus," "in Him," "by Him," "through Him," "in the Beloved," "together with Him," or "in whom." These are all synonymous for "in Christ."

This phrase, which expresses the basis of the Christian's hope and salvation, was first introduced by Christ Himself when He told His disciples, "Abide in Me." These are the undergirding words of the gospel. If we do not understand the expression "in Christ," we will never be able to fully understand the message of the gospel. A Christian, or believer, is one who is faithful in Christ—who stands reconciled in Christ and whose hope is in Christ. Everything the Christian experiences comes in Christ.

When Christians speak of the peace they have through justification, they say the change comes while they are "in Christ." Victorious, holy living that comes through the power of the Holy Spirit is accomplished "in Christ." The hope of transformation of this nature to incorruption and this mortal to immortality at the Second Coming of Christ remains alive only while we are "in Christ." We have nothing as Christians except what we have "in Christ." Outside of Christ we have nothing but sin, condemnation, and death.

The expression "in Christ" may at first be difficult to understand. Just as "you must be born again" boggled Nicodemus's sophisticated Jewish mind, the concept of being "in Christ" is difficult for the Western mind. This happens because the phrase "in Christ" is based on biblical corporate oneness, whereas the Western mind thinks in terms of individuals.

The question is often raised "How can I, an individual, be in someone else? How can I be in Christ, who lived 2,000 years ago?"

We read in 1 Corinthians 1:30 that God puts us into Christ. How can He put us into Christ 2,000 years before we were born? It makes no sense, so we tend to skim over this phrase, though it crops up time and time again.

What does Scripture mean when it tells us that we were together with Christ in His death, burial, and resurrection and are now sitting in heavenly places in Christ (Ephesians 2:5 and 6)? As we read them, we sense that an understanding of the gospel somehow hinges on the significance of these two vital words "in Christ."

The "in Christ" motif is based on the biblical concept of oneness. To understand this we must accept three fundamental facts.

The first is that God created all men in one man. God did not make us individually. He created the whole human race in one man. Genesis 2:7 describes how God created our first father, Adam. He made him of the dust of the ground and breathed into his nostrils the breath of life. In English Bibles, the word "life" in Genesis 2:7 appears in the singular. But in the Hebrew original, the word "life" is plural. God breathed into Adam the breath of lives. God called him "Adam," for the word has a collective significance. It means mankind. While it is true that the plural in Hebrew can mean singular, the word "Adam" has a single meaning—the many in one.

Later, the New Testament in Acts 17:26 says that God created all men—the whole human race, all nations—out of one man. So the human race, by definition, is really the multiplication of Adam's life.

The second important fact is that Satan ruined all men in one man. We read in Romans 5:12 that sin entered the world—the human race—in one man. We see this clearly in Romans 5:12-18. In verse 18 Paul tells us that through one man's disobedience, condemnation unto death came to all men. We are told in 1 Corinthians 15:21 and 22 that one man brought sin to the human race—Adam. Paul says in 1 Corinthians 15:22 that in Adam all die.

The third biblical concept central to understanding the words "in Christ" is the unconditional nature of the good news of salvation—the gospel which Jesus commissioned His disciples to preach to every nation, tongue, and people. God redeemed, reconciled and justified all men in one Man. The New Testament is full of "universal texts," and the Bible clearly teaches that Jesus Christ is the Savior of all men. In 1 John 2:2 we read that Christ is not only the propitiation of the sins of the believer, but of the whole world. John 3:16 is another universal text, "God so loved the world that He gave His only begotten Son."

But we must not take these universal texts and fall into the heresy of Universalism, which teaches that all men will be saved because Jesus died for all men. Remember Paul's statement in Romans 5:12-21 that the gift of God to mankind—the righteousness of Jesus Christ—must be accepted.

Unfortunately not all accept the gift. But God redeemed, reconciled, and justified all men in one Man.

These are the three biblical corporate-oneness facts we must accept to fully understand the term "in Christ." Just as God created all men in one man, so at the incarnation God put all men into Christ to enable Him to save all men. Thus in 1 Corinthians 15:45, Paul can refer to Christ as the last Adam.

First Corinthians 1:30, 31 puts it well: "But of Him you are in Christ Jesus who became for us wisdom from God and righteousness and sanctification and redemption. As it is written, he who glories (*boasts*) let him glory (*boast*) in the Lord."

In verse 30 Paul is talking about three different people. "Him" refers to God the Father. "You" in its plural form refers to the human race. Jesus Christ, the Son of God and second in the Godhead, is the third.

Paul is saying that God took the human race at the incarnation and put it into Christ. By doing this, Christ became our wisdom. This word "wisdom" simply means "special knowledge."

Jesus says in John 8:32, "You shall know the truth and the truth shall make you free."

Paul tells us in Romans 10:17 that faith comes by knowing the truth. The truth is what God did to us in Christ. God put us into Christ.

The Paper in the Bible

Let's try an illustration. Hold an open Bible in your hand. Then take a small, single sheet of paper and place it over the pages of the open Bible and close the book. Now the paper is hidden among the pages of the Bible. The two have become one.

This is what took place at the incarnation when Christ's divinity was united with our corporate humanity and Christ became the second Adam—the second humanity. Just as the paper and the Bible became one because one is in the other, so Christ and the human race became one.

Now suppose we take the Bible with the piece of paper in it, wrap it in a brown paper and mail it to someone who is teaching college in China. Because China is a Marxist country at this time, however, it is still illegal to import Bibles. So when the Bible arrives at the post office and the clerk opens the parcel to examine its contents, he discovers a Bible. Since it is illegal to import Bibles, he takes it outside and burns it.

Now, what happens to the paper in that Bible? Yes, it burns up with the Bible. When the Bible went to China, the paper went with it to China. And when the Bible is burned, so is the sheet of paper.

Because God put the human race into Christ (just as we put the piece of paper into the Bible), Christ and mankind became one at the incarnation and the history of Christ for the next 33 years becomes the history of mankind. His perfect obedience was our perfect obedience because we were "in Him." His death on the cross was our death.

True Biblical Substitution

Second Corinthians 5:14 says that when one died, all died. This is the true meaning of biblical substitution.

Many Christians have yet to understand the biblical concept of substitution. For Christ to be our substitute—for Christ to be our representative—He had to first qualify to be our substitute. The way God qualified Him was to unite Him with us in the womb of Mary. Without this unity—without this identification—the gospel becomes unethical. The Bible never teaches that when Christ died, one Man died instead of all men. Yes, the Bible does use the term "in place of," but only in the sense that Jesus stands for us "instead of" Adam!

When Jesus died on the cross, all men died in that one Man. This is true Biblical substitution. So the good news of the gospel—the good news of "in Christ"— is that in Jesus Christ God gave all men a new history. This new history places us in perfect stead before Him and His holy law. In Christ mankind has fully met the positive demands of the law. In Christ mankind fully meets the justice of the law, so in the doing and dying of Christ He fully satisfies the law for us. The only reason it can be legally ours—the only reason we can lawfully be justified by the obedience and death of somebody else—is that we were "in Him" when He obeyed the law and died on the cross.

Biblical substitution becomes lawful and ethical, in other words, because of the corporate oneness between Christ, the second Person of the Godhead, and the human race He came to redeem. This is why we must identify the humanity of Christ with the humanity He came to redeem. The moment we make any distinction between the humanity of Christ and the humanity He came to redeem, we are preaching an unethical gospel.

Having explained this, Paul says that when God put us in Christ, He gave us a new history. By His perfect life Jesus met the positive demands of the law; by His death He met the justice of the law. When a Christian accepts this, he accepts God's gift to man. The moment a person accepts that history as his by faith; the moment a person surrenders his will to the holy history of Jesus Christ, God accepts that person as if he had never sinned. God accepts him as if he himself had paid the wages of sin along with His Son. And just as they are not guilty (responsible) for Adam's sin which condemns them, likewise they get no credit for Christ's obedience that justifies them.

Christ is the "End"

Paul makes a wonderful statement in Romans 10:4: "For Christ is the end of the law for righteousness to everyone who believes." The word "end" can have two meanings. Since Paul is dealing in this passage with Jews who were trapped in legalism, it could mean, "Jews, when Christ died on the cross, he brought legalism to an end. He terminated salvation by the works of the law."

Another possible meaning of "end" is that Christ is the fulfillment of the law for righteousness to all who believe. Those who accept Christ receive Christ's obedience as their obedience and His death as their death. So Christ is the fulfillment of the law for righteousness to those who believe as well as the end of legalism. Whichever way we look at it is correct.

Every Christian needs to know this. When Paul sends his greetings to those 26 people by name, he says in effect, "These are my fellow believers in Christ. These are the ones who will share eternity with me, not because they are good or I am good, but because we have accepted God's holy history in Jesus Christ which we can legally, lawfully claim."

The Blessings of Acceptance

Let us look at some of the blessings that come from this wonderful truth. First, the moment Christians accept their history in Christ, they have peace with God. Romans 5:1 says, "Being justified by faith, we have peace with God." Why? Because there is no longer a barrier between a holy God and sinful man when they accept the holy history of Christ as theirs.

Paul in Romans 8:1 tells us there is no condemnation for those who are in Christ— not because they are not sinners but because, in Christ, they have fully satisfied the demands of the law.

Second, they receive full forgiveness of all sins and are seen by God as holy and blameless.

As we read Ephesians 1:3-6, we discover that all the verbs are in the past tense: "Blessed be the God and Father of our Lord, Jesus Christ, who has blessed us (*past tense*) with every spiritual blessing in the heavenly places in Christ, just as He chose us in Him (*God chose us 'in Christ' before the foundation of the world*) that we should be holy and without blame before Him in love."

We are holy and without blame in Christ, though in ourselves we are sinners. Luther, the great Reformer, made this wonderful statement about believers: "A Christian is 100 percent a sinner and 100 percent righteous at the same time." A born-again Christian is 100 percent a sinner, not by performance but in nature—in himself. But he is 100 percent righteous in Christ.

"Having predestined us to adoption as sons by Jesus Christ...."

The words "by Jesus Christ" form another variant of the "in Christ" phrase. Through Jesus Christ we have become adopted sons and daughters of God. John says in 1 John 3:1: "O, what manner of love God has bestowed upon us that we should be called sons of God."

Because we are sons we are joint heirs with Christ. We shall reign with Him. Ephesians 1:6 says, "To the praise of the glory of His grace, by which He has made us accepted in the Beloved."

Turning to Ephesians 2:5,6, we read as Paul explains the wonderful truth of what happens to humanity "in Christ." According to these two verses, we were made alive together with Christ, we were saved together with Christ, we were resurrected together with Christ, and are now sitting together with Christ in heavenly paces. All the verb tenses are in the past historic tense. These all point to an objective truth that took place some 2,000 years ago in the holy history of Christ. And the key word in all these facts is the word "together."

What a wonderful message this gospel is! No wonder Luther describes Romans as the clearest gospel of all.

In closing, let us read again those opening lines of Paul's letter to the Romans, in chapter 1, verse 11: "I am writing you and expounding you this gospel that you may be established in Jesus Christ."

Now as he closes his letter in Romans 16:25-27, he gives this benediction—the longest one he ever writes: "Now to Him who is able to establish you according to my gospel and the preaching of Jesus Christ, according to the revelation of the mystery which was kept secret since the world began but now has been made manifest, and by the prophetic Scriptures has been made known to all nations, according to the commandment of the everlasting God, for obedience to the faith to God, alone wise, be glory through Jesus Christ forever. Amen."

May God bless all who respond to this gospel.